Bankers and Borders

The Case of American Banks in Britain

Bankers and Borders

The Case of American Banks in Britain

Janet Kelly

This book was written under the auspices of the Center for International Affairs, Harvard University

Ballinger Publishing Company • Cambridge, Massachusetts
A Subsidiary of J.B. Lippincott Company

This book is printed on recycled paper.

International Standard Book Number: 0-84410-459-1

Library of Congress Catalog Card Number: 76-43350

Printed in the United States of America

Library of Congress Cataloging in Publication Data

Kelly, Janet.
Bankers and borders.

Includes index.
1. Banks and banking, American—Great Britain. I. Title
HG2988.K38 332.1'5 76-43350
ISBN 0-88410-459-1

To my father

Contents

List of Figures

List of Tables

Preface

In 1969, as a briefly employed research assistant at the Federal Reserve Bank of Philadelphia, I spent many hours studying huge maps with special dots all over them representing all of the bank branches in an area. My job was to decide whether banks wishing to merge should be allowed to do so—whether the proposed merger would be good or bad for local competition. I found myself a champion of the forces of the future, of ever bigger banks and ever expanding services. This point of view agreed not only with the desires of the applicant banks, but also with the thrust of the economics courses I had taken in college. In my years at graduate school, the questions of competition and control, of freedom and authority, constantly intruded so that when I returned to the study of banks, my conclusions were somewhat different from what they had been some years before.

Along the way, I have been both inspired and helped by David Calleo, Raymond Vernon, and Joseph Nye. Useful criticisms came from Stephen Krasner, Jonathan Aronson, Peter Katzenstein, Charles Pearson, Hans Schmitt, and, especially, from Gustavo Escobar. I have received support from the Council for European Studies, the Johns Hopkins School of Advanced International Studies, and from a Rockefeller fellowship for the study of Transnational Relations which permitted me to spend a year at the Center for International Affairs at Harvard University. I have benefited particularly from the stimulation of my colleagues at the Center. Beverly Davenport typed the final draft. To these, to the many who helped me in London, Washington, and Cambridge, my sincere thanks. Needless to say, the responsibility for the final result is mine.

Janet Kelly

Introduction

Not long after World War II, a historian of American international banking said:

> One thing was certain: this nation clearly was destined to assume again the leading role in the rebuilding of Europe and Asia, and even more than before the war New York would have to function as the chief international banking citadel.[1]

No one would have argued with this statement in 1951, and in a sense it still holds true today, American finance does reign supreme in the Western world; American banks dominate. But the real growth of American banks abroad did not come until the 1960s. And an odd fact remains. Despite the relative decline of Britain, London has retained its position as the leading international money center of the world. American bankers may pull the strings in international finance, but to a large extent, they pull them in London. Almost one half of all assets of foreign branches of American banks can be found in London while 56 percent of all American bank credits to foreigners were arranged outside of the United States in 1974. London might have been called the international banking citadel of the 1960s and early 1970s, but it was manned heavily with New York and other American bankers.

By any measure, the growth of American banking in Britain is astounding. The volume of deposits at the branches of American banks there illustrates most clearly the changes which have taken place. These were less than a billion dollars in 1960, just over $3 billion in 1965, and over $70 billion by 1975. Meanwhile, the number of American banks operating in Britain skyrocketed as more and more bankers took interest in the City, as the London financial center calls itself.

The growth of American banking in Britain and the regeneration of London as a financial center is more than an interesting footnote. An understanding of the transformation of Americans into international bankers can help to answer more general questions about multinational corporations, governments, and the problems of world finance. Most studies of multinationals have focused on some or all of these concerns—why do companies go abroad, how do they interact with the governments which regulate them, and how do they affect the system in which they operate? These questions are extremely broad and no one answer would be correct if applied to all multinationals. Oilmen differ from bankers; Botswana from Britain. Nevertheless, both the questions and the answers remain important and must be asked in specific cases. The power of American banks in Britain is so great that it cannot be ignored or subsumed in aggregate studies of multinational enterprise.

One does not, of course, embark on a case study without some ideas about general truths the case may illustrate. My principal contention is that the study of multinational corporations must be integrated with a study of politics—that an understanding how the multinationals act demands an understanding of the political systems in which they operate. Economics and politics should perhaps be restored to their former connection, to borrow the old name of political economy. This book examines the relationships between the growth trends of the last decade or so, and (1) the structure of the international system, (2) American and British government policies, and (3) the character and stability of the banking systems in the two countries. The exploration of these three relationships will in turn allow several goals to be met: description, explanation, and prescription.

The growth of American banking in Britain is itself a complex phenomenon. At the most general level, it means the increased volume of American business as seen above, and the increased number of American banks operating in Britain. The number of banks has changed from seven commercial banks there in 1960 to tenfold that number in 1976. This growth, however, must be taken in a qualitative as well as quantitative sense. Individual banks have increased the scope of their activities to such an extent in Britain, that even if the absolute numbers starting British operations in the 1960s had not increased so much, the change in the quality of the operations of banks already in existence there would also be significant. The growth of operations in Britain has changed in character, in that the range of customers has also grown. We could say that American bankers abroad were "international" in the sense of providing the international services demanded by American clients abroad. But many banks in Britain now engage in "multinational" business, servicing clients from many countries. The nature of the growth will of course be presented in greater detail below, and we will see that distinct factors produced the increased numbers of banks in Britain, while other factors contributed to the increased scope of their activities.

Just as "growth" itself is a complex phenomenon, its relationship first to the structure of the international system, second, to government policies, and third, to changes in the international banking system is also multifaceted. Both economic and political aspects must come in to play. For instance, to seek the sources of the growth of international banking in terms of specific corporate economic motivations only, is to miss the larger political question of the relationship between corporate action and the political or policy environment which promotes that action. Some studies of multinational corporations find that companies pursue markets or profits where they are greater abroad without telling us *why* they are greater. On the other hand, political studies of multinationals may err in assuming overly simplistic connections between governments and corporations. In trying to characterize government-corporate relations, a single rule is often asserted to describe an essentially shifting interaction. The dominant interest here will be to see to what extent governments *do* control: are the multinational banks really beyond the nation-state? Need they be? This book shows that the banks do not operate in a static world faced with textbook-writer options, but rather in a dynamic environment where government policies have proved crucial factors in influencing bankers' decisions to move to Britain.

Other examples show how economics and politics can be joined. The economist, for instance, tells us that certain barriers to trade, such as tariffs, encourage direct foreign investment. He interests himself in how this relationship works given various tariff levels. But tariffs are set by governments, not by markets. For the political scientist, the important relationship is between the direct foreign investor and the tariff-setting government. Did the government achieve its end by setting the tariff? If it wanted to encourage domestic employment in a certain industry, the answer might be yes. If it wanted to promote autarky, the answer might be no. This is why in the case of banks, growth abroad will be related to government policies and purposes rather than to actual economic factors only. For instance, the question of the relationship of bank growth abroad to capital controls at home will be examined—but examined particularly in the light of the goals of the government in putting those capital controls in place.

In the case of the relationship of the growth of American banking in Britain to the structure of the international system, an eclectic approach is useful again. Economists have shown that direct foreign investment usually takes place in oligopolistic industries and generally involves the exploitation of some market advantage by the foreign investor.[2] It will be found that banking supports the economists' rules. That is interesting in itself—but not the full story. American bankers' chief competitive advantage abroad lies in the fact that they are the world's dollar bankers. They possess this advantage not by any accidental process, but because the structure of the international monetary system places the dollar in the premier position as a transactions, reserve, and vehicle currency. This fact has as much to do with politics and power as it has with the "blind" laws of economic science. Liberal analysts (including both economists and political scientists) often fail to examine the importance of the structure of power for outcomes. For them, it seems that a liberal structure is simply a fact, created by no one in particular. Marxists have not missed the significance of structure, but can ignore the complex ways in which events actually occur. It is not enough to go from the primacy of the dollar to the existence of Indiana National Bank in London.

Analysis should be an aid to prescription. An understanding of international banks will improve our ability to control them intelligently. The growth of American banking has affected the banking and monetary systems in Britain and the United States, and in the world, for that matter. The changes have in turn prompted alterations in government policies as policies have been adjusted to facts. None of the changes in America or Britain has been geared to reverse or even slow down the growth of American banking and of American financial power, but only to mitigate the more unpleasant side effects. These policies indicate that both governments—if for different reasons—actively approved of, or encouraged, that growth. These responses by both the American and British governments will tell us a great deal about the larger goals of the leaders in both countries—again bringing us to the heart of political questions.

A convincing grand theory of multinational corporations has yet to be constructed, and perhpas never will be. I have tried to avoid the pitfalls of overgeneralization by confining this book to one industry in one place. In this way, the full range of variables and actors can be included. As the most important instance of international banking growth, however, the case also avoids the charge of triviality. Its findings do have broader significance for other industries and other countries, particularly developed countries.

If this study differs from prevailing opinion, it probably diverges most of all in its emphasis on the primacy of the state. The actions of states determine the conditions of corporate activity; the state is the only agent we have which represents the collective interest, regardless of how well or badly it does so. Other theories generally stress the ways in which states fail to represent the collective interest by being too weak to control multinationals. Either the growth of interdependence limits governments' freedom of action or the nature of the capitalist state means that the government only serves particular (corporate) interests. Both of these assertions are sometimes true—but beside the point. At least in the case of developed countries, and perhaps in the undeveloped as well, states have wide powers to deal with multinationals. Banks operate virtually at the whim of governments. That states do fail to control has much to do with the nature of the domestic political systems. Those who look to domestic political structures to explain international politics look, I think, in the right place.

Although the state will be assumed primary here as the agent of the collective good, this is not to say that state policy is autonomous. A free emigration policy would be meaningless if all other states outlawed immigration. Equally, banking policies in Britain and the United States jointly create the environment facing the banks. Examination of the interaction between home and host country policies forms an important part of this book. London would never have become such an important banking center had it not been for the peculiar conditions in the United States in the 1960s.

This study, then, attempts to do a number of things at once. It will add to our detailed knowledge of the multinational corporation and examine the rather murky subject of American international banking and of banking in general. It will support some of the propositions made about multinational enterprise, particularly examining the economic factors which have contributed to the trend to internationalize banking. This case also proposes to go beyond the usual confines of microeconomic studies of the multinationals. It seeks to explore the determinants of the environment in which banks operate; in other words, to put what first appears to be a purely economic phenomenon into its political context. We will see that politics plays the larger part.

NOTES TO INTRODUCTION

1. Siegfried Stern, *The United States in International Banking* (New York: Columbia University Press, 1951), p. 47.

2. See, for a review of this literature, Richard E. Caves, "International Corporations: The Industrial Economics of Foreign Investment," *Economica* 38 (February 1971): 1-27; Thomas Horst, "Firm and Industry Determinants of the Decision to Invest Abroad," *Review of Economics and Statistics* 54 (August 1972): 258-66.

Chapter One

Little Headway: American Banks in Britain Before 1958

In 1959 in Britain, the Radcliffe Report on the Workings of the Monetary System observed:

> We must emphasize that the overseas and foreign banks are diverse in their interests and experience; only their relative insignificance in the domestic financial scene can excuse our summary treatment.[1]

The following decade changed such perspectives radically, however, as the American banks increased their British operations to the point where they had indeed become significant in that country. This chapter traces the growth of American banks in Britain in the period before the 1960s to see the historical roots of the later movement, and to distinguish the factors important in earlier attempts at expansion abroad by American banks, from conditions of the more recent period. The international financial system before 1958 was very different from what it is today and thus the potential for foreign expansion was also different. Banks which did branch abroad, particularly in the interwar years, found the going extremely rough and few were successful. Most of the failures were associated with problems in the structure of the international financial system. The most important factors were the system of international exchange and trade and the competitive position of American banks vis-à-vis European bankers.

This chapter will show that certain conditions are necessary to a broad and successful movement of American banks into international banking—conditions which were lacking before 1958. Given a desire to expand abroad (and it will be seen that the *desire* has typically been present since as far back as 1900), the banks needed some competitive advantages. They had to be able to offer something which the dominant European banks of the day could not offer. British banks had long been successful because they had the advantage of size, because they could offer reliable trade finance in sterling, and because they were assured of a market for their services supplied by the fact of the importance of the British in world trade and investment. Their competitive advantages therefore flowed from the structure of the system of international money and trade of the nineteenth century. The experience they acquired over the years became another competitive advantage that American banks would also have to acquire if they wished to challenge the British bankers at their own game.

Certain associations can thus be established between the failure of American banks internationally and the structure of the international system before the Second World War. Before the war, international trade and the international exchanges were unstable. The Americans' postwar success took place after the creation of fully convertible currencies and increased trade and investment by U.S. firms. Prewar failures took place when the dollar was not fully established as an international currency, while postwar success occurred under conditions of a large world demand for dollar finance.

After 1945, American banks gained competitive advantages which they did not possess before. Until 1913, the national banking system did not even grant legal authorization for foreign branches, although some state systems did allow such expansion. But the government responded and changed the law not long after banks began to express interest in foreign branching. Given the legal precondition, however, other factors also had to be present. The banks needed potential customers first of all. The first wave of internationalization in the 1920s was not buttressed by as large a pool of domestic clients needing international services as would be available by the 1960s. (The fact that so many branches *were* established in Latin America follows from the fact that American business growth there was relatively concentrated. In Latin America, a larger number of bank branches was associated with a relative paucity of local finance and growing trade with the U.S.)[2]

In banking, size and investor confidence are also crucial advantages. A bank must be large to absorb the costs of doing business abroad, and it is generally considered that these costs are higher than costs of business at home.[3] The American banks which opened London branches were at first not so large as British banks. After the war, however, there were more American banks large enough to afford the international venture. The American banking system also lacked a reputation for stability, a reputation which fell lower with the crises of the 1920s and 30s.

A third advantage that American banks have had since World War II, and which was lacking before then, is the fact that they have the largest dollar resources when the dollar is the effective international currency. The dollar backing of American banks in the twenties was hardly the advantage that it is today. Thus, given what we know about the determinants of foreign direct investment, the failure of American banking in Britain before 1958 should come as no surprise. Current research on multinational corporations suggests that internationalization takes place only in oligopolistic industries by companies seeking either to protect their market position or to exploit some business advantage not held by competitors abroad.[4]

FIRST STEPS TOWARD INTERNATIONAL BANKING: TO 1914

London was the site of the first foreign branch of an American commercial bank in 1887. It occupied one room on Gresham Street. The Jarvis Conklin Mortgage Trust Company established this obscure branch, which eventually became the grandfather of Chase Manhattan's London presence.[5] In 1897, the Guaranty Trust Company opened its London branch. This bank later merged into J.P. Morgan and Company to become the Morgan Guaranty Trust Company. Morgan, however, traces its roots further into the nineteenth century when Junius S. Morgan (J.P.'s father) went to England to join another American banker named George Peabody. In fact, Peabody's old lunch box retains a place of honor in Morgan Guaranty's main London office today.

First National City Bank inherited its London office from a now-defunct company as well. In 1902, the International Banking Corporation established a branch in London. The National City Bank of New York acquired the branch in 1915 and merged later to form the First National City Bank. The Farmers Loan and Trust Company of New York opened an office in 1906. It later became part of the Citibank empire. Finally, the Empire Trust Company of New York opened a branch in 1913 in London. Thus, by the start of the First World War, there were five American banks operating in London,[6] and only four were branches of domestic commercial banks.

Britain was a natural place for these branches to locate, given London's predominant role in world finance during this period. The few American bank branches compared with over 1,000 overseas branches of British banks. The United States, however, was beginning to emerge as a rival world economic power and American individuals and companies abroad began to require international banking services. There is little doubt, on the other hand, that the United States' banking system at the beginning of the twentieth century lacked the sophistication and resources to challenge Europe's financiers. America's need for capital at home precluded considering the needs of foreigners for financing. The National Bank Act, which regulated national banks until 1914, contained no provision for foreign branches of any kind, although some states, notably New York, did provide for foreign branches for state-chartered banks. In London, the offices of firms dealing mainly in securities (investment banks) were far more important than the branch banks established there.

In the early days of American international banking, branches of commercial banks were sometimes established abroad as arms of affiliated companies or investment banks. Laws did not clearly separate ownership of commercial banks from ownership of other financial and nonfinancial institutions until the 1930s. This was the case with Guaranty Trust Company, which was controlled by the Mutual Life Insurance Company—it was Mutual's decision that Guaranty Trust should set up in Britain in order to fulfill Mutual's desire to embark on a new venture. Mutual's venture was not very successful, but it does support a contention that early American banking abroad was ancillary to other activities.[7] Interlocking directorships among commercial banks and other businesses blurred the sources of decision-making power until commercial banking was definitively separated from investment banking and other financial interests. Commercial banks were also controlled by each other in complex ways.[8]

The story of the Farmer's Loan and Trust Company branch in Paris hints further at how intercompany connections worked. During the war, the Paris branch had been forced to move to Marseilles

> . . . where we had as street neighbors the French representatives of the *Standard Oil Company* . . . The years 1915 and 1916 saw a rapid growing of the Bank. Deposit accounts grew rapidly. This was partly due to the new conditions, but it was also evident that a good number of new friends had been made during the (1914) regime.
>
> During the year 1915, our deposit accounts increased to over 400 accounts, and the total reached the sum of over Frs. 22.000.000. Our New York office secured for us the accounts of some of the leading New York banks, including the *National City Bank* and a few of their South American branches that they had just opened.[9]

The nature of early American banking in Europe was therefore limited before World War I. American banking at that time was so domestically oriented that only after 1900 was it common for national banks to offer foreign exchange facilities at home. Many European banks had New York branches and they likely supplied Americans most foreign services. For American banks, the functions of a London branch were to act as correspondent for the parent bank, service domestic clients abroad, and facilitate the extension of trade by knowledge gleaned locally.[10] Their lack of experience hampered even these activities. While the international business of U.S. banks came mostly from Americans abroad, there is evidence that those American businesses which made direct investments in Britain negotiated the finance of their foreign trade at British banks, so that early American direct foreign investment may have lessened the business of U.S. commercial banks. This, however, is somewhat speculative, and does not apply to Latin American or Far Eastern investors.[11]

American investment banks, with their ties to European bankers, had a far more international outlook than the commercial banks.[12] Their main function was to draw capital *into* the American economy by floating securities abroad for public and private U.S. finance—a role eschewed by commercial banks. Such was the case with J.S. Morgan and Company which was opened in London in 1837. Morgan's, however, was one of the few American banks to transcend the usual parochial attitudes prevalent before World War I. J.P. Morgan (son of J.S.) really derived power from his control of sectors of the domestic economy. What success American finance did have abroad before the First World War was thus not really in commercial banking but rather flowed from connections between the banks and the "barons" of the day. These international connections, coupled with questionable domestic activities, in the end aroused mistrust rather than pride in America. The fear developed that only a few financial entrepreneurs could concentrate overwhelming power among themselves, a fear reflecting a tradition of American resistance to bankers going back to the incorporation of the First Bank of the United States. There grew a desire to encourage legitimate American international banking without domination of the field by a few individuals. National banks, after all, were not even permitted foreign branches at that time, so competition was weak. The banking panic of 1907 spurred action. In the wake of that panic, investigations exploring the power of American finance capital produced new rules to curb the growing monopolistic elements in finance[13] and wheels were set in motion to create the Federal Reserve System which granted in 1913 international banking facilities to all national banks and organized regulation at the national level.

THE FIRST WAR AND THE INTERWAR YEARS: NEW YORK v. LONDON

The First World War established precedents in the United States as the government assumed far greater responsibilities than ever before and as America suddenly found herself a world power. When Britain prohibited foreign loans in 1915, the United States remained for a time the only possible world financier of note, and New York became the preferred depository of foreign capital for those seeking a currency guaranteed in terms of gold.[14] In addition, Britain, France, Germany, and others placed bond issues in New York. The war favored banks with foreign branches to some extent. Guaranty Trust and Farmers Loan and Trust expanded British facilities to service American troops after the United States entered the war.[15]

Given these opportunities during and after the war, banks made a clear play to expand their international business, a move facilitated by changes in the U.S. banking laws. We have seen how financial crisis and fear of monopoly in the early 1900s gave birth to pressure for reform. By 1912, the National Monetary Commission had reported on the monetary structure with its reform proposals, arguing *inter alia* that foreign trade was being hampered by the lack of international branching by American banks.[16] The Federal Reserve Act (1913), remedied the situation by permitting foreign branches to member banks; that is, to all national banks and to those state-chartered banks which chose to be members of the system. The Act also encouraged trade finance in dollars by authorizing national banks to accept drafts. During the war, Congress recognized that to grow internationally, American banks could benefit from a further liberalization of the law. The Congress permitted (through the 1916 and 1919 amendments to Section 25 of the Act) participation by banks in special subsidiaries for foreign trade and financing, the so-called "Agreement" and "Edge Act." corporations.[17] The Edge Act of 1919 allowed joint ownership of these subsidiaries so that smaller banks might also be able to afford foreign ventures. The legal changes came, not surprisingly, with real changes in America's world position. The flowering of new foreign branches and subsidiaries after the war was clearly associated with the growth of American foreign trade and with America's new role as a creditor nation.[18]

With the incentives to American confidence which accompanied the war, American banking attempted to internationalize itself in several ways: by branching abroad, by forming Edge Act corporations, by foreign lending, and by building up New York as a financial center. Unfortunately for the bankers, they usually failed. Despite a better legal environment, economic and political conditions at that time were not suitable for long-term expansion and the bankers lacked the expertise and financial power necessary to fulfill their hopes.

Despite the establishment of European branches which had already taken place, most of the post-World War I expansion occurred in Latin America and the Far East. American traders saw a bottomless market for their exports in South America. The Latin American countries were considered natural areas for U.S. trade and banking expansion because of their proximity and relative underdevelopment (even though the British already had about 70 South American branches and the Germans 40). In addition, manufacturers pressed for accompanying finance.[19] National City Bank responded for instance by placing a commercial agent in its branches who would explore markets for American exporters.

The branching movement in Latin America soon produced big losses for parent banks. Stern notes that there was actually insufficient business there, in addition to "overexpansion and lack of sound banking judgment."[20] Noyes called the branches "hastily arranged and imperfectly equipped."[21] From seventy-five Latin American branches in 1921, the number fell to 46 in 1922. One contemporary textbook cited the disappointing development of the foreign branches and subsidiaries of banks in the 1920s.[22]

The corporate affiliates and subsidiaries of the 1920s formed under the Edge Act did no better. Between 1919 and 1929, eighteen foreign banking and financing corporations were formed. By the 1930s, sixteen of the eighteen had been either liquidated or absorbed.[23] Thus, in 1921, there were more U.S. banks involved in foreign banking corporations than there were even in 1958. These early Edge Act corporations, however, did provide an initial taste for international banking—a taste which would not be satisfied for many years.

The passage of the Federal Reserve Act and the formation of branches and Edge Act subsidiaries reveal much about the goals of American bankers by the 1920s. The Edge bill, like the Federal Reserve Act it amended, was meant "to broaden the market for the American producer, manufacturer, agriculturist, or whoever has goods to sell "[24] The actual formation of the branches and companies reveals: (1) the desire of *many* banks to develop international business; (2) the inability of most banks to go it alone abroad;

(3) the lack of experience of Americans in foreign banking. While the branches belonged only to several of the largest banks, most of the early Edge Act corporations were jointly owned by groups of American banks. Seven banks were involved in the Mercantile Bank of the Americas, at least thirty in the American Foreign Banking Corporation, and many small cotton belt banks in the Federal International Banking Company. Most of the failures came when the volatile Latin American commodity markets went into sharp decline and the inexperienced Americans were left holding vastly depreciated goods. While the framers of the Edge Act law had envisaged use of the law to form foreign banking corporations for direct competition with European banks, the banks chose to operate in Latin America because it seemed easier to break the Europeans' hold over trade financing far away from the competitive worlds of London and Paris.

The move to Latin America was an "end run" to avoid a frontal assault on the Europeans. It belied the real hope of American bankers: to supplant London bankers' control over the finance of trade and to supplant the pound as the premier world currency. This was the most ambitious undertaking by the Americans. While before World War I, a London branch seemed logical because of the importance of London as the center for international finance, now American attitudes demanded independence from London. This may explain the lack of effort in the 1920s to open London offices. The British were aware of the challenge to their leadership and made serious efforts to reconstitute London's supremacy, which had been tarnished in the war. Only two American banks opened in London in the 1920s and there was some expansion of trust facilities by the banks already operating there.[25]

The second effort against London took the form of competition against London's position as international lender to governments. While Americans tried to get a share of British markets in Latin America, investment bankers floated New York loans for Europeans. The resulting friction of the interwar period has already been well documented; the British saw as their prime target the return of London's financial supremacy, while the United States financial community remained eager to acquire that supremacy for itself.[26] William A. Brown argues that one of the main flaws of the international financial system in the interwar period was its lack of a fixed center.[27]

American bankers struck out on their own in these efforts with the government's interested and benevolent approval.[28] Feis catches the mood of the times well, as well as the laissez-faire attitude of the government:

> Yet with what a lively urge, with what bright hopes we had entered this first era of the diplomacy of the dollar.
>
> For most Americans our participation in the First World War was an arousing experience. It was the first time that their lives and thoughts were touched by events abroad. . . . The investment and banking houses had sensed the temper and grasped the chance. . . . The authorities in office in the main shared these sentiments and judgments. . . . As stated by Secretary of State Hughes in August, 1923: "It is not the policy of our Government to make loans to other governments, and the needed capital if it is to be supplied at all, must be furnished by private organizations."[29]

Secretary of the Treasury Mellon announced that financing Europe from the U.S. would produce "progress and increasing prosperity here."[30]

Bankers started to shed their isolation. Foreign issues taken up by Americans averaged about $800 million a year between 1920 and 1924 and grew even more in the later 1920s.[31] The Dawes Loan negotiations put the New York/London struggle into sharp relief. While the United States government stood officially aloof, J.P. Morgan and Company filled the gap by having their partners on the Committee of Experts on Reparations in 1924. Paul Warburg attests to the consciousness American bankers had of the connection between such negotiations and the future of American finance. He said in a cable to Owen Young in 1924:

> I understand Dr. Schacht is in Paris. Is it not advisable to point out to him the importance of resting his credit on stable gold instead of fluctuating sterling? Incidentally, it would be invaluable advantage for American discount market if as a result of America's entering the field now substantial portion of future German gold reserve were invested in dollar acceptances. England realizes that and makes sacrifice to preserve predominance sterling market. Could not America be brought into the first line right now pari-passu with British banks? Pardon this cable but I am frankly alarmed at the thought that we may miss this unique opportunity for putting America's discount market on the map and complete our position as world bankers.[32]

Warburg's reference to "stable gold" hit directly at what Britain considered her weakest point at the time. Before 1925, "stable gold" meant only the dollar, since Britain had not yet returned to a fixed parity. And for Britain, the return to gold and the predominance of London were symbiotically related. To defend the position of London, the British had held the return to gold as a practically undisputed goal since the First World War. As the Cunliffe Committee on Currency and Foreign Exchanges noted in 1918, "there was no difference of opinion among the witnesses who appeared before us as to the vital importance of these matters." (i.e., the maintenance of the Gold Standard.) W.A. Brown reports that the decision to return to gold at the prewar fixed parity was made as soon as the exchange rate had diverged from it. The British were determined not to lose the position they had built up over the preceding century.[33]

A third means to take London's place as world banker, after inroads in foreign markets and in the international bond business, was the crusade for the development of an acceptance market in the United States—the argument being that no reason existed for London raking off profits from the finance of American trade. Until the passage of the Federal Reserve Act, national banks could not accept drafts. Trade finance from national banks consisted only in non-negotiable notes. Those banks which did accept bills could not market them successfully.[34] It was generally felt that American dollar acceptances would not become widespread until American banks developed foreign branch systems. For acceptances to become attractive investments the acceptor (the bank) must be well known. British banks' visibility world-wide contributed the needed confidence in their names. Thus, until they established themselves abroad, particularly in big money centers like London, American banks would remain obscure.[35] Paul Warburg said to the National Monetary Commission in 1910 what would be felt more generally in the twenties:

> It is impossible to estimate how large a sum America pays every year to Europe by way of commissions for accepting such documentary bills, and other bills with which we shall now deal, but the figures run into many millions. This annual tribute to Europe resulting from our primitive financial system is not merely a waste of money, but reflects upon the dignity of a nation of the political and economic importance of the United States.[36]

Thus the development of a market in acceptances would establish American self-sufficiency. Such a market might benefit from foreign branches for the service of *American* foreign trade, but activities of these branches would be limited to a supportive role. The volume of bankers' acceptances for international dealings did reach $1.4 billion in 1929, up from about one-third that level in the early 1920s.[37] There is, however, little reference in the 1920s to the idea that American banks might finance purely third-country trade, the way British banks had for years. Although American bankers wanted to supplant London, many had perhaps a more parochial view of what constituted full international banking than did their British counterparts. A sort of hierarchy developed in which big New York banks established European offices so that smaller American banks could use them as correspondents abroad who could be expected to be familiar with local names. This was the case with Bankers Trust which stated that one of its motives for a British branch was to service its correspondent banks in the United States.[38] The American banking movement thus remained hesitant and incomplete.

The interwar period thus far illustrates the general problems of internationalization for American banking. Entering new markets, a bank must be able to offer something more than its entrenched competitors. And it must offer it on terms that will not endanger the solvency of the bank itself. Most American commercial banks could not do this in Britain, nor even in Latin America in the 1920s. The field was more open to the south, but there, foolish investments were made. The investment bankers did compete successfully for big bond issues in New York, but in the end these too turned out to be unsound. Unsettled exchange and currency conditions made trade finance a risky business, while unsettled political conditions made big government loans chancy as well. The grand move quickly fell apart because the foundations were weak. The American government had supplied a *legal* basis for foreign expansion, and growing interests abroad did prompt a wave of foreign expansion: these were necessary, but not sufficient grounds for the expansion the banks desired. The failure of American commercial banks in the interwar years parallels the failure of the American governments of the day to seize leadership. Both still lacked an understanding of the interaction of economic and political factors. The failures of the twenties were followed by even greater setbacks in the thirties—but many lessons were learned during those difficult years.

THE GREAT CONTRACTION

The stock market crash brought an end to the grandiose international plans of the 1920s, and the depression which followed continued the drying up of American banking growth abroad and of international lending. In the 1930s few foreign branches were established and many were closed (Table 1-1). By 1939, there were only 92 branches of member banks, eleven of them in Britain.

The whole adventure in internationalism had fallen into serious difficulties. As A.C.L. Day says,

> Although New York came to share with London dominance in international finance, there were some spheres she never fully entered. Her

Table 1-1. U.S. Banks and Banking Corporations Operating Foreign Offices 1920-1937

Year End	*Numbers of Banks and Banking Corporations*	*Number of Foreign Branches*
1920	12	181
1926	12	107
1933	9	132
1937	11	108

Source: Tamagna and Willis, "United States Banking Operations Abroad," p. 1289.

> attempts to establish overseas banking connexions were mainly unsuccessful.... The entry of New York into a position of partnership with London made the system harder to work, partly because of the very fact of partnership, partly because of serious inadequacies in New York's technical equipment.[39]

These problems of so-called "technical equipment" surely contributed to the domestic failures of the 1920s and 1930s as well. The record of bank failures was catastrophic, reaching 4,000 in 1933.[40] Defects permeated the banking structure itself. Galbraith attributes much of the weakness to the large number of independent banks at that time, which encouraged a "domino effect" of failures resulting from the failure of the weakest banks.[41] And it followed that a sick domestic banking system could hardly make headway in the international sphere. The domestic banking environment must also be stable in order for solid international expansion to take place.

The weaknesses of the American banking system were largely domestic and to a great extent, self-inflicted. American international banking had thus failed in several ways: it had overexpanded in Latin America, domestically it had linked itself to a basically unsound capital market by financing the boom in stocks, and it had made few inroads in important foreign centers such as London. With the decline in production and trade in the thirties, demand for international services dried up. It would not be until the 1960s that American bankers really moved abroad in force. The American banking system had to clean itself up before it would find real international stature.

The cleanup produced new forms of regulation: the Banking Acts of 1933, 1935, the creation of the Federal Deposit Insurance Corporation and the Investment Company Act of 1940. The process of self-purification carried out in the 1930s held up expansion abroad, since the new laws demanded a restructuring of the system. Long-run expansion would benefit, however, from the new rules by increasing world confidence in the American system. The Glass-Steagall Act (1933) for instance, severed commercial banking from investment banking.[42] This rule split some very prestigious financial companies down the middle and even today limits American banks' functions.

The stock market and the later banking crash damaged the American image abroad. Bankers were accused (some with justice) of outright criminality. Their prestige fell precipitously as hearings before the Senate Banking Committee proceeded.[43] Banking circles abroad expressed shock at the improprieties confessed to and they placed direct blame for many of their own problems on the men they had formerly respected. For instance, *The Economist* of London noted with admiration Morgan's participation in the Dawes Loan negotiations, (where Morgan representatives effectively determined the terms of the loan) but it also saw on the list of personal loans made by Morgan in the 1920s, General Dawes himself, and on the list of "preferred clients," many important American government officials under Wilson and Hoover. Something was wrong, and Morgan's and other large banks were a part of it all.[44]

Until the Second World War, then, American banking necessarily kept a low profile at home and in Europe. The commercial banks dropped their securities affiliates in 1933, as the new law of that year required, and attempted to regain the public's trust. Most investment houses chose to give up deposit banking since they had operated mainly in corporate finance and would have less to lose this way. The years between 1933 and 1935 witnessed a scramble as companies split up and re-formed. It was a time of general retrenchment with few thoughts of expansion abroad. American international banking, despite its ambitions after the First World War, had not got very far by the start of the Second. But a firmer domestic base was slowly built up in the forties and fifties and confidence seeped back into the system. This satisfied another necessary condition for foreign expansion and the war would supply the rest.

THE SECOND WORLD WAR AND A SECOND CHANCE

While World War II accomplished what the First had failed to do in establishing the United States as the foremost financial power, the actual conduct of the war provided hard times for American international banking. Britain was the only European country where branch operations could continue freely, since French offices were effectively lost until the Liberation. Even though Britain remained as a bastion in Europe, American sights again directed themselves toward Latin America during the war. Most transactions across the Atlantic were government-directed. In England, severe restrictions hemmed in the ability of the branches to act. They were prohibited from making any transfers of money abroad, except with the approval of the Bank of England. But wartime activities were largely of a personal nature: cashing checks and transmitting funds for United States army and navy personnel. American government organizations also established important accounts with the London branches—the War Shipping Administration, the Post Exchanges, the Chief Disbursing Officer of the Treasury Department, and the disbursing clerks attached to the State Department and the Navy.[45]

The loss of international business during the war was made up to some extent by the transfer of a certain amount of business to the United States. Purchasing missions of foreign governments were established in the United States, although the Federal Reserve Bank of New York was the principal agent for handling their dollar disbursements for war and other supplies. By 1945, there were only 78 foreign offices of American banks and banking corporations, a decrease of about 30 from the start of the war.

The 1950s brought about a reconstitution of the former position, however, fairly quickly. Many banks had planned for the peace with the idea of foreign expansion. The new world position of America and the dollar made the difference. The government planned as well during the war, trying to create as open a system as possible for American trade and investment. The banks determined to open their sights, having lost the residue of parochialism which had obstructed their view between the wars. The Bank of America, for instance, studied its own possible postwar role. It had by that time a London branch, European correspondents, and its branch system in Italy through the Banca d'America e d'Italia. Yet the Bank of America at that time could not compare internationally with banks such as Chase or National City. Its first postwar branch was established in the Pacific, rather than in Europe. But Bank of America had no intention of leaving the Atlantic system to the New York banks. Mario Giannini, head of the bank, said in 1949:

> We don't like to see exports from San Francisco financed by New York lines of credit. We expect to build the position of the Bank of America in the international field to a point where it will be comparable to the bank's position in the domestic field. We feel we owe it to the country, to our state, to our customers, and to the stockholders.[46]

Before a real expansion could come, however, general convertibility of currencies would have to replace the highly regulated system of exchanges in Europe. In London, the scope of American bank activities remained limited by lack of a strong deposit base. As Table 1-2 shows, no new banks entered London between 1945 and 1958.

European exchange controls also choked off expansion and the banks contented themselves with the more traditional and less innovative functions usual to foreign branches. They invested a substantial portion of their sterling deposits in British short-term government bonds and left the peculiarly domestic (U.K.) business to the domestic banks. Dollar deposits in the foreign offices were usually transferred to the head offices and often invested in U.S. Treasury bills or dollar acceptances.[47]

By the end of 1957, the total deposits of the branches of American banks in the U.K. amounted to only $318.9 millions, compared with $41.0 billions by December, 1972.[48]

The banks lagged behind the general trend of spreading American investment abroad. Other kinds of American foreign investment outstripped investment in financial enterprises. By 1953, in comparison, there were 303 American manufacturing establishments in Britain alone, against the limited activities of the six banks there. By 1959, manufacturers had grown to almost 700.[49] Only seven commercial banks had foreign branches anywhere by 1958. Total foreign branches numbered 119, and five Edge Act corporations were still in existence. This did not compare with the many hundreds of foreign branches, subsidiaries, and affiliates of British banks, most of which were in the old empire. By 1958, the stage was set for renewed outward movement. The banks had achieved size, stature, and experience; the dollar had become the dominant international cur-

Table 1-2. American Banks in Britain Before 1958

Bank	*Entry*	*No. of London Branches*
First National City Bank of the City of New York	1902	2
Chase Manhattan Bank	1887	2
Bank of America	1931	2
Bankers Trust Company	1922	1
Hanover Bank	1925	2
Guaranty Trust Company	1897	2

Source: Tamagna and Willis, "U.S. Banking Organizations Abroad," p.1289. Names of banks are as of December, 1956.

rency; U.S. trade and investment abroad was booming; currencies were made convertible; and the play could begin.

The history of United States banking does show the early concern of at least the biggest bankers to internationalize and to increase the stature of New York as a financial center in the years before the Second World War. And those banks which have expanded most in Britain since World War II are the same banks which managed to get a toe-hold there before the war. Banking is to a large extent a cumulative business in which financial power breeds even more financial power. This will become more obvious in later chapters. After World War II, the unfavorable conditions of the interwar period were reversed and the world was calling for the dollar. United States bankers no longer felt that the world should come to them: they would go to meet the world. As George S. Moore, then president of First National City Bank said in 1963:

> With the dollar the leading international currency and the United States the world's largest exporter and importer of goods, services, and capital, it is only natural that the United States banks gird themselves to play the same relative role in international finance that the great British financial institutions played in the nineteenth century.[50]

It might be argued that even George Moore underestimated the role that American banks might play.

NOTES TO CHAPTER ONE

1. Great Britain, Parliament, *Parliamentary Papers* (Commons), Cmnd. 827, 1959, "Report of the Committee of the Workings of the Monetary System," (The Radcliffe Report), par. 197.

2. By 1929, the U.S. carried on twice as much trade with Latin America as did Britain, the second most important trader. This was a strong reversal of the pre-1914 pattern. William C. Wells, "The Situation in South America," American Academy of Political and Social Science, *Annals* 94 (1921): 12.

3. On banking, see Charles P. Kindleberger, "Size of Firm and Size of Nation," John H. Dunning, (ed.) *Economic Analysis and the Multinational Enterprise* (London: George Allen and Unwin, 1974), p. 348.

4. See Raymond Vernon, *Sovereignty at Bay: The Multinational Spread of U.S. Enterprise* (New York: Basic Books, 1971); Stephen Hymer and Robert Rowthorn, "Multinational Corporations and International Oligopoly: The Non-American Challenge," in Charles P. Kindleberger (ed.), *The International Corporation* (Cambridge: M.I.T. Press, 1970).

5. Jarvis Conklin failed in the Panic of 1893, but its London office was taken over by the North American Trust Company, by the Trust Company of America, and finally, by the Equitable Trust Company in 1912. Clyde William Phelps, *The Foreign Expansion of American Banks* (New York: The Ronald Press, 1927), pp. 133-34.

6. Excluding London branches of American investment and private banks. Frank M. Tamagna and Parker B. Willis, "United States Banking Organizations Abroad," *Federal Reserve Bulletin* December (1956): 1286.

7. Morton Keller, *The Life Insurance Enterprise: 1885-1910, A Study in the Limits of Corporate Power* (Cambridge, Harvard University Press, 1963), p. 150. Keller shows how insurance companies were perhaps the most powerful American financial institutions in the early twentieth century. They were also the first companies to penetrate European markets on a large scale with European-based operations.

8. Before the First World War, the important banking organizations in the United States had tended to coalesce into only two groups: one centered on Rockefeller interests, one on Morgan. The Citibank (Stillman)-Standard Oil (Rockefeller)-Harriman connection, for instance, presented a powerful challenge to Morgan.

9. Proof copy of the *History of the Paris Office of the Farmers Loan and Trust Company from the Opening in 1906 to the End of 1920* (Baker Library, Harvard Business School). (Italics added.)

10. Siegfried Stern, *The U.S. in International Banking* (New York: Columbia University Press, 1951), p. 183.

11. Mira Wilkins, *The Emergence of Multinational Enterprise* (Cambridge: Harvard University Press, 1970), p. 68; Phelps, *The Foreign Expansion*, pp. 80-81.

12. Wilkins, *The Emergence . . .*, p. 21.

13. House of Representatives, 62nd Congress, 3rd Session, *House Report 1593*, "The Money Trust" (1913). J.P. Morgan appeared before the Pujo Committee of the House and denied his power to affect the United States economy, without entirely satisfying his interrogators. The outcome of the hearings was a series of recommendations, some of which led to the Federal Reserve Act, while others were embodied in the Clayton Antitrust Act of 1914. The Clayton Act prohibited interlocking directorships in banks and trust companies with resources of more than $5 million and forbade private bankers from serving on the boards of directors of national banks. This 1914 restriction was weakened, however, by a 1916 amendment—and interlocking directorships had to be curbed again later in the fiasco of the 30s.

In New York, laws were also passed prohibiting insurance control over banks and trust companies. Keller, *The Life Insurance Enterprise*, p. 258.

14. Alexander D. Noyes, *The War Period of American Finance: 1908-1925* (New York: G.P. Putnam's Sons, 1926), pp. 106-7.

15. *Ibid.*, p. 112; Henry Wynsham Lanier, *A Century of Banking in New York: 1822-1922*, Farmers' Loan and Trust Company edition (New York: Gilless Press, 1922), pp. 287-96.

16. See the speech made by Nelson Aldrich, Chairman of the National Monetary Commission before the Annual Convention of the American Bankers' Association, New Orleans, November 21, 1911 (as reported in Paul A. Samuelson and Herman E. Kroos, *Documentary History of Banking and Currency in the United States* (New York: McGraw Hill, Chelsea House Publishers, 1969), pp. 2100-2106). Aldrich says of the Commission's recommendation:

> The plan authorizes the organization of banks in foreign countries to assist in the extension of our international trade. . . . I ask you if it is not worthwhile to take the banking institutions of the United States out of condition of dependent helplessness and place them, where they belong, in a class with the best and strongest banking institutions in the world? There is not a particle of reason why prime sterling bills should forever remain the highest form of credit.

Thus, the desire to supplant London's position preceded the First World War in some circles. Yet the war itself, and Britain's final dependence of the United States in the war, doubtless increased the suspicion that Britain had begun to decline and that America was the logical heir to England's world position. Harry Magdoff dates the first American hopes to replace London in the Boer War when London finance faltered for a time. (*The Age of Imperialism* (New York: Monthly Review Press, 1969), p. 81).

17. For further details, see Chapter 5.

18. A review of current opinion from 1914 to the 1920s reveals constantly the concern of the U.S. for increased exports—and export finance. See especially articles on this in American Academy of Political and Social Science, *Annals*, 59 (1915); 94 (1921).

19. Noyes, *The War Period*, p. 389; Carl P. Parrini, *Heir to Empire: United States Economic Diplomacy 1916-1923* (Pittsburgh: Pittsburgh University Press, 1969), p. 86.

20. Stern, *U.S. in International Banking*, p. 9.

21. Noyes, *The War Period*, p. 389.

22. Harold G. Moulton, *The Financial Organization of Society* (Chicago: University of Chicago Press, 1930), pp. 391-93. See also H. Parker Willis, John M. Chapman, Ralph West Robey, *Contemporary Banking* (New York: Harper and Brother, 1933), p. 502.

23. In the process of absorptions, the present-day First National City Bank seems to have been the chief beneficiary. In 1924, it (at the time, the International Banking Corporation) bought the Asia Banking Corporation with 12 offices. Meanwhile, the Bank of Manhattan Company acceded to the International Acceptance Bank—which had a representative in London and a subsidiary in Holland. Chase National Bank also profited by buying the Equitable Banking Corporation with 3 Far Eastern branches.

24. Statement of Walter Edge, U.S. Congress, Senate Committee on Banking and Currency, *Hearings on S. 2472*, 66th Congress, 1st Session, 1919, p. 20.

25. Trust companies in Britain must be separately incorporated, so most new subsidiaries were merely trust departments for already existing branches.

26. This is the thesis of Parrini, *Heir to Empire*. He says: "In reality the American plan was to replace the faltering leader of the previous century, Great Britain." (Idem, p. 248). The Federal Reserve stated in its Annual Reports that the purpose of the Edge Act was specifically to compete with British and continental banks. (*Annual Reports*, (1919), p. 59; (1921) p. 24). This goal was also repeated by bankers, businessmen and bureaucrats. For a good contemporary account, see Paul Einzig, *The Fight for Financial Supremacy* (London: Macmillan, 1932).

27. W.A. Brown, *The International Gold Standard Reinterpreted* (New York: National Bureau of Economic Research, Inc., 1940). See particularly Part II, "What was Restored, a Decentralized International Financial System."

28. Actually, some influential bankers thought that the government should help out in providing finance to European countries with debts after the First World War. The Treasury, however, did not agree and the lender's role was thus to some extent thrust on the private banking community. See Joan Hoff Wilson, *American Business and Foreign Policy: 1920-1933* (Boston: Beacon Press, 1971), p. 14. Wilson documents a split of opinion among American bankers about the exact strategy they should use in their expansion. The Morgan-Chase group felt that American banks should not try to compete with British banks all over the world, while the National City Bank-Rockefeller group stressed the importance of branch banking and direct investment abroad. The Morgan group thought that American dominance would come naturally anyway and Morgan's had a close working relationship with the British as the agent of the British government in the U.S. The Rockefeller group was eager to invest in areas long controlled by the Europeans. But as Wilson said, "The ultimate goal of both factions was the same: 'an independent American system' which would dominate world trade and finance in the wake of the war." (Idem, p. 16.)

29. Herbert Feis, *The Diplomacy of the Dollar: First Era 1919-1932* (Baltimore: Johns Hopkins Press, 1950), pp. 3-6.

30. *New York Times*, 3 December 1924.

31. U.S. Department of Commerce, "The Balance of Payments of the United States in 1924," p. 26.

32. As reported in Stephen Clarke, *Central Bank Cooperation: 1924-1931* (New York: Federal Reserve Bank of New York, 1967), pp. 61-62. Warburg was one of the original members of the Federal Reserve Board, and became Chairman of the International Acceptance Bank in 1921. He was a keen advocate of the development of the American banking system and had a part in the drafting of the Federal Reserve Act. See his book, *The Federal Reserve System: Its Origin and Growth* (New York: Macmillan, 1930) for his views.

33. Great Britain, Parliament, *Parliamentary Papers* Cd. 9182, 1918, "First Interim Report of the Committee on Currency and Foreign Exchanges after the War," p. 5. The Committee said that without the gold standard mechanism, Britain might handicap its industry, its position "as an international financial centre" and its "general financial status in the eyes of the world."; Brown, *The International Gold Standard*, p. 221. See also Sir Henry Clay, *Lord Norman* (London: Macmillan and Co., 1975), pp. 159-160; Lester V. Chandler, *Benjamin Strong: Central Banker* (Washington: The Brookings Institution), pp. 86-94; 294; Sidney E. Rolfe and James L. Burtle, *The Great Wheel: The World Monetary System* (New York: McGraw Hill, 1973), p. 28, for the supporting views by the Bank of England, Winston Churchill, the New York Federal Reserve Bank.

34. Though the United States banks were undoubtedly eager to engage in international banking after the passage of the Federal Reserve Act, they were on the whole rather inexperienced in the field. A history of Brown Brothers and Harriman, the private bankers, illustrates the lack of sophistication among

American bankers at the time. When the Federal Reserve Act finally permitted the issuance of acceptance credits by national banks, few knew quite what to do with them. Often, a banker would forward credit to a customer and then fail to see the possibilities of the negotiability of the instrument, locking it away securely until the date of payment. See John A. Kouwenhoven, *Partners in Banking* (Garden City: Doubleday and Co., 1968).

35. A credit was not useful to an American importer unless a foreign merchant immediately recognized and completely trusted, the issuing house. Edwin J. Perkins, *Financing Anglo-American Trade: The House of Brown 1800-1880* (Cambridge: Harvard University Press, 1975), p. 11.

36. Paul M. Warburg, *The Discount System in Europe* (for the National Monetary Commission, *Miscellaneous Articles* 20 (Washington: 1911), p. 9.

37. American Acceptance Council, *Bulletin* 7 (1925) 6; 12(1930)1.

38. Phelps, *The Foreign Expansion*, p. 150.

39. A.C.L. Day, *The Future of Sterling* (Oxford: Clarendon Press, 1954), p. 32.

40. Board of Governors of the Federal Reserve System, *Banking and Monetary Statistics* (Washington, 1943), p. 283.

41. J.K. Galbraith, *The Great Crash* (Boston: Houghton Mifflin, 1961), p. 161.

42. For the significance of those limits, see Chapter Five.

43. There was a series of investigations in 1932 and 1933, but by far the juiciest in terms of uncovering the sins of big bankers was the Pecora Investigation of the U.S. Senate. Committee of Banking and Currency, *Report on Stock Exchange Practices*, S. Rept. 1455, 73rd Cong., 2d Sess., 1934.

44. *The Economist*, 16 June 1933, p. 1232; 27 May 1933, p. 1123.

45. Stern, *The U.S. International Banking*, p. 192.

46. Marquis James and Bessie James, *Biography of a Bank* (New York: Harper and Row, 1954), p. 479.

47. Stern, *The U.S. in International Banking*, pp. 183-84.

48. Bank of England, *Quarterly Bulletin.*

49. John H. Dunning, *American Investment in British Manufacturing Industry* (London: George Allen and Unwin, 1958), p. 91. Vernon, *Sovereignty at Bay*, p. 62.

50. From George S. Moore, "International Growth: Challenge to U.S. Banks," *The National Banking Review*, September 1963, p. 6.

Chapter Two

The Rush to London: American Banks in Britain After 1958

The Radcliffe Report notwithstanding, American banks in London are now an important factor in British banking.

Since the advent of convertibility in 1958, the expansion of American banks has changed the face of the City. The expansion continues today and will probably continue in the future, despite the belief of some doomwatchers. A walk around the City of London is interesting in this respect: surrounding the American bank branches (and they are not hard to find) there is often a flurry of construction to make room for the newcomers or to expand for more firmly entrenched and successful banks.

The purpose of this chapter is first of all to catalogue this growth of American commercial banking since 1958 and to establish its nature and pace. We can then become familiar with the most important actors in this case and will be able to get a general idea of the scope of the American banking establishment in London. It will be helpful to distinguish among the various kinds of banks and to see that there are distinct differences in the way they function. Earlier entrants to Britain have large organizations and varied lines of business; later entrants, on the other hand, have much smaller London operations and more limited holdings there. The differences among the activities of the banks are crucial to an understanding of the motives of different classes of banks for coming to Britain in the first place.

A second objective of the chapter is to take a brief look at some of the simpler hypotheses which have been suggested by prior work on multinational corporations. Two of these are supported by the aggregated data below. The hypothesis that size is the best indicator for whether or not a company expands through operations abroad applies in the case of the banks which have opened offices in Britain. Size is associated with the probability that a bank has opened a London branch or subsidiary; size is also associated with *how soon* the branch was established and with how extensive a bank's British operations are.

Another hypothesis is that some movement to international operations is of a defensive nature: if one participant in a domestic market moves abroad, his domestic competitors will follow his lead in order to preserve the stability of market shares. This is evidenced by the patterns of London entry by banks from certain U.S. cities—what has been called "follow-the-leader" investment.

This chapter will set the stage for a fuller analysis of the movement of banks to Britain by introducing all of the participants and their origins. Later chapters will reveal the specific conditions of the movement, the role of governments in it, and the effects of the movement on both parent and host countries. Here, we will find out just what has been happening since 1958.

THE RECENT RECORD

There are various ways in which a bank can establish itself in Britain. A bank may first open a representative office which cannot itself take in deposits or offer loans. It often represents a preliminary stage which a bank undertakes in order to explore a market before it actually goes into business there. For full business, a branch is needed. Banks can also choose to establish banking subsidiaries instead of branches, but these have certain disadvantages because the more limited capital base of a subsidiary will support less business by the foreign office. Finally, banks can either enter into joint banking ventures or take minority interests in other financial companies. All of these methods have been used by American banks in Britain.

At present, thirty-seven banks possess either a branch or a wholly-owned subsidiary; seventeen more banks have representative offices; some forty banks participate in joint ventures and several more have minority interests in British financial institutions. Thus, almost one hundred banks have entered Britain in one way or another. Most of this activity was initiated in the last ten years, as is evident when the numbers are compared to American bank activity in Britain in former years.

Table 2-1 shows the rapid growth of branches of American banks in Britain in the last fifteen years.

Table 2-1. Number of Branches of Member Banks in the U.K.

1958	10	1962	14	1966	21	1970	41
1959	10	1963	14	1967	24	1971	45
1960	13	1964	17	1968	32	1972	49
1961	13	1965	21	1969	37	1973	52
						1974	55

Note: (Most large United States Banks are members of the Federal Reserve System.) These figures represent the branches of fewer than 55 banks since some have more than one British branch. Includes Franklin National Bank and Republic National Bank. Franklin's assets are now controlled by a foreign banking group (European American Banking Company) and Republic is affiliated with Swiss bank.

Source: From the Board of Governors of the Federal Reserve System, *Annual Reports.*

Equally dramatic is the growth of business carried on by these banks: total deposits grew from about $350 million in 1958 to over $60 billion in 1974. A select number of the American banks far outweigh all the others in importance. The names of these more important banks will reappear constantly. They arrived first in London, have the greatest number of employees, the most deposits, and a proliferation of subsidiaries and affiliates. They are household names in America as well as in London. The peak year for new banks entering London was 1968. While fewer American banks are entering London now compared with 1968, enough interest continues in the London market to justify some new entrants.

As of 1975, the American commercial banks with branches in the United Kingdom are shown in Table 2-2 (by order of total world assets of holding company as of 31 December 1974).

Banks with representative offices only are listed in Table 2-3. For the most part, these are second-ranking United States Banks with relatively limited world assets.[1] The average is less than $2 billion. They are, however, large enough to conduct a fair amount of international business and perhaps have ambitions to extend themselves internationally more than they have. The addition of six new representative offices in 1974 shows that interest in international business has continued among the less important American banks, but the three closures in 1975 reveal that some smaller banks have found the going rough. Most of the banks with London representative offices already have at least one foreign branch in the Bahamas or the Cayman Islands, cheaper havens from which they can participate in the offshore dollar business without taking on London's higher costs. Seven of these banks also have access to London through participation in consortia or through minority ownership of

Table 2-2. American Banks with U.K. Branches

	Assets (000's)
1. Bank of America	60,376
2. First National City Bank (Citibank)	57,839
3. Chase Manhattan Bank	42,532
4. Morgan Guaranty Trust Company	25,963
5. Manufacturers Hanover Trust Company	25,754
6. Chemical Bank	22,175
7. Bankers Trust Company	20,387
8. Continental Illinois National Bank and Trust Company of Chicago	19,798
9. First National Bank of Chicago	19,139
10. United California Bank	18,727
11. Security Pacific National Bank (San Francisco)	15,487
12. Marine Midland Bank	12,665
13. Irving Trust Company	11,343
14. Crocker National Bank (San Francisco)	10,290
15. Mellon Bank (Pittsburgh)	9,919
16. First National Bank of Boston	8,714
17. National Bank of Detroit	7,586
18. First Pennsylvania Bank	6,883
19. First National Bank in Dallas	5,792
20. Seattle First National Bank	4,625
21. Republic National Bank (Dallas)	4,382
22. Bank of New York	4,191
23. Harris Trust Savings Bank (Chicago)	4,102
24. First City National Bank of Houston	4,067
25. North Carolina National Bank	3,897
26. Northern Trust Company	3,789
27. Texas Commerce Bank	3,684
28. Girard Bank (Philadelphia)	3,541
29. First Wisconsin Bank of Milwaukee	3,503
30. Bank of California	3,047
31. Fidelity Bank (Philadelphia)	3,015
32. Detroit Bank and Trust Company	2,984
33. Ranier National Bank (Seattle)	2,492
34. American National Bank and Trust Company (Chicago)	1,488
35. City National Bank of Detroit	946

Note: Bank of Tokyo Trust Company and Republic National Bank of New York are to be excluded for our analysis because of their association with foreign banks, the Bank of Tokyo and the Banque pour le Developpement Commercial, Geneva, respectively. Philadelphia National Bank has no direct branch, although its Edge Act subsidiary does. Wells Fargo, rather than establishing a branch, set up instead a banking subsidiary based in London, Wells Fargo, Ltd.; PNB and Wells Fargo can for practical purposes be included among commercial banks with U.K. branches.

Table 2-3. American Banks with London Representative Offices

1. Central National Bank of Cleveland*
2. Commerce Union Bank of Nashville
3. Fiduciary Trust Company of New York
4. First National Bank of Atlanta
5. First Union National Bank of North Carolina
6. Hartford National Bank and Trust
7. Houston Citizens Bank and Trust*
8. Indiana National Bank
9. International Bank (Washington, D.C.)
10. Lasalle National Bank (Chicago)
11. Manufacturers National Bank of Detroit
12. Maryland National Bank
13. Midatlantic National Bank (Newark)
14. National City Bank of Cleveland
15. Northwestern National Bank of Minneapolis*
16. South East Bancorporation of Florida
17. State Street Bank and Trust Company (Boston)
18. Trust Company of Georgia
19. Union Bank of California
20. Union Commerce Bank (Cleveland)

*Closed in 1975.

some other London financial institution. But because representative offices do not conduct a "banking business" in the true sense, their impact on the British banking system is only peripheral. The staff at a representative office in London usually varies from 2 to 5 employees, so that the amount of business transacted (mainly of an advisory nature) must necessarily be limited.

The branching movement peaked in 1968, but the movement to establish subsidiaries and affiliates may only be beginning. It provides new opportunities for diversification for banks already in England. These subsidiaries and affiliates take the form of "merchant banks,"[2] multibank consortia, leasing, factoring and consumer finance companies, and a host of others.

Most banks have set up their newer merchant bank arms to take over the longer term business formerly carried out by the branches. Some specialties claimed by these banks are:

acceptance credits
eurobond underwriting
eurocurrency finance

syndicated operations
take-over and merger advice
property and shipping finance
investment management
equipment financing

Of course, not all merchant banks offer all of these services, nor are they limited by the above list. The merchant bank can itself have subsidiaries for specialties such as leasing. The crux of the operation, however, lies in the fact that commercial banks are prohibited from underwriting corporate securities in the United States. With a merchant bank subsidiary, an American commercial bank can obtain this facility at the international level, as long as the securities are not sold in the United States. One disadvantage of a subsidiary compared to a branch is that the branch has the full capital backing of its parent and is thus capable of extending larger loans than is the subsidiary.[3]

The banks which have a majority share in a London banking subsidiary are:

1. Bank of America-Bank of America International.[4]
2. First National City Bank-Citicorp International Bank Ltd.
3. Chase Manhattan Bank-Chase Manhattan Ltd.
4. Manufacturers Hanover Trust Company-Manufacturers Hanover Ltd.
5. Bankers Trust Company-Bankers Trust International Ltd.
6. Continental Illinois Bank and Trust Company of Chicago-Continental Illinois Ltd.
7. First National Bank of Chicago-First National Ltd.
8. Wells Fargo Bank-Wells Fargo Ltd.
9. Marine Midland Bank-International Marine Banking Company Ltd.
10. First National Bank of Boston-First National Boston Ltd.
11. First National Bank in Dallas-First International Bancshares Ltd.

The names, of course, reveal the character of the banks in this group. All but one rank among the fifteen largest banks in the United States. Each has more than $5 billion in assets. Wells Fargo is the only one among them without a London branch, thus its banking subsidiary functions as its local branch as well. Excluding Wells Fargo and First National Bank in Dallas, all of the banks had a London presence by 1964.

Manufacturers Hanover was the first to establish a merchant bank subsidiary in 1968.[5] This movement, therefore, is relatively recent and still somewhat limited. Staffs are fairly small at these merchant banks, the largest being about 60 at the end of 1972, and 110 at the end of 1973. They are considerably smaller than their British counterparts. Growth, however, is likely. In an interview with *The Banker* in 1971, Sir Kenneth Keith, chairman of Hill, Samuel at the time, named the American banks as the most serious banking rivals in Britain. He said, "Obviously, international banking is now a highly competitive business. The big internationally-minded American banks are probably our main competitors, and I suspect the other merchant banks would say the same."[6]

Most of the American merchant banks are wholly owned by the parent banks, or holding company.[7] All were established *de novo* except Bankers Trust International, which was formed after Bankers Trust bought into Rodo International.

Aside from majority-owned merchant banks, there are several merchant banks owned in part by American banks. Some of these have engaged in lending to British secondary banks involved in the property market (Texas Commerce, First Maryland) while others have stronger connections. Morgan Guaranty, for instance, owns about one-third of Morgan Grenfell, an important British merchant bank. Citibank has a strong interest in William Brandt's Sons and Company, Ltd. (It owns 40% of National and Grindlays Bank which in turn owns Brandt's.) The banks with merchant bank affiliates are:[8]

Texas Commerce National Bank-35 percent in Burston and Texas Commerce Bank Ltd. (formerly London Burston Howard de Walden Merchant Bank).

First National Bank of Maryland-25 percent in First Maryland Ltd. (formerly Heller and Company).

Philadelphia National Bank-8 percent in Arbuthnot Latham.

Fidelity Bank-10 percent in Henry Ansbacher.

Wachovia Bank and Trust Company, N.A.-10 percent in Henry Ansbacher.

Morgan Guaranty Trust Company-32 percent in Morgan Grenfell and Co., Ltd.

Multibank consortia are jointly owned banks similar in function to the new merchant banks.[9] In the case of American participation in consortia, the tendency is for the smaller banks to join together in such groupings while larger banks more often choose to go it alone by setting up their own independent merchant banks. The exceptions to this rule are Chase Manhattan and Bank of America. Chase Manhattan belongs to a consortium, the Orion Bank, while Bank of America also participates in a consortium of European, Japanese, and Canadian banks with subsidiaries in various countries. Both banks, however, also own their own merchant bank subsidiaries. Most other American consortium members are the smaller American banks which cannot afford subsidiaries—in many cases they cannot afford their own London branches.

At the end of 1975, there were twelve multinational consortia based in London with at least one American member. In addition, Allied Bank International is a New York-based consortium which maintains a London branch. There was virtually no American participation in consortia before 1967, although First National City Bank claims to have started the ball rolling when it bought into M. Samuel (now Hill, Samuel).[10] Table 2-4 displays the thirteen consortia with United States members based in London, or with a London branch and American members.

The table shows that more American banks have London access through consortium membership than through branch expansion. Admittedly, the advantages of having a branch are lost, but consider-

Table 2-4. London Consortia with U.S. Members (1975)

Bank	*No. of American Participants*
Allied Bank International (New York)	18
Atlantic International Bank	2
Brown Harriman and International Banks	3
International Commercial Bank	2
International Energy Bank	1
Iran Overseas Investment Bank	2
London Interstate Bank	5
The Orion Group	1
Rothschild Intercontinental Banks*	3
Saudi International Bank	1
United International Bank	1
Western American Bank	3
Wobaco Investments**	1
	43

*Rothschild sold this consortium to American Express International in 1975.

**Wobaco, a Bank of America affiliate, is a subsidiary of a Luxembourg consortium, the World Banking Corporation.

ing the costs of a London branch, smaller branches can profit from such minority participation.

Most other subsidiaries and affiliates in Britain are owned by big banks in addition to their branches or merchant banks. This is true for the fields of factoring, leasing consumer finance, and other specialized financial activities. The banks in the factoring field thus far are:

Bankers Trust Company	Bankers Trust Factors Ltd.
Bank of America	BankAmerica Finance (Factors) (A)
	Bank of America-William Glyns Factors (A)
Continental Illinois National Bank and Trust Company	H & H Factors (A)
First National Bank of Boston	International Factors, Ltd. (A)
First National City Bank	Midland-Citibank Factors (A)[11]
Philadelphia National Bank	Arbuthnot Factors (A)

The banks directly involved in leasing subsidiaries and affiliates are:

Chase Manhattan Bank	Equipment Leasing Company Ltd.
First National Bank of Chicago	First Chicago Leasing International Inc.
First National City Bank	Citicorp Leasing International
Marine Midland Bank	IMB Ltd.
Chemical Bank	Chemco Financial Services Ltd.
North Carolina National Bank	Carolina Leasing Ltd.

Citicorp Leasing is now expanding into Birmingham. Of course, as mentioned above, other banks engage in leasing without a special subsidiary for the purpose.

The banks now involved in consumer finance are:

Bank of America	Bank of America Finance
First National City Bank	Citibank Financial Trust Ltd.
Morgan Guaranty Trust Company	HFC Trust Ltd. (in affiliation with Household Finance Company)
Bankers Trust Company	Kinghurst Financial Trust
Philadelphia National Bank	Philadelphia Credit Holdings Ltd.[12]

Imagination places practically the only limit on the variety of financial subsidiaries American banks can incorporate in Britain. Those above represent the most important, but others include international banks, investment companies, trust companies, insurance and mutual funds (or unit trust companies) companies, and more. (See Table 2-5.)

Table 2-5. Other British Affiliates of American Banks

Bank	*Subsidiary or Affiliate (A)*
Bankers Trust Company	Kinghurst Securities (A) Cybernetics International
Bank of America	European Brazilian Bank Ltd. (A)
Chase Manhattan Bank	Standard and Chartered Bank (A)* International Investment Corporation of Yugoslavia (A)
Crocker National Bank	Standard Industrial Trust
First National Bank of Chicago	Commercial Bank of Wales Ltd.
First National City Bank	Grindlays Bank Ltd. (A) National City Trust Citicorp International Capital Ltd. Computer Projects Ltd.
Girard Bank	Penn Investments (London) Ltd. Girard Financial and Investment Ltd. Penn Computer Services Ltd. Penn Sharp Associates Ltd.
Manufacturers Hanover Trust Co.	Anglo-Romanian Bank (A) Commercial Export Credit Company Ocean Acceptances (London) Ltd.
Mellon Bank	Lloyds and Bolsa International Bank (A)** First Boston (Europe) Ltd. (A)
Morgan Guaranty Trust Company	Morgan Guaranty Investment Services (UK) Ltd.
Northern Trust Company	Europension Ltd.

*Chase was directed to divest itself of its 14 percent share in this affiliate in 1973, because Standard and Chartered's United States operations in California effectively allowed Chase to operate in more than one state, in contravention of American banking law. See *The Times*, 5 July 1973, p. 19.

**Mellon agreed to sell its share in this affiliate because of the limits the connection placed on the expansion of Lloyds within the United States. Mellon had used this connection with Lloyds in establishing its London branch. Lloyds acted as a sort of sponsor. See Francis A. Lees, *International Banking and Finance* (New York: John Wiley and Sons, 1974), pp. 76-77.

Banks and holding companies without direct London branches also have varied subsidiaries such as:

Philadelphia National Bank	Philadelphia International Investment Corporation (branch in London)
Union Bank (California)	Unionamerica Management Co., (Ltd.)
	Unionamerica Insurance Company (branch in London)
	Anglo-Continental Investment Ltd. and Finance Company Ltd.
American Express Company[13]	Amex Bank, Ltd.
	American Express International Banking Corporation (branch)
	LB/AMEX (A)
	Bowmaker Leasing (A)
	Crusader Insurance (A)
	Amex International Ltd.
International Bank of Washington[14]	Moneycare Ltd.
	Security Trust Company of Birmingham Ltd. (A), (sold, 1975)
	Security Trust Investment Ltd. (A), (sold, 1975)
	Taurus Finance Ltd.
	Kliklok International Ltd.

The above lists describe the full scope of American commercial banks' activities in Britain. Practically all of the subsidiaries and affiliates have been established in the last five years, and ownership shifts are common. It is likely that more changes will come about as banks reassess their European strategies.

GENERAL CHARACTERISTICS

What can be said thus far about this sudden growth of American banks in the United Kingdom? Several patterns emerge from the record which can be illustrated here. First of all, size is the best predictor of whether a bank goes to Britain. Second, the size of the bank also seems to be closely related to the timing of its entrance into London banking. Thirdly, the size of the bank is also closely associated with the size of its organization and hence with the approximate extent of its business in Britain. Size, however, is not an absolute predictor. Market characteristics also seem to play a part in banks' decisions to move to London: banks which compete in the same U.S. banking markets tend to move abroad in tandem, competitors following the lead of the first banks from an area to open in London.

Size of Bank

If the best predictor of whether a bank will operate a British branch or subsidiary is size, a list of the largest U.S. banks should read the same way as a list of U.S. banks with British branches. This is in fact the case, with few exceptions. Of the thirty-five largest banking corporations in the U.S., only four lack branches or fully owned subsidiaries and only two (or 3 percent) have no offices or affiliates in Britain. One of these is a multibank holding company in which no individual member bank has more than $900 million in assets. The other is Cleveland Trust, which is, in this case, the exception for the rule. For the next fifteen largest banks in the U.S., the percentages change dramatically. While 73 percent of these do have some British interest, mostly in the form of minority participation, only three (or twenty percent) have branches.

Size has also been significant in determining when a bank has decided to move to Britain. Smaller banks have come later, most in the late sixties or early seventies.

Figure 2-1 shows the relationship between the size of the American banks which have built British branches and the timing of the banks' moves.

We can see that only the very largest banks in the United States maintained London branches before 1964. All of these early entrants have assets today of more than $15 billion. The relationship between the size of the entrant and the date of entry becomes less clear after 1967, but the relatively smaller assets of later entrants is evident. Geographical considerations account for many of the odd cases. For instance, larger banks which have entered Britain relatively late tend to be midwestern and western banks.

Figure 2-2 shows the pattern that emerges among banks with London branches. It shows expansion trends for the banks according to their assets. As a rule, banks with assets of more than $5 billion have over one hundred employees in their branches while the "smaller" banks usually have fifty or fewer. This is not terribly significant except in learning that the biggest banks must be a far more important factor than their smaller American competitors and that we will have to distinguish in the future among the various classes of banks in Britain. The dotted lines group the banks according to size and staff levels. In terms of London operations, and the place of American banks in the financial scene there, we can

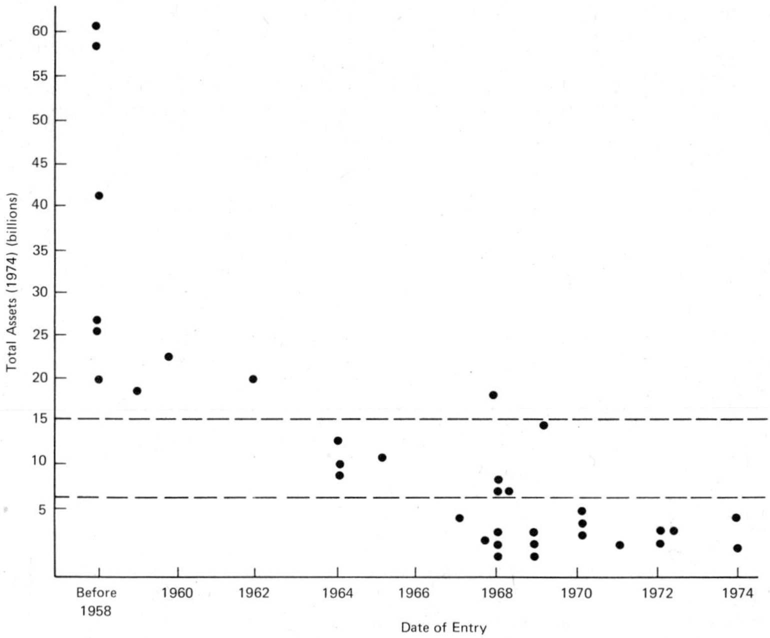

Figure 2-1. Assets and Date of Entry

actually separate three distinct groups: six banks with assets over $15 billion and London staff of more than 300, ten banks with between $8 and $15 billion, generally employing over 100 in London, and nineteen banks with less than $8 billion, and usually fewer than 50 employees in London. By looking once again at Figure 2-1, we can see that these largest banks practically all came to London before 1960, the middle group generally came between 1964 and 1968, while the smallest weakest London residents, tend to have arrived since 1969. Just as the patterns of entry and expansion for these three groups have been distinct, so we will see later that the factors making London offices seem like attractive investments for the different groups have also varied.

Market Charecteristics

Another aspect of the recent movement of American banks to Britain can be seen in aggregate figures, and that is a pattern of what has been called "follow-the-leader" investment in Britain. The nature of domestic American banking markets promotes such patterns. A classic tendency of oligopolists has been to do exactly what fellow

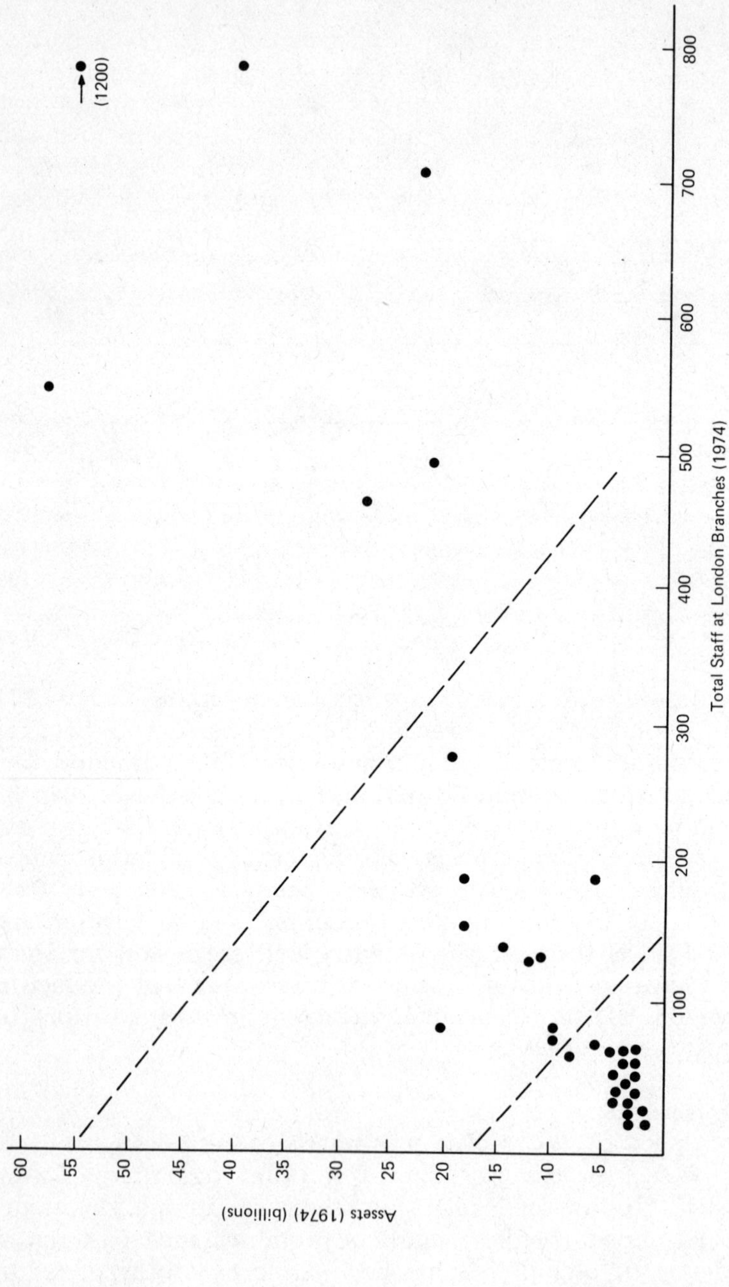

Source: Staff levels from *The Banker*.

Figure 2-2. Assets and Staff Levels

oligopolists within a market do. This behavior promotes market stability and discourages individual firms from such activities as price cutting or market poaching. The problem in banking is to decide the extent of a domestic market and the competitors in it. The American banking system is not one oligopoly but rather is divided into many separate oligopolies across the country. For our purposes, two kinds of market are relevant. The first could be called the national banking market. It is a market in which the largest U.S. firms are serviced for their national and international trade and investment needs. Only the biggest U.S. banks can answer these needs and the competition for the big clients crosses state and regional lines: Bank of America in California competes in this sense with First National Bank of Chicago and Chase Manhattan in New York. We have seen that all of the big banks in the "national" market have London offices and have had them for some time.

The less obvious follow-the-leader effects can be seen among regional banks. Below the national market are submarkets, or regional markets. Such regional markets center on the most important U.S. cities. The markets remain distinct because of the prohibition against nation-wide branching in this country. Again, the biggest banks in a regional market compete for the biggest customers in that market and while the number of banks may be large, only a few banks (usually 2-3) will be important enough to handle the big firms' financing needs. They act very much like oligopolists under these circumstances. Should one of these banks from a regional market go to Britain, or elsewhere, there is a high probability that other banks of comparable size will move as well.[15] It has been rare to see only one bank from a definable regional U.S. banking market in London: competitors, if they exist, seem to follow close behind. They are afraid that local customers will prefer a bank with a foreign branch; they are afraid of losing a market share; afraid of losing face.

We have already seen that with more than $3.5 billion in total assets, a bank will be likely to have a London branch, since in fact, 31 of the thirty-five banks in that category do have London branches. The figures reverse themselves quickly when the next fifteen largest U.S. banks are examined: only three of these fifteen banks have London branches. Moreover, only three of the remaining 14,000 or so American banks which are even smaller have such branches.

In explaining why a bank not ranked among the top thirty-five U.S. banks goes to London, we can turn to the follow-the-leader hypothesis. Once we are dealing with these smaller regional banks, characteristics of local American banking markets can produce expectations about which banks are most likely to move to Britain. If a follow-the-leader phenomenon works, then we would expect banks to be more likely to go to Britain if another bank from its home market has also done so. With rare exceptions, banks which have London interests have in excess of $1.4 billion in assets and this is close to the minimum level necessary for such a move. If we take the universe of 39 U.S. banks in the potential pool of entrants of medium size, that is, with between $1.4 billion and $3.5 billion in assets the follow-the-leader pattern should be evident. With certain exceptions, it is, as of December, 1975.

Fourteen of these banks have absolutely no London interests, of which nine originate in home markets where no local competitor has a London branch or representative office established before 1974. Conversely, fifteen of the 39 banks do have representative offices or branches and all but two face domestic competitors which also have some branches, affiliates or representative offices in London.[16] Even among banks with small holdings in London-based consortia, the pattern persists.

Is there any explanation for the few exceptions to the general tendency? A particularly aggressive management may make a difference for a smaller bank, and this seems to be the case with one of our exceptions, Hartford National Bank, which has both a representative office and an affiliated consortium. Hartford's aggressiveness was evidenced, for example, by its efforts to create an international consortium particularly designed to enable smaller banks to compete abroad.

What of the four banks which have *not* gone to Britain even though they are all (1) large enough and (2) in competition at home with international banks? These four share a peculiar characteristic. Although they are large enough to have gone to Britain in an objective sense, they are relatively weak in their domestic regional markets. Both National Bank of North America and a Newark bank, First National State Bank of New Jersey must compete against the New York giants for big firms' business—and have decided not to do so. Pittsburgh National Bank is less than one-third the size of its next largest competitor, Mellon Bank. Pittsburgh National chose to open a Paris branch instead, probably to avoid the more intense London competition. Similarly, Bank of the Southwest, Houston, is significantly smaller than its two Houston competitors, as well as two aggressive Dallas banks in Texas. Thus domestic competition acts as a spur to foreign expansion as long as a bank sees itself as a viable competitor in the foreign market.[17]

Finally one other exception remains to be accounted for: the

Southeast First National Bank (Miami). Southeast National is in an opposite position to that of the banks facing extremely powerful competitors at home. This Miami bank opened a London representative office without any domestic competitive spur. But it is the *only* Florida bank with resources of more than $500 million[18] and thus is the only bank capable of servicing local Florida business abroad.

These exceptions thus modify the follow-the-leader hypothesis by confirming the phenomenon generally but adding that another factor comes into play. A bank does react to moves by local competitors, but also takes into consideration its power relative to those competitors at home and abroad.

We have seen thus far how the scope of American banking in Britain has grown since 1958. All of the indicators illustrate this expansion—number of branches, representatives, subsidiaries and affiliates; volume of business; levels of employment; lines of business. We have also found a pattern of London entry which supports the proposition that domestic competition in the United States influences a bank's decision to go to London—some banks have reacted in a defensive way to the foreign expansion of their home competition.

These findings are useful in assessing the overall character of the movement of American banks in London. The following chapters will investigate the deeper causes which derive from the political and economic environment facing the banks in the sixties and seventies.

NOTES TO CHAPTER TWO

1. Today a bank must show total assets of more than $1 billion before it will get Bank England approval to open a British branch. The limit may now be about twice that amount, since this rule of thumb was unofficially announced by the Bank of England in 1972.

2. Thomson's *Dictionary of Banking* gives this explanation of merchant banks in England today:

> The great merchant banking houses of today have evolved from the merchants who, coming to this country in the early or middle years of the eighteenth century, built up their business by lending their names to bills financing particular transactions and by accepting such bills made the first-class bills freely discountable. In their estimate of credit-worthiness of their customers they were often helped by their local knowledge of their countries of origin. As their banking activities grew, they became specialists in the granting of long-term finance for projects abroad, and they added to their business of foreign acceptance the issue of foreign loans. In modern times their specialization in any particular class of financial business varies considerably and includes, in addition to normal banking transactions dealing in foreign exchange, the investment of funds and safe custody of securities for clients in this country and abroad, the carrying

out of merchanting transactions, the issue and placing of shares and debentures, the advising the management of take-over bids, and marine and other insurance business.

3. While Britain permits all forms of organization to foreign banks, many countries do not. As will be seen, tax considerations as well as local and domestic regulations also affect the decision on whether to open branches, agencies, subsidiaries, affiliates, or representative offices.

4. Merged in 1974 into its Luxembourg-based Banque Ameribas (Lux) to form Bank of America International (Lux), with participation of Banque de Paris et des Pays-Bas and the British merchant bank, Kleinworts.

5. With the participation of Rothschild Nominees (10%), Riunione Adriatica di Sicurta (10%), and Long-Term Credit Bank of Japan (5%).

6. "Merchant Banking: A Survey," *The Banker* 121 (December 1971): 1566.

7. The exceptions are Bank of America, Ltd., held 25 percent by Kleinwort, Benson, a large British merchant bank, and Manufacturers Hanover, Ltd., held 25 percent by a combination of banks as noted above.

8. First National City Bank formerly held about 10 percent of Hill, Samuel, but sold out in 1968 when its share fell to 8.1 percent after a take-over. See *The Banker* (November 1968): 1054. First National Bank of Maryland took a loss on its investment in its merchant bank—reported as over $2.2 million in the second quarter of 1974. The merchant bank, with connections in the property market, was affected by sharp declines in real estate values. See *The Washington Post*, 15 June 1974. Texas Commerce had similar problems. Texas Commerce announced it would buy the remaining 65 percent of Burston and Texas Commerce when the Burston Group got into financial difficulties in 1975. See *The Economist*, 8 February 1975. Similar problems faced First National City in 1975 when Brandt's got into trouble in the property market. Citibank announced it would increase its stake in Grindlay's in order to shore up the troubled financial group. (See *The Economist*, 20 September 1975).

9. Generally, consortia are banks with three or more members in which no one participant owns more than 50 percent.

10. See interview with W.B. Wriston, president, FNCB, in *The Banker*, May 1971, p. 476. That venture does not fit our definition of consortia, despite Citibank's usual claim to have done most things first. Today, Citibank is one of the least likely banks to join consortia, preferring instead its policy of independence except under special circumstances.

11. *The Times*, 8 March 1973, p. 19, announced that Midland Bank would buy out Citibank's share in this company. Citibank, of course, does factoring independently as well.

Most of the information for this section is originally derived from *Who Owns Whom: International Subsidiaries of U.S. Companies* (London: O.W. Roskill and Co., 1972). But because ownership changes are frequent, the entries have been checked as far as possible against reports in periodicals and newspapers, Annual reports and bank directories such as *Polks* and the *Bankers Almanac*. Most inconsistencies arose with respect to whether an institution is a subsidiary or affiliate. *Who Owns Whom* uses "affiliate" to describe ownership of 10 to 50 percent, while "subsidiary" means more than 50 percent ownership. This is a sound definition for most purposes (although control can certainly be maintained in many cases with less than 50 percent ownership) and is the one I have adhered to. Unfortunately, this definition is not universal, and companies have sometimes characterized their subsidiaries as affiliates or vice-versa.

12. It was announced in January, 1974 that the Philadelphia International Investment Corporation made an offer for control of Western Credit Holdings while Arbuthnot Latham would retain its 22 percent share. Western Credit was a Plymouth-based banking and finance company whose subsidiary, Western Trust and Savings is in the money shop business. (See *The Financial Times*, 10 October 1973, p. 33, and 10 January 1974, p. 19.) Western Credit thus became Philadelphia Credit when PNB took control.

13. In 1968, American Express established the American International Banking Corporation to carry out the banking portion of Amex' business. Although known principally as a dispenser of travellers' checks, American Express ranks as an important bank in London. American Express itself has a large source of funds from its travellers' checks. LB/AMEX is a joint subsidiary of American Express and Lazard Brothers which acts as an agent for its owners in their common syndicated medium-term lending. See *The Banker*, November 1971, p. 1445.

14. The International Bank of Washington is a District of Columbia holding company which has a variety of financial and industrial subsidiaries in the United States and abroad. It also has a London representative office. IB owns a 22.4 percent interest in a bank holding company, Financial General Bancshares. The Federal Reserve has determined that this holding constitutes effective control and would thus necessitate registration by IB as a banking holding company subject to federal regulation. IB has decided instead to sell. See William H. Jones, "D.C.'s Mini-Conglomerate," *The Washington Post*, 23 September 1973, p. G1; *Annual Report* (1975); *Wall Street Journal* 27 May 1976.

15. F.T. Knickerbocker has found similar patterns of investment by manufacturing firms. Where an industry is relatively concentrated, or oligopolistic, participants in the industry are more likely to follow the lead of their fellow competitors in foreign investment. See his *Oligopolistic Reaction and Multinational Enterprise* (Boston: Division of Research, Graduate School of Business Administration, Harvard University, 1973).

16. A Chi-Square test shows that such differences would occur by chance less than one percent of the time.

17. More recent events further confirm this tendency to follow the actions of close competitors only. Of the three banks which closed representative offices in 1975, this pattern emerged:

Houston Citizens Bank and Trust closed. It was the smallest American bank in London (assets less than $500 million). It is far smaller than the other Houston bank in London (assets over $4 billion).

Central National Bank of Cleveland closed. Close competitors do have London representatives, but the largest Cleveland bank has no London outlet, lessening the prestige value of the office.

Northwestern National Bank of Minnesota closed. With no very powerful lead bank owned by the holding company and no local competitors in London, the pressure to continue the office was probably slight.

18. Some holding companies have resources of over $1.4 billion, but no members of the holding companies individually possess such assets.

Chapter Three

Government Goals—Government Policies

The last chapter showed that American banks have used the Atlantic as a bridge instead of a barrier in the last fifteen years. Predisposed as we are to suspect that government action played a role, the obvious question arises: what role? What happened in the United States in the 1960s and 70s to provoke the mass exodus of banks; what was London's attraction for the emigrants? Did the movement of American banks to Britain take place because of, or in spite of, the policies of the American and British governments?

At the outset, it was conceded that individual banks perceive their own actions in terms of microeconomic factors, seeking to maximize their profits, revenues, market power, and so on. The record will show, however, that government actions in both Britain and the United States affected the outlook of the banks to such a degree that establishing a British outlet became a logical choice for any bank pursuing the maximization of those values. For the most part, American government policies created problems for the banks at home, forcing them to look abroad. British government policies, on the other hand, were such that Britain appeared to be the best place to go, at least for any bank wealthy enough to do so.

Whatever their actual policies, both the American and British governments shared the view in the 1960s that the development of American banking in Britain was a healthy thing. Either government could have short-circuited the banks' attempts to expand in London, but neither made an attempt to do so. The growth of American banking in Britain was in fact congruent with the goals of both countries. We shall not find, however, that the American government pursued a specific policy to encourage its banks to go to Britain. But policies in other sectors did promote this result, and the fact that the result was, on the whole, perceived as "good" meant that no counterpolicies would be initiated. A review of British actions will, in contrast, reveal explicit promotion of American banking in the U.K., since such action seemed directly to support important aspects of national policy.

THE HEAVY WEIGHT OF BRITISH HISTORY

In the years since 1964, Britain has seen government shifts from Labour (1964-70) to Conservative (1970-74) and back to Labour again in 1974. The Bank of England, an important and somewhat independent power, also underwent several changes of leadership. While overall policy did vary with power changes in Britain, the aims of banking policy remained remarkably stable. There was virtual unanimity throughout the period that the United Kingdom should encourage the development of London as an international financial center, welcome American investment in Britain, and retain good relations with the United States in general.

That a Labour prime minister should come to the same conclusion as a Tory leader or a Bank of England governor may come as a surprise to those who read Labour party manifestos, but in many ways, Harold Wilson and Edward Heath read their options in identical terms when it came to matters of high finance. As they saw it, the City of London, the financial center, supplied jobs and foreign exchange income to Britain and the presence of American banks enhanced its ability to do both. In fact, to these leaders, the City regrettably appeared to be the only dynamic sector of the British economy—to limit it was ridiculous; to bolster it, sensible. The Tories found such perspectives not only reasonable but also attractive. Labour found them at best reasonable but also distasteful. The historical experience in Britain shows how these perspectives evolved.

How did the two parties come to a common position? The weight of history hangs over all British governments. The present they deal with is loaded with the past. England grew up around the City of London so that the financial center became an integral part of her culture, her politics, and her interest. The policies of British governments toward the City in the 1960s were a continuation of past policies, and amounted to natural efforts to preserve what already existed.

The whole complex of financial activity is entwined with Britain's industrial and political development in the nineteenth century. The growth of industry, of empire, of trade, finance and class was a coordinated whole in the last century to which the political system gradually adapted itself. Whereas once the great landed and aristocratic classes could be seen as politically separate from the rising mercantile and bourgeois classes, the evolution of Britain tended in the 1800s to produce a sort of consensual system with domination by commercial interests.

The aristocratic and entrepreneurial elites came closer to each other in their promotion of the nation as a world power based on its competitive edge in both military and economic arenas. The British navy and the pound sterling dominated the world. This happy conjuncture resulted in a certain coherence such that one was engaged in mutually supportive activities whether one worked as an investment banker, a military man, factory worker, or a diplomat at the foreign office.[1] Along with the increasing complexity of British industry and the relative decline of British agriculture particularly after 1846, of course, the new class of politically important urban workers expanded. The working classes' interests created a potential social split in that high employment was their first priority.[2] High employment could at times conflict with policies designed to maintain the value of sterling, the mainstay of finance. In the meantime, a second potential split between domestic industry and international finance developed. New elements claimed that the world-wide tentacles of the nation only drained resources from the home country.[3] The First World War created the conditions which would make these potential conflicts real.

The economic decline of the 1920s and 1930s crystalized the lines of opposition in Britain. Domestic deflation in the service of sterling came to be seen by Labour as a *class* policy, one which benefited only the elites while depriving home industry of jobs and income. The young Labour Party in these years had few solutions to the economic problem: it rejected more radical alternatives as offered by a Keynes or even a Mosely.[4] Basically without power after the defection of McDonald in 1931, the Labour Party and the unions took up a position of resentment and opposition to the status quo. This opposition found its practical application in general dislike and distrust of the City and its financial interests.[5] Meanwhile, the Conservative Party provided the home of those City elites, even though the Tories still attracted men imbued with Disraelean sensibilities and somewhat progressive, if paternal, tendencies.

The Labour Party, despite its avowed purpose of redirecting the nation toward domestic, as opposed to international development, has not yet found a way to skirt the problem faced by Ramsey McDonald in 1931: how to fulfill socialist ideals without precipitating financial disaster. Collective effort within the framework of British politics would require acceptance of a policy by all societal groups, and important Conservative and City interests would not support a Labour abandonment of traditional financial principles, including principally the defense of London's international status. Just as McDonald found that he had to accede to the perceived necessity of wage cuts and deflation in 1931, so postwar Labour governments would find that their projects depended on the confidence of the financial elites.

The City existed in fact. Defection by City interests, particularly by the banks, could make governing impossible. This is, at least what Labour leaders believed. As the printer of a major international currency into the 1960s, Britain lacked the option of doing as it pleased internally because every attempt at expansion seemed to produce yet another crisis of the pound. The specter of sterling withdrawals has hung over the head of every government, Tory and Labour alike, since the First World War. Regardless of its historical aversion for international finance, therefore, the Labour Party has seen no choice but to preserve stability by guaranteeing a flow of income from the operations of the City through a policy of noninterference with the existing City structure. When the City has demanded an uncompromising defense of sterling, the Labour Party thought it had to be the defender. And when the City has argued for the maintenance of the City as a largely unregulated international financial center, Labour has put aside its preference for control.

The balance of payments has thus acted as the principle constraint on Labour Party policy. Labourites have engaged in symbolic action to prove their devotion to traditional socialist ideals—they nationalized the Bank of England, for instance, the symbol of City power independent of government control—but they have hardly ever tried to stand in the way when the City has made real demands.[6] Typically the City has had its way and Labour politicians, as in the thirties, have amounted to a Disraelean anomaly: Labour government, Tory policies.

City demands have evolved away from a strict defense of sterling since the 1967 devaluation. With the decline of the pound and the rise of the dollar, bankers in Britain perceived slowly that the important thing was to have trade and investment financed in London, regardless of whether sterling provided the financial vehicle. Since American banks in Britain contributed to the importance of London as a world dollar center, British bankers began in the 1960s to put more emphasis on changing laws to facilitate international banking there. Labour policy has in the end supported the goal of preserving and extending London and the City and by implication, welcoming the entrance of American banks in the "square mile." The Labour government, beyond defending sterling, served the financial institutions by changing laws which had limited the growth of the Eurodollár market in the 1960s. More recently, the Wilson government backed down in its attempts to tax foreigners' wages more heavily. In effect, Labour has only been able to exercise its distrust of the City through symbolic action, producing a gap between its words and deeds. Its first priority, to stay in power, seemed to necessitate financial policies in support of City institutions for which it felt little affection.

The Tories feel no such schizophrenia. The Conservative Party has taken a fairly consistent stand in support of British finance based mainly on an ideological belief in the invisible hand and on the very business and financial background of its membership. Prominent Conservatives from Disraeli to Edward Heath have stressed the Tory responsibility for the working class and the need to make capitalism "civilized" and to encourage home employment. Their emphasis nevertheless rests on free markets, noninterference, and support of the international character of the British economy. These perspectives find their application in the Conservatives' financial policy. Thus, at the same time that Heath's government abandoned the pound, they were in the process of overhauling the domestic banking system in such a way as to increase the role of foreign banks in it.

It has often been charged that the Conservatives have placed too much emphasis on the defense of sterling, but in fact, Tory policy has been in defense of trade and finance. Defense of sterling was only an instrumental goal in the service of international business. When the defense of sterling seemed necessary to the City, the pound was backed; but when the City found in the 1960s that it could survive quite well without a fixed pound, the Conservatives proved even more willing than their Labour counterparts to abandon a fixed parity.[7]

The City of London thus finds that it can call upon any British government to support it. As a uniquely successful sector, it holds an almost irreversible claim on its governors. If the environment for American banks in Britain has been attractive, it is because of this almost complete agreement, willing or unwilling, that the City depends on its open and international character and that Britain depends on the City.

AMERICA AND THE WORLD

While British governments have been eager hosts to American banks in the City of London, American governments have been accommodating parents, glad to see the children making their mark in the big world. But how can one assess the significance of American government support for the internationalization of banking and how can it be documented? To a large degree, the U.S. government encourages its multinationals today by means of nondecisions—that is to say, by refraining from action which would limit foreign expansion. Given the natural profit- and revenue-maximizing tendencies of business, international expansion follows naturally if environmental factors are sufficiently satisfactory.

It is nevertheless the case that decisions of the American government at crucial times in this century have contributed to the internationalization of American business and of American banking. As Chapter One showed, American policy directly facilitated foreign expansion by the banks in the years before the Second World War. In the postwar period, American policy has focused mainly on creating an optimal international structure for the outward movement of banks and business. Of course, the United States' overall power to determine the character and rules of the international system had been vastly expanded by the war itself.

Once having constructed a system to its liking, very little in the way of direct policy would be needed to foster the world-wide spread of American companies. As for the banks, they could be expected to follow their customers in the way that British banks had long ago followed in the tracks of the British investor and the British army. As in the British case, all administrations have shared common views about the gains from international business. Again as in the British case, both government and business enjoyed a convergence of views in this respect. Even when the American government would be faced with hard choices in later years, it would always try to devise solutions which would leave intact the freedom of American business to grow abroad.

The United States' almost romantic attachment to this freedom of investment was a devotion which developed out of past experience. In the twenties, America had worked in various ways to encourage international business and had tried to foster the use of the dollar in international trade. Many of these efforts were piecemeal, however, and most came to naught with the 1929 crash. But the "lessons of the thirties" proved significant in a redirection of American foreign economic policy. The words "beggar my neighbor" became a code word for what the United States thought was wrong with the prewar system. It was no longer sufficient for *one* country to allow open exchange and trade. Rather the whole world should be convinced that Ricardo was right: every country's welfare would increase if every country opened its door to trade and capital flows.[8] Not only would economic welfare increase but by some magical process, peace would result. America's policy might be interpreted as idealistic—a world system benefiting all—or as self-interest, but it is closer to the truth to say that the two points of view were taken to be synonymous.

It can be argued at the least that the policy was not a simplistic effort to support American business abroad although that was indeed the outcome. The effort was, however, purposeful, intended to create a proper world environment for increasing economic contact and realizing the expected benefits of interdependence. It is a clear example of one part of our original descriptive model: governments determine the environment in which businesses function. Business decisions, trade, and capital flows respond to market forces—but governments must allow those forces to work. Normally, such government action might be in the nondecision arena, but given the closure of the thirties, positive policy was necessary to free up the markets and destroy the barriers.

The United States started in 1934 with the Reciprocal Trade Agreements Act. The Tri-partite Agreement of 1936 was a step toward currency stabilization, then thought necessary for the growth of trade. Multiple efforts were made during the Second World War to dismantle the British imperial system of preferences, create a stable monetary system in the IMF, lower tariffs through an International Trade Organization (realized in the GATT) and later, to encourage freer capital movements through the OECD Code on the Liberalization of Capital Movements. In addition, it can be inferred from the historical record that the U.S. efforts to make the dollar the world's principal reserve currency were carried out in the knowledge that American business, trade, and finance would benefit.[9] Had not the U.S. been frustrated in the 1920s by the limits on American trade finance resulting from continued use of sterling? The United States also worked to dismantle exchange controls, a process completed by the late 1950s in Europe. The Roosevelt, Truman, and Eisenhower administrations all worked in the same direction, not so much because these presidents understood what they were doing, but more because the entire bureaucratic, business, and academic world had become convinced of the rightness of the policy.

Of course, all of this was relatively easy in the forties and fifties. U.S. power was so unquestioned and the U.S. economy so dominant and successful that no challenges from outside really existed in the noncommunist world and no internal forces had reason to oppose the policy. Events seemed to confirm the conviction that an open economic world produced benefits for all participants. The scarcity of the dollar in the fifties created a dreamlike situation for the U.S. balance of payments in that capital outflows were consistent with international monetary needs. American foreign investment in Western Europe seemed to benefit the other parties as well. It was only in the 1960s, in fact, that American foreign economic policy became more complex. It is in the 1960s that we see conflicts, particularly with respect to balance of payments problems. There was no longer a harmonious congruence among the various goals of American policy. Capital outflows, for instance in the form of direct investment abroad, began to appear inconsistent with the perceived goal of defending the dollar.

The record of the 1960s, under the Kennedy, Johnson, and Nixon administrations gives a clearer insight into the priorities of the American government. It was one thing to *allow* direct foreign investment at a time when capital outflows produced only positive effects; it was quite another to protect the ability of American companies to invest abroad when such a policy was problematical. It was one thing to *allow* American banks to expand abroad when their activities were relatively insignificant; it has been quite another to permit such expansion when their business abroad affected domestic monetary control and international stability.

Various threads of U.S. policy can be interwoven to indicate the importance of foreign business expansion among American priorities in the 1960s. Other goals, of course, were of higher rank: domestic growth, national defense, world prestige among the most important. Defense of the dollar might have been seen as an instrumental goal of primary importance. Within these policy parameters, however, the American government did always attempt to apply policies which would in no way limit foreign business expansion. And it may be no accident that balance of payments policies actually encouraged foreign investment by American banks. Actions by the Kennedy, Johnson, and Nixon administrations support this view.

President Kennedy's dominant interest appeared to be in the area of stimulating domestic growth which would presumably "trickle down" and benefit everyone.[10] His efforts in this direction were two-pronged in that he promoted a tax cut and low interest rates. Like it or not, however, Kennedy was also faced with a balance of payments problem which seemed to call for higher interest rates to increase capital inflows. An alternative might have been some form of control of American foreign investments to decrease capital outflows.[11] The solutions attempted illustrate the Administration's priorities. First, American capital outflows for direct investment were *not* limited by the interest equalization tax, a tax which only affected foreigners' borrowings from the U.S. for spending abroad. Second, domestic long-term interest rates were kept as low as possible (to promote domestic investment) while allowing short term rates to rise through so-called "Operation Twist." Third, various attempts were made to discourage spending abroad by tourists, to devise better cooperative crisis arrangements among central banks, to promote exports, and to hold down domestic wages and prices. Finally, official foreign dollar holders were provided with a preferential investment yielding a higher, subsidized rate so that foreign countries would continue to hold dollars as reserves rather than cash them at Fort Knox. Thus while domestic prosperity was Kennedy's first priority, his Administration preferred a host of alternatives to limiting American business expansion abroad.[12]

President Johnson faced a more difficult situation than his predecessor because he wanted to do more: spend in Vietnam, spend on the Great Society, avoid higher taxes, and also follow Kennedy's lead in keeping interest rates low and the dollar at par.[13] Kennedy's arsenal of technical adjustments was insufficient to achieve all of these goals: for the first time American direct foreign investment from the U.S. was limited, having been bumped down a few rungs on the ladder of priorities. L.B.J. placed voluntary controls on foreign investment in 1965 and made them mandatory in 1968. American banks' lending to foreigners was also limited through the 1965 Voluntary Foreign Credit Restraint Program.[14] It is interesting to note, however, that the controls on direct investment and foreign credits had little or no effect on American business growth abroad. It seemed to have increased it instead in the case of banks because many banks moved their foreign operations abroad where limits did not apply. American investors, meanwhile, found they could finance their foreign operations by borrowing in the Eurodollar market based in London. New York's power as international lender was curbed pending dollar recovery.

Can we say that the government knew in 1965 that its controls on foreign investment and on bank lending to foreigners would not impinge on foreign investment? Certainly, some businessmen feared that they would be constrained when the 1965 rules were proposed. Cairncross argues that foreign investment controls were made possible by the existence of foreign finance potential. More importantly, Secretary of the Treasury Fowler stated explicitly in May 1965 that the controls would not "militate in any substantial way against the upsweep of investment income over the long-term future."[15] It should also be noted that the controls of 1965 were not mandatory.

That they were voluntary instead points to a certain tentativeness on the part of the government, an unwillingness to make things too difficult, and a feeling that at least the U.S. should see what would happen. The government would have the option of flexibility in the administration of the controls, just because they were voluntary.[16]

In fact, the program pleased the government since both banks and business found they could get along well under it. By the time the controls were made mandatory in 1968, it had become obvious that Eurodollar financing was an adequate substitute for domestic credits for foreign use and that the banks were surviving, even flourishing, by transferring their foreign business to branches and subsidiaries abroad. One problem did develop: foreign branches could lend dollars to their parents in periods of tight money, thus making the control of credit more difficult for U.S. monetary authorities. The Johnson administration took no action on this problem.

The case of the Johnson administration thus lends further support to the argument that the U.S. government does whatever it can to facilitate foreign expansion by American business and, in pursuing other goals, it seeks to limit that expansion as little as possible.

The Nixon administration, not surprisingly, also supported business expansion abroad. Along with his political supporters from the business world, Nixon placed the freedom to invest even higher than did his Democratic predecessors. Trumpeting the traditional Republican laissez faire tune, Nixon had promised in his 1968 campaign to remove capital controls and did make some early moves to ease them a bit. But Nixon shared at least one goal with Johnson—the pursuit of the war in Vietnam. The large government expenditures that the war required made it difficult to meet subsidiary goals. Given the volatility of world capital markets between 1969 and 1973, a removal of capital controls might have invited a concerted and uncontrollable attack on the dollar as speculators would judge that the U.S. was unwilling to defend it.

By the end of 1973, conditions had changed so much that the removal of capital controls began to be consistent with other U.S. goals. Nixon could now finally fulfill his earlier promise. What had changed? First of all, the 1973 transition to a system of floating exchange rates took much of the pressure off the dollar so that capital flight was not expected. The 1973 oil price rises had in fact strengthened the prospects for the dollar, making it once again valuable to hold. Secondly, it was thought that the government actually *wanted* to allow the rate for the dollar to fall—banking authorities were reported to want to take "some of the wind out of the dollar."[17] Removal of capital controls might encourage some movement out of the dollar.

A third reason why the Nixon administration could find the removal of capital controls a good prospect is more complex and speculative. Up to that time, it had been felt that the capital controls had functioned relatively well. That they had resulted in the growth of American banking abroad could be considered as a lucky positive outcome. Yet there was something about the concentration of international finance in London which irritated those who thought New York should not be deprived of her rightful place at the center. It was all very well that American banks had developed international connections, but the time had come to remove some of New York's handicaps. There is no statement to this effect by the American government, but it was obvious to anyone who understood international finance that American capital controls had in effect been free protection for London. The British newspapers were filled with fears for London's future on the announcement that capital controls would end. Andrew Brimmer of the Federal Reserve had assuaged some of these fears in a speech in London predicting that while New York would increase its international lending, London would keep much of its Eurodollar business anyway.

The Nixon administration, along with the Ford administration which proved to follow the same policies, showed in other ways its desire to restore the United States as an international financial center. Besides removing capital controls, proposals have been made to eliminate the American withholding tax on interest paid to foreigners, to reform the treatment of foreign banks operating in the United States, and even to allow special treatment of foreign bank deposits in the United States in a way which would erase the difference between New York deposits and Eurodollar deposits. The law regulating foreign banks met initial success in Congress, and future administrations may be expected to continue to move in the direction of liberalizing the regulation of international finance in the United States.

While American administrations have done what they could to foster international business and banking by Americans, this is not to say that they have followed such a policy in a vacuum. The Nixon administration, for instance, seemed to approve of the growing number of foreign branches of American banks, but not to the extent that these branches interfered with domestic monetary policy, with domestic political support or with foreign policy objectives. In 1969, for instance, the money flows between foreign branches and American parent banks became disruptive. As will be seen in Chapter Five, action to limit these flows was quickly taken. This control was consistent with the Republicans' early attempts to follow monetarist principles of limited domestic monetary expansion.[18] Again, however, no attempts were made to curtail American banking or business expansion abroad, even in the face of growing labor disenchantment with international business.[19] In the meantime, Nixon's actions on the international monetary front tended to work to the advantage of the dollar as an international currency, buoying up the postwar structure which had served both business and government so well.

What does this review reveal about the attitudes of the American and British governments toward the movement of American banks to Britain? Accepting tentatively that their actions regarding capital flows and banking regulations made it rational for American banks to go to Britain (as will be shown more fully below), we can say first that government policy must be deemed as crucial to the movement. The environment was indeed shaped by the governments, either directly or indirectly.

In the British case, direct and conscious influence is evident. Judging by actions rather than words, we can conclude that both Labour and Tory governments pursued an explicit policy of encouraging foreign bank entry, the most important component of which was American.

In the American case, less can be said definitively. Certainly, American regulatory actions on capital flows induced the banks to open up shop abroad—but the evidence indicates that these policies were conceived with different ends in mind. But the fact that the movement was in no way obstructed reveals a passive acceptance or approval of the movement. This relatively passive approval parallels general U.S. policy toward multinational enterprise, a stance which has in fact had a positive effect on the multinational spread of American business.

Big powers, of course, need not intervene daily to achieve their goals. After the First World War, it took some initiative to get American businessmen to go abroad—but by 1945 all that was needed was a safe and open system, a structure congenial to world-wide operations. The United States secured that system and could then sit back and let events take their course. Some action was necessary to maintain the dollar as the central currency and, after some delay during the turbulent 1960s, this was achieved. Thus, the structure was set, and it was favorable. The British and American government had worked to make it so.

NOTES TO CHAPTER THREE

1. E.J. Hobsbawm, *Industry and Empire* (New York: Random House, 1968), p. 108; Albert H. Imlah, *Economic Elements in Pax Britannica* (Cambridge: Harvard University Press, 1958), pp. 156-193; Asa Briggs, *Victorian People* (Chicago: University of Chicago Press, 1970), p. 200.

2. The Labour movement in Britain grew at the end of the century perhaps spurred by less favorable economic conditions for the country. See Bernard Semmel, *Imperialism and Social Reform* (Cambridge: Harvard University Press, 1960); E.J. Hobsbawm (ed.), *Labour's Turning Point* (Cranbury: Associated University Presses, 1974), p. 19; Robert Gilpin, *U.S. Power and the Multinational Corporation* (New York: Basic Books, 1975), p. 62.

3. The split between industry and finance produced exponents of protectionism for British industry, in opposition to what the City saw as its interest in free trade. See Julian Amery, *Joseph Chamberlain and the Tariff Reform Campaign* (London: Macmillan, 1969), v. 5, pp. 284-317; Hobsbawm, *Industry*, pp. 201-206.

Other opponents of City finance focused on the effect of foreign investment on domestic investment. These included Chamberlain, as well as MacKinder, Hobson and others. See J.A. Hobson, *Imperialism: A Study* (London: Secker and Warburg, 1902) and Hobson, *An Economic Interpretation of Investment* (London: Financial Review of Reviews, 1911), p. 79.

The anti-foreign investment argument has been disputed by Peter Mathias (*The First Industrial Nation* (London: Methuen and Co., 1969), pp. 330-34); also by Charles Kindleberger, *Economic Growth in France and Britain: 1851-1950* (New York: Simon and Schuster, 1969), pp. 61-67. But while the system may have made economic sense in Mathias' and Kindleberger's analyses, a national system dependent on foreign investment and stable capital flows was undoubtedly less resilient in the face of external dislocations such as the First and Second World Wars.

4. Robert Skidelsky argues forcefully that Labour's lack of an alternative policy resulted from its commitment to a "nebulous socialism"—a point of view which precluded acceptance of a policy involving interventionist capitalism. See his *Politicians and the Slump* (London: Macmillan, 1967), p. xii.

5. The City of London supported the maintenance of sterling at its prewar parity, to which it had returned in 1925. The reason this policy had class implications was that it was perceived that wage cuts would be necessary to maintain that level. To get a loan in New York, Labour Prime Minister MacDonald accepted a demand for benefit cuts, precipitating mass resignations by his cabinet. The party split over the issue—but it should be emphasized that Labour did not itself have an alternative monetary policy at any time up to that point. See D.E. Moggridge, *The Return to Gold 1925* (Cambridge: Cambridge University Press, 1969); on Labour resentment, see Hugh Dalton, *Call Back Yesterday* (London: Frederick Muller, 1953), p. 276; L. MacNeill Weir (M.P.) *The Tragedy of Ramsay MacDonald* (London: Secker and Warburg, 1938), p. 565.

6. Examples of the Labour problem abound in the 1960s under Prime Minister Wilson. His policies in support of the City will be examined further below. These include most importantly his defense of the pound and legal changes during his tenure which facilitated the development of the Eurodollar in London. See his memoirs, *The Labour Government 1964-1970: A Personal Record* (London: Wiedenfield and Nicolson, 1971); also William Davis, *Three Years Hard Labour* (Boston: Houghton Mifflin, 1970); Henry Brandon, *In the Red: The Struggle for Sterling* (London: Andre Deutsch, 1966). For interesting,

if biased views, George Brown, *In My Way* (London: Victor Gollancz, 1971); Cecil King, *The Cecil King Diary: 1965-70* (London: Cape, 1972).

7. The change of heart in Conservative policy on sterling was first made obvious in Chancellor of the Exchequer Anthony Barber's Budget message of 21 March 1972 when he said: "It is neither necessary nor desirable to distort domestic economies in order to maintain unrealistic exchange rates, whether they are too high or too low. Certainly in the modern world, I do not believe there is any need for this country, or any other to be frustrated on this score in its determination to sustain sound economic growth."

8. The American devotion to free trade paralleled British ideas from the nineteenth century, especially those of Ricardo (*On the Principles of Political Economy and Taxation*), Richard Cobden, and John Bright. On this development in America, particularly the influence of Secretary of State Cordell Hull, see Arthur M. Schlesinger, Jr., *The Coming of the New Deal* (Boston: Houghton Mifflin, 1958), pp. 253-260; Richard N. Gardner, *Sterling-Dollar Diplomacy*, (Oxford: Clarendon Press, 1956), pp. 12-23; Cordell Hull, *Memoirs* (New York: Macmillan, 1948), v. 1, p. 81; John Evans, *The Kennedy Round in American Trade Policy* (Cambridge: Harvard University Press, 1971).

9. The development of American policy toward the postwar monetary system was, in its specifics, a one-man show conducted by Harry Dexter White in the Treasury. The general principle of the New Dealers, including Roosevelt, Secretary of the Treasury Morganthau and White was (in Morganthau's later words to Truman) to "move the financial center of the world from London and Wall Street to the United States Treasury." (Quoted in David Rees, *Harry Dexter White: A Study in Paradox* (New York: Coward McCann and Geoghegan, 1973), p. 138). The compiler of Morganthau's diaries said, "White sought openly, with the Secretary's approval, to make the dollar the dominant currency in the postwar world." See *From the Morganthau Diaries* (John Morton Blum, ed.) (Boston: Houghton Mifflin, 1967) v. 3, p. 123.

10. See Arthur M. Schlesinger, Jr., *1000 Days* (Boston: Houghton Mifflin, 1965), p. 620; p. 624. Also, Kennedy's speech to Congress of 6 February 1961, "The Balance of Payments and Gold Outflow from the United States," in Richard P. Stebbins and Elain P. Adam, (eds.), *Documents on American Foreign Relations* (New York: Council on Foreign Relations, Harper and Bros., 1962), p. 26.

11. Theodore Sorensen (*Kennedy* (New York: Harper & Row, 1965), p. 409) maintains that Kennedy himself would have felt little compunction over decreased foreign investment, but that his advisers considered it out of the question to control direct foreign investment. Kennedy's speeches always made the traditional point that the U.S. was committed to free flows of capital. See "The Balance of Payments: Message of President Kennedy to the Congress," 18 July 1963, *Department of State Bulletin*, 12 August 1963.

12. Of course, this choice can be interpreted as rational and not ideological. There is evidence that direct investment produces net positive effects on the balance of payments. Also, the Kennedy Administration saw the balance of payments problem as a temporary one, so that drastic measures were not necessary to solve this short-term imbalance.

13. Johnson's memoirs, *The Vantage Point* (New York: Holt, Rinehart and Winston, 1971), reveal these priorities clearly just in the amount of space accorded to each.

14. It could be argued that Johnson cared little for the traditional concerns of foreign investors anyway. With his background, he felt freer to ignore their lobby. Kennedy had never called himself a populist—LBJ had.

15. Sir Alec Cairncross, *The Control of Long-Term International Capital Movements* (Washington: The Brookings Institution, 1973), p. 28; U.S. Congress, Joint Economic Committee, *Balance of Payments—1965, Hearings* (pt. 2), 89th Cong., 2d sess., p. 1047. The government immediately encouraged business to continue foreign investment by borrowing on foreign capital markets. See the Press Conference of Secretary of Commerce Connor, 17 August 1965.

16. There are actually two ways of viewing this point. Although the guidelines were nominally voluntary, they were treated as if mandatory by both companies and government. But the tentative nature of the guidelines is supported in the case of Canada. Here market unrest led to a Canadian exemption after the fact. The 1965 Guidelines were left ambiguous vis-à-vis dollar flows—in part to pressure the Canadian government to cooperate. See Gerald Wright and Maureen Appel Molot, "Capital Movements and Government Control," 28 *International Organization* 4 (Autumn 1974), pp. 676-78.

17. *Wall Street Journal*, 30 January 1974; *New York Times*, 30 January 1974.

18. For statements on the Administration's monetarist views, see U.S., Congress, Joint Economic Committee, *1969 Economic Report of the President, Hearings*, 91st Cong., 1st sess., 1969. Also Sherman Maisel, *Managing the Dollar* (New York: Norton, 1973), p. 228; p. 265.

19. Labor's opposition came in the form of resistance to foreign imports and to the "export of jobs" via U.S. direct foreign investment. In an important sense, the need to placate labor influenced the Nixon Administration's imposition of an import surcharge in 1971. The call for a devaluation of the dollar big enough to bring about a trade turnaround of $13 billion was another plank of the same effort.

Chapter Four

Why Bank on Britain?

It is one thing to want to run the world's financial center, but quite another to succeed at it. Having acted as world banker in the past, Britain enjoyed a natural edge over her competitors. Only New York possessed an equal potential. Since New York was largely closed off to foreigners because of American capital controls in the 1960s, London found at least temporary protection from her most serious rival. In the meantime, the British followed a conscious policy of promoting London as the premier international money capital.

How did they do it? Chapter Three showed how the value of sterling came to be associated with London's importance in world trade and finance. Successive governments fought to maintain the pound's parity, ostensibly in order to protect the international bankers and businessmen in the City. We will see that this policy continued even though London's importance decreased with respect to the diminishing role of sterling.

A second prong of British financial policy had far more important effects on the fate of the City: the pursuit of maximum freedom in the regulation of international banking. In former days, this freedom had worked to the benefit of the powerful British bankers themselves and now the relative freedom drew bankers from abroad. British banks realized that the competition from the newcomers would be stiff, but the alternative might have been a total loss in favor of some other financial center. Thus, both domestic and foreign banks were united in ensuring that the authorities would continue their liberal policies.

Foreign banks are attracted by the British method of regulation, one which provides sympathetic regulators and relatively lax rules. The institutions of regulation are such that the regulators themselves approve of and promote the further internationalization of the City. Since sterling was made convertible in 1958, the British have often limited the activities of foreign banks in the domestic U.K. economy, but they have rarely interfered with purely international, or entrepôt, functions. This discriminating and lenient approach extends to virtually all areas of regulation: authorization, inspection, taxation, exchange control, and credit control.

This road has not been without bumps. While our original formulation stressed that governments determine the regulatory and economic structure, it also indicated that governments react to structural changes. The open system created by British governments proved extremely inviting to foreigners—so inviting, in fact, that the influx of American and other banks essentially changed the workings of the system itself. To deal with the system, regulatory changes became necessary to keep the level of control constant. Such changes as did come about, however, were once again carefully designed to maintain the freedom of the international bankers.

THE REGULATORS AND THEIR METHODS

Although the British government determines overall banking policy, the Bank of England carries it out. The Bank is more than just a conduit of official directives—it has wide discretion at the practical level to run the banking system as it sees fit. As a result, the character of the Bank of England is important in determining the relative stringency of banking regulation. Three aspects combine to make the Bank's regulation unique: the leadership at the Bank, its technique of regulation and its independence.

In a strictly legal sense, the Bank of England should not be considered independent. But history in England can be stronger than law. The Bank of England was born as a private institution in 1694 and remained private until 1946 when the Labour government nationalized it. The nationalization act[1] subordinated the Bank to the Treasury with subtle language (sec. 4(1)):

> The Treasury (that is, the Government) may from time to time give such directions to the Bank as, after consultation with the Governor of the Bank, they think necessary in the public interest.

The Labour government (1946-51) had wished to reverse the historical situation in which the Bank could do as it chose—and sometimes even dominate the government. The Macmillan Committee in 1931 had described the powers of the Bank in this way:

> . . . it is a private institution practically independent of any form of legal control save in regard to its powers of issuing bank notes and granting loans to the state. . . . The restrictions, so far as there are restrictions, under which the Bank works in its operations are restrictions which the Bank has imposed upon itself and which of course, it has the power to alter. (Q.71)[2]

But it is generally agreed that the act of nationalization did not make much difference.[3] Harold Wilson complained bitterly in the 1960s that the Governor of the Bank could force his government into undesirable policies by dint of its financial power.[4] One Labour M.P. said later that the Bank "brought undue pressure to bear on this Government during those two years when they had a small parliamentary majority, to change their financial policy abroad and social policy at home."[5]

The point of view of the Bank is sympathetic to the City on the whole. Although the Bank does take its regulatory role most seriously, it is also seen as a sort of lobbyist for City interests. The Governors have, in recent years, openly supported the policy of maintaining regulations at a minimum, in effect keeping government out of the banking system. The three most recent heads of the Bank of England have all favored development of the Eurodollar market, the increase of foreign banks in Britain, and the removal of limits to competition.[6] Traditionally, Bank of England Governors have themselves been bankers.

Lord Cromer, a merchant banker and Governor (1961-1966), called for more international business, a stable pound, fewer exchange controls, more competition, favorable tax treatment of foreigners, and development of the Eurocurrency markets.[7] His successor, Leslie O'Brien, shared most of these views.

O'Brien presided over the Bank of England during the greatest of influx of American banks, the general overhaul of banking regulations of 1971-72, and the sharp buildup of the Eurodollar market in London. The *Financial Times* said on his retirement that O'Brien's name would be associated with the development of international finance in London.[8] His speeches between 1966 and 1973 reflected (1) his growing awareness of the importance of the eurocurrency markets in London and the declining importance of sterling, (2) his acceptance of the constraints which international money markets impose on domestic monetary control, and (3) his conviction that the benefits of running an international center outweigh the costs. He often stressed the City's contribution to invisible exports and supported the formation of a permanent committee to monitor these invisible accounts.[9] In short, like Cromer, O'Brien approved almost anything which would increase London's international character (and earnings). He joked in 1969 that the City had "the most comprehensive banking community in the world and one that is ready to welcome newcomers. American banks join it nowadays almost as often as American airlines are hijacked to Cuba."[10]

As O'Brien's difficulties as Governor increased, he became somewhat critical of the eurodollar market, but not seriously so. He said in 1971, ". . . do we, after all, really like the consequences of it?" But he concluded that controls on foreigners should only be "very skillfully" and "sparingly" applied.[11] He was not about to kill the goose. He thought that if Britain tightened controls, the market would simply move elsewhere, the world would be no better off, and Britain would forfeit its lucrative business to another country.[12] After his retirement, he remained a supporter of the Eurocurrency market.

O'Brien resigned his post in July, 1973, and then moved into the presidency of the British Bankers' Association in early 1974, as well as becoming an official adviser to Morgan Guaranty and Morgan Grenfell. On his resignation, the Heath government returned to the merchant banks to find a successor, Mr. Gordon Richardson, chairman of Schroders.

Richardson knows the City well as director of companies such as Rolls-Royce, ICI, Legal and General Assurance, and Lloyd's Bank. In his first public speech he defended the new, freer regulatory system installed by his predecessor.[13] Later, he pointed to opportunities to Britain resulting from surplus oil funds in the Middle East by saying that the U.K. should welcome the sums seeking profitable investment opportunities.[14] Bank of England policy has thus been constant and can be expected to continue to promote the international character of the City.

While the substance of Bank policy is crucial, its technique of regulation is also important. Unlike the American Federal Reserve Board, the Bank of England relies largely on a sort of "old boy" network to let its wishes be known. It avoids very specific directives and expects the banks it regulates to use their judgment and discretion in complying with the spirit of the Bank's directives.

Yet the Bank has full power to regulate the foreign as well as the domestic banks.[15] It is probably the knowledge of this power which keeps the banks in line rather than explicit or detailed rules.[16] The foreign banks acknowledge the Bank's authority and admire its methods. All are attracted by the absence of rigid procedures—there is no battery of bank examiners or constant statements to be assembled. Recent years have necessitated increased supervision of banks in Britain, but even the most recent reforms, proposed in August 1976, seek to give the Bank of England the maximum discretion possible consistent with a sound banking system. The Bank's touch is personal; each bank must locate an office convenient to the Bank of England so that the club remains close. On the whole, American bankers have found the Bank of England to be surprisingly accommodating to their needs.

REGULATIONS

The actual regulation of banking in Britain is relatively simple, at least from the American point of view. The main areas of regulation are:

authorization
solvency
taxation
exchange control
credit control

Authorization

For an American bank, authorization to operate in Britain is no problem as long as the bank is relatively large. The British were so vague about authorization in the past that no law actually required a potential banker to do *anything* official before setting up his shop. As the number of banks increased, however, some clarification was necessary. The Companies Act of 1948 contained a provision which read:

> In this paragraph the expression "banking or discount company" means any company which satisfies the Board of Trade that it ought to be treated for the purpose of this Schedule as a banking company or discount company.

Section 429 of the Act said that any banking company of more than ten persons was required to register with the Registrar of Companies. A variety of different classes of banks emerged, depending on how the bank was registered, but for American banks, two things have been necessary: (1) registration as a company (which allows reporting exemptions[17]) and (2) authorization from the Bank of England for the purpose of dealing in foreign exchange. Whether or not the

Bank grants authorization for foreign exchange operations depends again on the Bank's discretion. The Bank will consider the size (assets) of a bank, the country of origin, the expertise of its personnel, the probability of compliance with local rules (whether the new bank is properly "socialized" into City attitudes). Although a bank from a smaller country than the United States would face a different standard, American banks must now probably have assets of nearly $2 billion in order to be considered.[18] Banks usually find a sponsor among local institutions to support their application. It is not unlike joining a country club.

Solvency

In the United States, banks are closely and constantly scrutinized. They make multiple reports, face frequent examinations, and must comply with a myriad of regulations. There was once a time in Britain when only the barest of reports was required and the Bank of England got most of its information from the grapevine and informal consultations. The growing number of banks in Britain, coupled with an increase in banking failures in the last few years have necessitated more reporting—but still much less than in the U.S. The government proposed new rules in late 1976, but the British goal is still to minimize interference and promote stability through flexibility and good sense. As Jeremy Morse, a former Bank official said:

> The Bank of England has been talking to the banks about it—and I guess the outcome will be something of a halfway house, in which the Bank will not go to full regulation on fixed arithmetical rules but will consult, probe and advise more frequently and more specifically about capital adequacy, profitability and the general conduct of banks' affairs.[19]

In discussing regulation of foreign banks in Britain, branches must be distinguished from subsidiary banks, merchant banks, or consortia. As integral parts of parent banks, branches are technically solvent as long as the parent bank is solvent. Should an American branch bank get into trouble, its lender of last resort would be its parent, and hence, the Fed. This is not the case for subsidiaries, except insofar as the parent bank feels a responsibility to support its offspring. Who, then, is the lender of last resort for subsidiaries and affiliates?

For many years, no determination was made on this question. Some have put forward the argument that the lack of a lender of last resort to offshore banks is a weakness of the current system. A recently reported agreement among central banks states that each Central Bank should be responsible for defaults occurring within its national territory—but the "ultimate responsibility" would still lie with the country of origin of international banks.[20] On the other hand, the Federal Reserve clarified its position: it feels that the country of origin should take responsibility for branches while the country of incorporation should take responsibility for subsidiaries if the parents cannot solve the problem.[21] The Bank of England, however, feels this puts too heavy a burden on Britain. The Bank, after its custom, probably prefers to leave open the question of its responsibility—thus allowing it to use its discretion should problems arise. It did call for assurances from banks with British subsidiaries that such subsidiaries would be fully backed by parents. American banks complied—although there is no way for the Bank to enforce this agreement should the need arise.[22] The Group of Ten industrialized countries (plus Switzerland and Luxembourg) organized a joint committee led by George Blunden of the Bank of England to increase communication for the prevention of further financial panics at times of crisis.

The question of responsibility for the solvency of foreign banks in Britain remains unclear. In this fluid situation, confusion could result. Clearer acceptance of responsibility would reduce the dangers inherent in the present system.

Taxation

American banks, of course, are subject to British taxation. They must be sensitive to the taxation factor because it affects their income directly. In the case of multinational businesses which have the option of operating in a variety of countries, decisions to locate in one country or another can be motivated by costs. Taxation certainly accounts for an important portion of costs.

Of course, other benefits found in a country may outweigh tax considerations. Professor Lee Remmers' study of multinational corporations showed that of thirty American companies, only one quarter assigned highest priority to taxes in making the decision to set up shop abroad.[23] His study did not look at financial companies in particular, so it may be that the findings do not apply in this case. But so many other conditions in London make a branch there desirable that it becomes impossible to focus on the tax motive alone.

British governments undoubtedly suffer from mixed feelings about taxation, and Labour and Conservatives tend to approach taxation from differing points of view. Tax policy reflects party philosophy in its details (i.e. in what is taxed) although *both* parties have imposed a fairly heavy tax rate on the whole.

Labour has sometimes tried to show its independence of City interests by its tax policy. Wilson imposed the Selective Employment Tax (SET) in 1966 which fell particularly on the service sectors, including banking. Services were seen as enterprises which fail to produce dynamic economies as employment increases. The Conservatives removed the tax (as much because of its impact on small retailers as because of its effect in other areas). More nationalistic wings in both parties would seek to derive as much revenue as possible from foreign sources operating in Britain—to "fleece" the Americans, or at least to discourage the repatriation of income. Others argue for encouraging American investment as a fillip to the economy. Finally, other groups see the income of the City as dependent on its primacy as an international financial center. They point to the City's contribution to the balance of payments through its supply of invisible exports. Some more ardent groups say that to continue as an international center, the City needs the presence of foreign financial institutions. Foreigners should therefore be welcome; favorable taxation being one means of such welcome. For instance, the Inter-bank Research Organization, which represents this last point of view, said:

> It is suggested . . . that London may compare unfavorably with other European financial centers. If such disparities exist they could persist for some time unless government action is taken to remove them or unless the progress of European harmonization is much accelerated . . . the government should review, and keep under review, the comparative advantages and disadvantages of London and other European financial centers in respect of tax and other important factors. For the time being it may be wise to err on the side of generosity to institutions conducting international financial business in London.[24]

Generally, all governments have tended to agree with this point of view, despite occasional Labour efforts to the contrary. Labour has backed down in the face of City opposition to some of its tax proposals. After coming back to power in 1974, the new Wilson Labour government decided to raise taxes on foreigners working in the United Kingdom. In his budget of March 26, 1974, Chancellor Healey announced plans to apply British income tax on as much as 90 percent of the earnings of foreigners residing in Britain, even when earned abroad, say, in the United States. Foreigners had been paying U.K. taxes only on income remitted to Britain, and, even then, could get that income through nontaxable dodges.[25] For anyone who worked in Britain for more than five years, the difference would have been considerable under the proposed changes.

The Labour government, however, would have pursued its policy of increased taxes on Americans only at its peril. Within two days of the budget, the *Financial Times* claimed that such action might endanger London's attractiveness and send foreign investors to the Continent.[26] In April *The Economist* said, "Mr. Healey should make a concession to (the foreigners) in the Finance Bill."[27] There was a report in *The Overseas American* that a poll of Americans in Britain showed that 69 percent would consider leaving the country if the Labour proposals went through. The American Chamber of Commerce entered the fray on behalf of its members.[28] An anonymous American bank was rumored to have postponed plans for a $60 million investment in the United Kingdom. Conservatives also expressed their displeasure with the move. Faced with such opposition, the Labour government had little choice but to capitulate. The final Finance Bill dropped the "infamous" Clause 18, although foreigners would be liable to U.K. tax on 50 percent of their earnings from foreign employers for services performed while in the U.K.[29] The extent of the campaign against the clause—and its early success—show the difficulties of taking any action specifically directed at multinational corporations in Britain.

The chief liability of American banks in the U.K. is the corporation tax. The United Kingdom tax applies to both subsidiaries and branches, branches being treated for tax purposes as if they were independent entities in Britain.[30] The main difference of treatment has been with respect to repatriations. Until 1973, the dividends paid by subsidiaries were subject to withholding tax so that branching tended to be favored over incorporation in Britain. The nature of banking itself also favors branching over incorporation because the direct capital backing of the parent in the branching case endows the branch with greater lending capacity and a larger claim to confidence. The incidence of American taxes also falls differently on the two: branch income is taxed currently in the U.S. while subsidiary income is taxed only on repatriation. This advantage to having a subsidiary under U.S. tax law seems to have been swamped by the advantages of having a branch in other respects. Some big banks, of course, have both branches and subsidiaries to get the advantages of each simultaneously.

Corporation tax had been introduced in 1965 by the Labour government, replacing income taxes on companies analogous to those on individuals. Originally set at 45 percent, the rate subsequently declined under the Conservatives to 42.5 percent in 1970 and 40 percent in the 1971 budget. Even though the American rate was higher, the advantage of having a subsidiary (but not a branch) because of the differential has not had much significance.[31] The factors mentioned above which favored branching were more important.

The chief feature of the original corporation tax was its bias toward discouraging the distribution of profits. Under it, dividends were subjected to double taxation—once at the source, and once in the hands of the shareholder.[32] U.S. tax law has the same feature, so this provision would not seem onerous to American companies. The Conservatives (like the Republicans in the United States) had long objected to this method of taxation. Heath's government announced in 1972 its intention to alter the system by giving a credit to shareholders to reduce taxation on their income received in dividends. The new law read:

> The company continues to pay corporation tax at a single rate on all its profits whether distributed or undistributed, but to mitigate the loss to revenue by the tax credit to shareholders this rate will be higher than it has been in the past.[33]

The overall rate of corporate taxation was now raised to 52 percent, and the method of taxing repatriations from foreign subsidiaries in Britain was changed. Although the old withholding tax on dividends was eliminated, dividends of subsidiaries to their parents abroad now demanded early payments of corporation tax called advance corporation tax, or ACT. U.S. companies complained that the new rules discriminated against foreign subsidiaries because of the way in which credits were given to U.K. companies—but not to non-U.K. companies.[34] Such discrimination went against previous double taxation treaties between the U.K. and the U.S., and against the O.E.C.D. standards of taxation.[35]

It took some time to straighten out the charges against the new tax system in Britain. The point is that foreigners were unhappy with it. The American authorities became involved in the re-negotiation of the double taxation agreement with Britain. As could be expected, given the typical British desire to satisfy foreign investors, a new treaty was worked out which tended to equalize the tax burden between foreigners and native companies. Credits were to be given the Americans which would in effect keep overall taxes from rising above U.S. levels. Branches, however, would still have some advantage over subsidiaries in the timing of their taxes since ACT does not apply to their repatriations.[36] In return, the U.S. reduced its withholding tax on British companies in America.

The British have manipulated the tax system in other ways which have benefited American banks. The Labour Finance Act of 1968, for instance, abolished the withholding tax on interest paid on certificates of deposit of over one year, thus permitting the growth of the long-term CD market in which American banks dominate. The Labour government also eased tax regulations in 1968 and 1969 to facilitate, at least for a time, Eurodollar borrowing by British corporations. Despite their heavy domestic tax burden, therefore, British governments have sought to structure the system as much as possible to favor London's international business.

Exchange Control

Exchange control limits the activities of American banks perhaps more than any other British regulation of banking. But the British are careful to see that in their purely international (non-British) business, the banks remain free. In order to foster London's predominance as a financial entrepôt while discouraging sterling outflows, they have written the rules very carefully. Exchange control discriminates between residents and nonresidents of the Sterling Area, between movements of long-term and short term capital, and between Sterling Area and non-Sterling Area currencies.[37] But dealings among nonresidents in nonsterling currencies are unregulated—and in this sphere the banks have carved the flourishing Eurocurrency business. Exchange control has generally worked in favor of the use of the dollar as an international currency, in large part because of limits on the use of sterling by those who held it.

The current system of exchange control originated in 1939 with the Defence (Finance) Regulation under the Emergency Powers (Defence) Act. Authority was consolidated in the Treasury by the Exchange Control Act of 1947 and delegated to the Bank of England. The Bank in turn delegated authority over day to day transactions to "authorized banks."[38]

The rationale for exchange controls, of course, was to conserve central bank reserves and to protect the value of sterling. From the beginning, a third goal was included: to preserve London's international banking function. At least until the 1960s, (and often after) the general consensus held that London's position depended upon the use of sterling. During the period when general sterling convertibility remained impossible, Britain attempted to preserve the pound as a trading currency by encouraging its use within the Sterling Area.

Benjamin Cohen noted that exchange controls were viewed as imperative in light of the emerging dollar shortage, but that "... it was also regarded as imperative that the pound's international monetary functions be preserved." Accordingly, from the beginning, the Government chose to operate exchange control around the whole group of sterling-associated countries, rather than around the United Kingdom alone.[39] Efforts to protect the pound's position as an international currency thus lay behind most British exchange policies. Limitations on the use of sterling were viewed as short-term measures to ensure its long-term acceptability. But it was never clear whether the British supported the City in order to defend sterling or whether they defended sterling in order to support City business.

Ironically, the very measures instituted to preserve sterling's future role helped to establish the use of the dollar in London.[40] The British were slow to recognize the fluke. In 1958, the Treasury defended the Sterling Area on the argument of the profitability of the City's transactions which were based on the international character of sterling.[41] Even as late as 1967, the Bank of England stressed the connection between Britain's position in world finance and the strength of her foreign exchange reserves.[42] Susan Strange described the English befuddlement well:

> It is this confusion between the function of the place and the function of the currency that has persisted longest and has confounded so much discussion of British economic policy.... Thus when distinguished foreigners sometimes tried to express their appreciation of London as a financial forum and their admiration for the skills of its bankers and brokers, their remarks were often misinterpreted in Britain as conveying admiration and support for sterling.[43]

In fact, the weakness of sterling discouraged its use for reserves or for trade finance. But because the exchange control rules were not meant to protect any currency other than sterling, the regulation of *other* currencies was far more liberal. London became a strong international financial center, but a center based on the dollar, not on the pound.

The Conservatives (1970-74) finally acknowledged the independence of the City's fortunes from sterling's sagging position and they virtually eliminated the distinction between Sterling Area and non-Sterling Area currencies in 1972 Exchange Control regulations. Yet Britain is no happier today to let the value of its floating currency fall, when currency depreciation means more inflation. Exchange control with regard to sterling remains an important element in the regulation of American banks. How do the British pursue the two goals of protecting a weak currency while preserving an open center for international finance?

The United Kingdom Exchange Control regulates both individuals (including corporations) and "authorized" banks and brokers.[44] In effect, the authorized banks regulate the individuals because all foreign exchange deals must include banks as intermediaries. Section 5.2 of the Exchange Control Act sets the general rule that U.K. residents may not buy, sell, or hold foreign currency without Bank of England permission. Authorized banks may therefore deal with residents only against certain permitted transactions, although they may deal freely with other authorized banks and with nonresidents.[45]

Limits on residents' dealings are clearly meant to minimize outflows of sterling which could eventually be presented to the Bank of England. Freedom of nonresidents' dealings, on the other hand, provides British compliance with the I.M.F. provision for current external convertibility and allows the continuance of international banking in London.

Sterling receives some protection because of controls over outflows from residents, even though nonresidents retain the freedom to sell sterling.[46] In addition, the ability of authorized banks to take open positions against sterling is strictly limited. This regulation of the composition of banks' foreign exchange holdings constitutes the most significant aspect of exchange control of the banks. They must not only guard that their customers comply with exchange control, but also that they themselves are in compliance. Exchange control rules concerning banks are rigorous, although some loopholes do exist. Under exchange control rules, the first step for American banks is to gain "authorized" status from the Bank of England. Once authorized, banks are responsible for their own operations in the foreign exchanges and for the legality of their customers' operations.

On its *own account*, a bank must observe a specified limit on its total open position "both spot and forward together—to preclude banks taking up a large open position against sterling." In addition, there is "a limit on the total amount of exchange (all currencies that may be held against forward sales)—to ensure a degree of concentration of the national reserves in the hands of the central institution and to preclude large amounts being arbitraged out of sterling for short-term investment abroad."[47] In other words, a bank must observe quotas which limit strictly the degree to which it may speculate against sterling.

While Bank of England control in other areas has been described as rather loose, in the area of exchange control it is far more precise. At the end of every month, banks must submit returns showing their positions in every currency. As of November, 1964, they had to indicate weekly their open and covered holdings in dollar and nondollar currencies. Since 1969, some banks have had to make daily returns.[48]

Aside from the banks' responsibilities on their own account, authorized banks in the United Kingdom have a responsibility for their *customers' accounts.* They will question the propriety of customers' actions or orders, and there is every indication that banks do discourage orders which appear to be speculative in character. But there is a questionable area between compliance and noncompliance with exchange controls. Banks, after all, are financial advisers and can only be expected to advise a corporate customer to minimize (maximize) his holdings of a weak (strong) currency. Banks even offer advisory services to help their customers do just that.

Regardless of the technical problems associated with exchange control, banks must indeed take the regulations seriously. The reason why the presence of the controls bothers the international banks so little is that no government has ever used them to hamper the City's international business. Limits on residents' transactions in the foreign exchange market can be as strict or as lenient as necessity dictates, and the amount of control varies over time. American banks can operate quite freely in the meantime, dealing without controls in their large business with nonresidents of Britain. In dealing with residents or in sterling, the Americans may be constrained, but no more than any other financial intermediary. Oddly enough, the extensive currency reporting system in Britain may contribute to London's prestige by assuring foreign depositors that their funds are not being foolishly shifted about.

Credit Control

For good or ill, the British government has often found itself trying to restrict the supply of domestic credit in England. Famous for the invention of "stop-go" economic policy, they have turned to domestic restraint of lending whenever a "stop" was called for. As in the case of exchange control, the problem has been to devise a system of close control of residents without infringing on London's international banking industry. Again as in the case of exchange controls, regulations have been very carefully drawn to this end.

The separation of international from domestic business is easier on paper than it is in fact. The British found in the course of the sixties that the foreign banks' business had a domestic impact which could, at times, frustrate their credit control program. Until 1971, foreign banks were not included under normal credit control regulations. The response was to institute a totally new program of credit control which brought foreign banks into the system on an equal footing with domestic banks. This had the result that foreign banks were given greater freedom to compete in the domestic U.K. economy while the Bank of England theoretically gained greater control over their ability to influence the domestic credit supply. It was the Conservatives under Heath who extended in 1971 the foreign banks' freedom in the local banking market, but this freedom turned out to be short-lived and was again limited in the next "stop" regime.

The structure of British credit control before 1971 shows how the influx of foreign banks made the system increasingly unsuitable. The purpose of credit control is to give the government the power to limit *domestic* lending. It thus applies only to sterling credits to domestic residents (while exchange controls regulate foreign currency credits for domestic use[49]). Taking American bank branches in Britain alone, their total advances in all currencies to British residents in mid-1960 amounted to only $163 million. By the end of 1973, they were lending over $3.5 billion to U.K. residents in sterling alone. Thus, as the American and other nonclearing banks became more important, it was necessary for the government to consider their impact if it wished to limit domestic expansion.

Until May 1965, credit control applied principally to the six big British clearing (i.e. commercial) banks. These banks belonged to a formal cartel all of whose members charged the same rates and followed generally the same lending policies. The Bank of England in effect set the prime rate, since the cartel's joint lending rate was tied to the official Bank discount rate. Foreign and other banks were not considered important enough to worry about and they were at the time unaggressive in pursuing local sterling business.

But the foreign banks were growing in importance. Between May 1965 and September 1971, credit control was broadened; it was mainly imposed by means of quantitative ceilings on sterling lending and by increases in required reserves (called special deposits) on sterling deposits. Quantitative ceilings applied to *all* banks while special deposits were still only required from the clearers. The new system of September 1971 abolished the quantitative ceilings and the cartel, but extended the applicability of special deposit calls to all banks, foreign and domestic.[50]

The differences between the last two periods of control are interesting. The 1965-1971 regime typifies the British approach in that international business was left totally untouched by credit control but domestic sterling business was sharply curtailed for foreign banks. While they did not have to submit to most of the regulations the clearers did (such as interest rate restraints, balance sheet ratio rules,[51] or special deposits), they were completely cut off from developing U.K. sterling business. Under the quantitative ceilings, sterling lending could be increased only by a fixed percentage over the level of a base period. For instance, in May, 1965, the Governor of the Bank of England requested that advances to the private sector should not increase more than 5 percent in the twelve months to March 1966. He requested "a comparable degree of restraint" from *all* banks with sterling business in Britain.[52]

For American banks, the implications were clear: a five percent limit on growth in sterling lending precluded any serious attempts to penetrate the local market. They were forced to remain purely international in their London branches.[53] Paul Einzig said:

> It had been suggested that the Bank was inclined to fix the limits for new foreign branches deliberately low in order to encourage them to lend in terms of Euro-dollars or other Eurocurrencies. . . . Actually, the main consideration which keeps credit ceilings for new foreign branches at a low level is probably that it would be unfair to encourage their competition with British banks when the latter are prevented by their credit dwellings from lending to industry and commerce.[54]

Of course, the new banks entering Britain from America felt particularly thwarted by the system. For different reasons, perhaps, others in the U.K. also had reasons for wanting to devise a new regulatory system.

1. Heath and many Conservatives opposed lending quotas in principle; they work against the benefits of competition. With their devotion to competition, free market Conservatives wished to maximize the number of market entrants, even if they were foreign entrants. The Conservatives also tend to be more "monetarist" than Labour, and thus have less fear of rising interest rates.
2. The Bank of England wanted a new system for the same reasons as the Conservatives. The Bank also realized that the old system of interest rate control through the cartel was no longer effective.
3. Two important Parliamentary reports called for more competition and abandonment of the cartel of clearing bankers.[55]
4. The Clearing Banks wished to be free from the cartel so they could openly operate in the new financial markets in which the Americans, particularly, had pioneered. These included especially the markets for sterling certificates of deposit.

The new system of September 16, 1971 thus came as no surprise. It abolished the cartel and the old lending ceilings and brought all the banks (those registered as "Section 127" banks) under the same rules for reserve ratios and special deposits. Anthony Barber, Conservative Chancellor of the Exchequer said,

> The changes we are now making will be by any standards a milestone in Britain's monetary history. . . . We are breaking away from the old regime that relied on rigid quantitative controls over lending and adopting a new system which will give full scope for competition and innovation. . . . —a framework which will combine that effective overall control with much greater flexibility and freedom for individual banks and finance houses.[56]

The Economist reviewed the changes and how they had come about:

> . . . some would even say that the newly competitive philosophy behind all the developments in British banking in the last few years, not excluding last year's credit revolution itself, can be attributed to the influence of foreign banks. It should not be forgotten that Citibank first introduced to London the idea of a base rate, and that was back in 1969.[57]

The Economist also noted that the "main impact of the new credit control system has been felt in the volume of foreign banks' business." Table 4-1 shows how the American banks increased their sterling business significantly after September, 1971, after six years of virtually no growth. The sudden spurt of interest in local banking reveals that it was legal constraints which prevented their U.K. penetration rather than the lack of desire to do so.

It turned out that the new system of 1971 brought some new

Table 4-1. Sterling Advances to U.K. Residents (£ millions)

	By Clearing Banks	*By American Banks*	*American Advances as % of Clearer's Advances*
Oct. 1971	5,371	456	8.5
Dec. 1971	5,528	533	9.6
Jan. 1972	5,808	551	9.5
Apr. 1972	6,522	633	9.7
Sep. 1972	8,041	828	10.3
Dec. 1972	8,577	880	10.3
Jan. 1973	8,978	916	10.2
Mar. 1973	9,715	1,020	10.5
Sep. 1973	10,848	1,186	11.0
Dec. 1973	11,379	1,454	12.8
June 1974	12,510	1,387	11.1
Jan. 1975	13,242	1,702	12.9

Source: Bank of England, *Quarterly Bulletin.*

problems. In the two years after the end of 1971, sterling business grew in the British banking system generally. Inflation increased the need for bank loans and inflationary expectations increased the willingness of borrowers to pay high rates. Thus, the easing of credit restrictions was accompanied by a surge in demand. Now free from ceilings on sterling credits, the banks could bid for sterling deposits with higher rates to satisfy the loan demand. In 1972, sterling advances to U.K. residents from U.K. banks grew by 70 percent; in 1973 by almost 40 percent. (American banks' sterling advances grew 65 percent in both years, while their sterling deposits grew commensurately.) The money supply, broadly defined, grew 28 percent the first year and 28 percent the second. The rate of increase was inflationary and unacceptable to the Government. The Bank of England took several restrictive steps, and finally revised the credit control system in December, 1973, to impose greater control over the banks.

It is, of course, impossible to say to what extent the banks themselves contributed to the growth in the money supply by more active bidding for deposits and by aggressive lending. Table 4-2 below shows the sharp decline in the banks' increases in sterling deposits and advances as well as in the money supply in 1974, after the Bank of England had imposed its stricter controls on bidding for funds. It shows that American banks were extremely active bidders for sterling deposits in 1972 and 1973, but not in 1974. While the American banks were able during this relatively free period between 1971 and

Table 4-2. Competition and Credit Control: Before and After December 1973 Changes (£ million)

	1972		*1973*		*1974*	
Deposits (Sterling)						
All U.K. Banks	30,772	(40%)	41,125	(34%)	44,339	(7.8%)
Clearing Banks	14,923	(27%)	19,613	(31%)	22,785	(16.2%)
American Banks	2,536	(67%)	3,945	(56%)	3,920	(–0.1%)
Advances (Sterling to U.K. Residents						
All U.K. Banks	14,479	(70%)	20,057	(39%)	24,831	(23.8%)
Clearing Banks	8,577	(55%)	11,379	(33%)	14,185	(24.7%)
American Banks	880	(65%)	1,454	(65%)	1,788	(23.0%)
U.K. Money Supply (M_3)		(28%)		(28%)		(11.4%)

Note: Figures in parentheses are rates of growth from previous year.

Source: Bank of England.

the end of 1973 to increase their share of the British sterling market, the kind of aggressiveness they and other banks engaged in was associated with an inflationary trend.[58]

Recognizing the problems with its new program after 1971, the Government still wished to avoid the return to quantitative controls such as the Labour Government had used. In August, 1972, the Bank of England requested the banks to make credit "less readily available to property companies and for financial transactions not associated with the maintenance and expansion of industry."[59] In November and December and again the following July (1973) the Bank called for special deposits from all banks. Interest rates rose above 10 percent. In September, 1973, the Bank imposed a limit of 9.5 percent on interest payable on small deposits in order to prevent a runoff of deposits from the building societies which could not compete with the high rates.[60] In October, special deposits were made more costly to the banks when the Bank lowered by 25 percent interest payable on them. But advances had continued to increase, as Table 4-2 showed for 1973, so the Bank took a major step in December, 1973 to limit the expansion of domestic credit.

The new credit control system of late 1973 called for non-interest-bearing special deposits to be required on *increases* in the banks' interest-bearing eligible liabilities of more than 8 percent after a certain period at the end of 1973. The further such increases exceeded 8 percent, the higher the penalty would grow. Special deposits could potentially be as high as 50 percent on excessive increases in those liabilities.[61] This system of incremental reserves on growth in interest-bearing liabilities was not entirely original: the Federal Reserve had invented a similar system in the United States some months before.

The 1973 modifications to the credit control system did avoid to some extent the quantitative ceilings of earlier years and some of the distortions. Loans were not directly limited, in order to allow the banks greater flexibility. But competition was thwarted since all of the banks are forced to the same rate of growth in interest-bearing liabilities. The system was particularly hard on the American and other foreign banks trying to break into the sterling business. In 1974, for the first time since 1971, sterling deposits at American banks failed to grow. The Clearers had the advantage of attracting interest-free demand deposit accounts through their extensive branch systems—and these were unaffected by the new limits. The only way the Americans can in the long run expand their sterling business is to bid for interest-bearing sterling deposits. So the Clearers could under the new regime increase their sterling deposits as a whole more easily than non-Clearing banks such as the Americans. Once again, American banks faced serious obstacles to their plans for engaging in the domestic money markets of Britain. Their international business remained unobstructed, of course, and the special 1973 rules were suspended after little more than a year.

The record of British banking regulation leaves little doubt about what the government has been trying to do. Where other developed countries including the United States have slapped on banking controls whenever convenience dictated, the British have found it convenient to avoid controls. In every case reviewed here, regulations have delicately skirted the international domain of the banks. The only possible exception is that of exchange control. But even exchange control has its beneficial side effects in directing the banks' profit-seeking activities away from pure currency speculation.

What the regulatory system of the United Kingdom illustrates most clearly here is the extent to which governments can and do determine economic structures. These structures may change and government control may be weakened by externally-caused events, but governments still have the option to respond and to reassert control by altering the rules of the game. We can no more speak of the "invasion" of Britain by the international banking community in the 1960s and 1970s than we can speak of the invasion of Britain by the Hanoverian monarchy: both were invited by their hosts.

The 1971 changes in the Bank of England's credit control system further support this point. The growth of banks outside the clearing banks' cartel had resulted in inadequacies in domestic credit control. Because the British wished to regain monetary control while still encouraging foreign bankers, they redrew their rules to achieve just these effects. This is not to say that all governments can always achieve all of their objectives. In the first place, many governments lack the prerequisite of a political consensus which produces clear objectives and priorities. Chapter Three showed that Britain does possess a consensus when it comes to encouraging foreign banks. Secondly, some goals may be of such low priority that these goals must be subordinated to higher ends. (For instance, the United States might have wanted to develop New York as an international financial center in the 1960s, but it might have seen this goal as less important than controlling the balance of payments.) Thirdly, a government could lack the power to enforce its own rules because of a lack of monetary or other resources. This third condition may, for instance, apply to many underdeveloped countries, but does not (in most cases) apply to the developed world.[62] The fourth condition under which governments fail to achieve their objectives occurs by simple human error: the government, in good faith, applies the wrong solution to a problem. The last condition may be a serious one, but does not affect this case to any great extent. If the British government mistakenly undertook a policy which would tend to drive the foreign financial community away, they would surely be aware of the result before very long. This seems to have happened when the Labour government tried to raise personal taxes imposed on foreigners—and they quickly revised their policy. In 1976, another flap occurred when the tax authorities ruled that a method subsidiaries used to protect the sterling value of their capital backing would give rise to taxation.[63] A reversal of the ruling could be expected in the event that this ruling led to pulling up stakes by foreign banking subsidiaries in Britain. And despite these occasional lapses of good feeling, the fact that British banking authorities stress consultation and discretion in regulating the banks promotes informed decision-making.

We have seen now the role of the British government in the development of London as the premier international financial center. But another government has been closely involved in the movement: the American government. We will see in the next chapter how the American banks were led in parallel ways to seek outlets abroad. American government policy was as important in this respect as the British in luring the banks to London.

NOTES TO CHAPTER FOUR

1. Great Britain, Laws, Statutes, etc., *Bank of England Act*, 1946, 9 & 10 George 6, ch. 27.

2. Great Britain, Parliament, *Parliamentary Papers* (Commons), Cmnd. 3897, June 1931. "Report of the Committee on Finance and Industry" (The Macmillan Committee). For a Labour view, see Hugh Dalton, *High Tide and After: Memoirs 1945-1960* (London: Frederick Muller, 1962), pp. 32-34.

3. For instance, *The Midland Bank Review* said, "Indeed, it is arguable that, in this respect, the act made little difference to the pre-existing situation." See "Banking Regulation in Britain—By 'Suasion' not Statute" (November 1967). Reprinted in J.E. Wadsworth, *The Banks and the Monetary System in the U.K.: 1959-1971* (London: Methuen and Co., Ltd., 1973), p. 105; also Henry Roseveare, *The Treasury* (London: Penguin, 1969), p. 321.

4. See Wilson, *The Labour Government 1964-1970: A Personal Record* (London: Wiedenfeld and Nicolson, 1971), pp. 34-38, 131-32. According to Wilson, Cromer gave advice on November, 1964 about cuts in some government expenditures, including some of Labour's favored projects. When Wilson resisted and threatened an election, Cromer countered that an election would inevitably drain all reserves. Some argue that Wilson secretly agreed with Cromer, but used him as a whipping boy. That is difficult to believe, given the very real bitterness both have displayed on numerous occasions.

5. Great Britain, Parliament, *Parliamentary Debates* (Commons), 777, (1969), col. 1216.

6. For a similar view of the Bank's predilections, see Robin Pringle, *Banking in Britain* (London: Methuen & Co., 1973), pp. 113-114.

It might be expected that the City would have opposed the entrance of so many foreigners to London on the ground that competition would be too stiff. But British financial institutions recognized that the presence of foreigners was necessary to their *own* business. As one City lobbyist put it in an interview: "The American banks are the cement which holds the City together."

7. For Cromer's opinions, see his speech at Mansion House, October 21, 1965, in Bank of England *Quarterly Bulletin*, December 1965, p. 345. See also the Cromer Enquiry, a study done by Lord Cromer in 1967 for the Board of Trade, investigating the export effect of foreign investment. (*Export Business from Capital Projects Overseas*, Cmnd. 3516, 1968.)

Also, Lord Cromer, "On Reconstructing the Monetary System," in D.H. Barran et al., *Rebuilding the Liberal Order* (London: The Institute of Economic Affairs, 1969), p. 23; his statements in favor of freer capital movements at the conference of May 16, 1968, of the Per Jacobsson Foundation in M.M.W. Holtrop, *Les Banques Centrales et l'Integration Economique*. Cromer favored more flexibility in tax arrangements so that the City could draw a greater amount of foreign business. (Mansion House speech, November 3, 1964, in *Quarterly Bulletin*, December 1964, p. 288.) On London as a commercial center, Bank of England, *Quarterly Bulletin*, June 1963, p. 117.

8. June 28, 1973.

9. Speech given on October 26, 1966, reprinted in Bank of England, *Quarterly Bulletin*, December 1966, p. 383.

10. To the Overseas Bankers Club, February 3, 1969, in *Quarterly Bulletin*, March 1969, p. 74.

11. To the Bankers' Club of Chicago, April 27, 1971, in *Quarterly Bulletin*, June 1971, p. 226.

12. Montreal Speech, *Quarterly Bulletin*, June 1972, p. 236.

13. Speech at Mansion House, October 18, 1973. See *The Financial Times*, 19 October 1973, p. 44.

14. Speech at Financial Times Conference on World Banking. See *The Financial Times*, 16 January 1974, p. 1.

15. Great Britain, Parliament, *Parliamentary Papers* (Commons), *1968-69. Minutes of Evidence*, Subcommittee B of Select Committee on Nationalized Industries. Q. 275-77; 392.

16. At the end of 1973, what *The Financial Times* termed "the worst crisis in half a century" hit the secondary banking sector in London. The initial problem was solved by a joint effort of the Bank of England, large banks and other companies which joined to bail out those banks in trouble. The operation was typical of the *ad hoc* and cooperative nature of banking regulation in Britain. See Margaret Reed, "How the Bankers' Lifeboat Came to Rescue," *The Financial Times*, 29 January 1974, p. 2. As losses in the British property market spread more doubts in the City, other measures were instituted in 1975. American banks which had lent money, for instance to the Stern group, were

rumored to be resisting a proposed moratorium. The Bank, however, succeeded in getting the American banks to help out in the crisis. See *The Economist*, 9 August 1975, "Survey," pp. 34-5. As *The Economist* had said in June, "Those foreign bankers who wish to stay in London may be reluctant to antagonize the Old Lady" (14 June 1975).

17. See Overseas Companies (Accounts) (Exemptions) Order 1968, (S.I. 1968, no. 69); also, Great Britain, Parliament, *Parliamentary Papers* (Commons), Cmnd. 1749, June 1962, "Report of the Company Law Committee" (The Jenkins Committee), par. 406. The rationale behind banking exemptions was that earnings of banks fluctuate widely, and thus downward fluctuations could create a lack of confidence in the banking system unnecessarily. Banks do have to make half-yearly statements of share capital, assets and liabilities, but until 1970 could publish their profit figures after deducting reserves and provisions out of revenue—without telling how much was deducted. The market value of investments could be described simply "at or under cost"; banks did not have to disclose the method they used to value fixed assets or show depreciation allowed. Profits were published without revealing the amount of tax paid. See J.S.G. Wilson, "Regulation and Control of the United Kingdom Banking and Financial Structure," *Banca Nazionale del Lavoro* 22 (June 1969): 130-33; also the Jenkins Committee "Report," par. 400. Of course, these details were known to the Inland Revenue Board, but not to the public. American banks' *branches* do not publish separate reports; their accounts are consolidated with those of the parent bank. In practice, the U.K. accepts accounts from companies in the form required by their country of incorporation unless the latter is considered inadequate. See David Alhadeff, *Competition and Controls in Banking* (Berkeley: University of California Press, 1968), p. 519. After 1970, the Clearing Banks, the main British commercial banks, gave up this exemption in favor of greater disclosure.

To call itself a bank, a company had to be registered under Section 127 of the 1967 Companies Act. Section 127 banks observe Bank of England banking rules on reserves, etc. A lower class of bank, a so-called Section 123 bank, also exists, but this distinction will be abolished according to new rules. See George Blunden, "The Supervision of the U.K. Banking System," 15 *Quarterly Bulletin* 2. It will now be more difficult to get approval to use the word "bank" in the name of a financial institution.

18. This opinion was formed from a review of recent decisions on entrance and an interview with Roger Barnes at the Bank of England, 6 September 1973.

19. Interview with *The Economist*, 9 August 1975, Survey, p. 26. For the British White Paper on Licensing of Deposit-Taking Institutions, see *Financial Times*, 4 August 1976.

20. See *The Economist*, 20 July 1974.

21. Edwin Dale, Jr. "Fed Offers New Approach to Eurocurrency Market," *New York Times*, 3 September 1974. The Bank of England, by failing to help out the failing Israeli-British Bank in July, 1974, showed that it did not consider aiding foreign subsidiaries in London as within its responsibility. But Israel did not accept responsibility either. In mid-1975, the Israeli government did relent and agreed that the remaining assets of the London subsidiary could be pooled

with those of the Israeli bank in satisfying creditors. According to the *New York Times*, the policy shift resulted from pressure on the Israelis from American Congressmen and Senators with interested constituents, including several banks with London branches and affiliates. (Reported 26 June 1975.)

22. *The Economist*, 8 February 1975, p. 83.

23. See Remmers, H. Lee, and Brooke, Michael Z., *The Strategy of Multinational Enterprise: Organization and Finance* (New York: Longman, 1970), p. 73.

24. InterBank Research Organization, *The Future of London*, pp. 1-10, 1-13.

25. See *Financial Times*, 27 March 1974.

26. "Executives Count the Cost," *Financial Times*, 28 March 1974.

27. "Multi-man Mulched," *The Economist*, 13 April 1974, p. 119.

28. Reported in *Financial Times*, 23 April 1974.

29. Those resident in the United Kingdom for more than nine years would have to pay somewhat more. See *The Economist*, 3 August 1974.

30. See the supplementary protocol of March 17, 1966 amending the Convention on Double Taxation (Taxes and Income) of April 16, 1945 (17 U.S.T. 1254 TII A.S. 6089). Article III(2) says:

> Where an enterprise of one of the Contracting Parties is engaged in trade or business in the territory of the other Contracting Party through a permanent establishment situated therein, there shall be attributed to such permanent establishment the industrial or commercial profits which it might be expected to derive if it were an independent enterprise engaged in the same or similar activities under the same or similar conditions and dealing at arm's length with the enterprise of which it is a permanent establishment.

31. For the general rules of American taxation of business abroad, see Sections 901-906 of the Internal Revenue Code.

32. See "Hitting Dividends Sideways," *The Economist*, 14 November 1964, p. 768. "The discrimination against distributed income is among the attractions of a Corporation tax for Labour, which (like a good few company chairmen) sees dividends as an extravagance and retained profits as the real source of expansion."

33. *Palmer's Company Law* (Supp. January 1, 1973) Chapter 82A of the Companies Act, p. 896.

34. *The Economist*, 25 March 1972; *The Times*, 22 March 1972; *The Financial Times*, 26 March 1974.

35. See 17 U.S.T. 125, Art. 16(1); Organization for Economic Cooperation and Development, *Double Taxation of Income and Capital*, Art. 24, Sec. 1, (1974).

36. Reported in the *New York Times*, 6 November 1975. See U.S. Department of the Treasury, "United States and United Kingdom Sign Agreement on Income Tax Treaty," *News*, 6 January 1976.

37. On June 22, 1972, the Scheduled Territories of the Sterling Area (that is, those which receive maximum exchange freedom with Britain) were reduced in number from over 30 countries to just 5 areas—the U.K., the Channel Islands, the Isle of Man, the Republic of Ireland and Gibraltar. See Exchange Control

(Scheduled Territories) (No. 2) Order 1972. The former Scheduled Territories, now called the Overseas Sterling Area, lost many of the privileges they had held before with respect to sterling. Despite British entry into the Common Market, there has been little effort to extend exchange freedom to the EEC as yet.

38. "The U.K. Exchange Control: A Short History," Bank of England, *Quarterly Bulletin*, September 1967, p. 246.

39. Benjamin J. Cohen, *The Future of Sterling as an International Currency* (London: Macmillan, 1971), p. 81.

40. One early exchange control regulation which contributed to the use of dollars for international finance was the temporary ban on the use of sterling for trade finance between non-sterling area countries between September 20, 1957 and February 19, 1959. See I.M.F., *Ninth and Tenth Annual Report on Exchange Restrictions* (Washington 1958, 1959).

41. See Memorandum submitted by H.M. Treasury to the Radcliffe Committee, Principal Memoranda of Evidence, vol. 1, reprinted in R. Conan, *The Rationale of the Sterling Area* (London: Macmillan, 1961).

42. See Bank of England, "A Short History," p. 245.

43. Susan Strange, *Sterling and British Policy* (New York: Oxford University Press, 1971), pp. 202-203.

44. London currency brokers must be members of the Foreign Exchange and Currency Deposit Brokers' Association. London brokers deal only with banks, but are prohibited from dealing with banks abroad. Hence, I will refer only to banks here since they are the principal actors with which we are concerned.

45. See Bank of England, "The Foreign Exchange Market in Great Britain," in Robert Z. Aliber, ed. *The International Market for Foreign Exchange* (New York: Frederick A. Praeger, 1969), p. 88.

46. Since December 19, 1958. At that time, "sterling in non-resident accounts . . . was made freely convertible at exchange market rate." See for details and exceptions, I.M.F., *10th Annual Report on Exchange Restrictions* (1959).

47. Bank of England, "The Foreign Exchange Market," p. 88.

48. See Paul Einzig, *A Textbook on Foreign Exchange* (New York: St. Martin's Press, 1967), p. 202. Also his *Foreign Exchange Crises* (London: Macmillan, 1970), p. 56. For a complete review, "Limits on U.K. Banks' Foreign Exchange Positions," *Quarterly Bulletin* (December 1975), pp. 355-58.

49. Even if it wishes to restrict domestic credit, the government may, at the same time, encourage foreign currency credits for domestic use. When switched into sterling, the foreign currency borrowed has two effects: it expands the domestic money supply but also expands foreign exchange reserves.

50. For descriptions of British credit control see *British Financial Institutions* (London: H.M.S.O., 1971); J.E. Wadsworth, *The Banks and the Monetary System in the U.K.: 1959-1971* (London: Methuen and Co., 1973); Jack Revell, *Changes in British Banking: The Growth of a Secondary Banking System*, Occasional Paper No. 3 (London: Hill, Samuel and Co., 1968); Bank of England, *Competition and Credit Control* (May 1971); *Reserve Ratios and Special Deposits* (September, 1971); Dorothy B. Christelow, "Britain's New Monetary Control System," Federal Reserve Bank of New York, *Monthly Review*, 56 (January, 1974).

51. Interest rates were controlled for the clearers by custom, not by law. In effect, they were required to maintain both deposit and lending rates at a certain margin with respect to "bank rate," the Bank of England discount rate. This was technically done through the officially sanctioned Cartel of Clearing Bankers. Balance sheet ratios were similarly determined, although in the 1960s, it was clear that the Bank of England could require changes. (See Great Britain, Parliament, *Parliamentary Papers* (Commons) 1967-68, vol. 26, "Report of the Monopolies Commission on the Proposed Merger of Barclay's Bank, Ltd. Martin's Bank, Ltd. Lloyd's Bank, Ltd." par. 201.

52. Bank of England, *Quarterly Bulletin* (June 1965), p. 111.

53. See Richard Vokey, "The Impact of the U.S. Banks on British Banking," *The Banker* (October, 1969), p. 1053.

54. Paul Einzig, *Parallel Money Markets*, vol. 1 (London: Macmillan, 1971), p. 65.

55. Great Britain, "Report of the Monopolies Commission," National Board For Prices and Incomes, *Report No. 34, 1967* (The Jones Report on Bank Charges).

56. From *British Financial Institutions*, p. 75. The new Labour government in 1974 implied that it would make no significant changes in the system. (See Denis Healey's budget speech reported in the *Financial Times* 27 March 1974, p. 20.)

57. "The City Fights it Out: A Survey," *The Economist*, September 23, 1972, Vol. 244, p. 43.

58. For a good review of the problems of inflation and credit control, see Dorothy B. Christelow, "Britain's New Monetary Control System."

59. Bank of England, *Quarterly Bulletin*, September, 1972, p. 372.

60. See *the Times*, 12 September 1973 for text and discussion; Bank of England, *Quarterly Bulletin*, December 1973, pp. 445-46.

61. In April, 1974, new levels were specified. By January, 1975, the allowable rate of growth in interest-bearing eligible liabilities was limited to 17 percent above the level of October-December 1973. See Bank of England, *Quarterly Bulletin*, June 1974, p. 161. On 28 February 1975, in light of declining demands for credit, both the interest ceiling on small deposits and the supplementary special deposits were suspended.

62. Several areas do seem to elude the control of even developed countries. Drug smuggling, tax evasion, and prostitution are obvious examples.

63. "Bye-bye banks," *The Economist*, 3 July 1976, pp. 92-94.

Chapter Five

Meanwhile, Back at the Fed

Bankers in Europe have long thrown up their arms in horror when asked about banking regulation in the United States. American bankers share this reaction. It is even possible to say that American bank regulators themselves feel the same. Banking regulation in the United States is extremely bureaucratic; Parkinson might have substituted the system for the Royal Navy in drawing out the implications of his law. The heavy bureaucracy in the United States helped promote the movement of American banks abroad: bankers were beginning to feel strangled by its rules.

It was pointed out above, of course, that the American government has traditionally approved of direct foreign investments. With banking this has been equally true. The result has been a strange combination of foreign freedom for the banks and domestic restraint. So at the same time that banking regulations squeezed the banks at home, they also pushed the bankers across the domestic horizon in search of fewer rules. These positive and negative inducements will be reviewed in this chapter. In the process, the main outlines of American regulation of banks abroad should emerge.

In the case of American regulation of banks, an interesting comparison can be made with British regulation. The British, as has been noted, ran into problems as the number of foreign banks in London increased in the 1960s. Most difficult were control of the domestic British money supply and defense of the pound. The United States suffered similar dislocations—and like the British, the

American authorities did find themselves at least technically able to maintain control.

Because the American system is itself so Byzantine, the rules may at times be difficult to follow. There are many cases in the courts right now in which it is not clear to anyone how the law should be interpreted. The main point is to determine the impact of given rules on banks' decisions to open foreign branches or subsidiaries. Three main areas will be examined here: (1) regulation of bank powers by various authorities; (2) monetary policy; and (3) balance of payments policy. The only possible conclusion is that practically every aspect of relevant government policy in the 1960s and 1970s contributed to sending American bankers to foreign markets. Banks faced so many restrictions at home and so few abroad that their choice had become clear.

REGULATOR NUMBER ONE: THE FED

The Federal Reserve exercises the most important responsibilities for control of the American banking system, although it is only one among the many authorities governing the field. Today, it largely controls the ability of banks to establish foreign branches and subsidiaries; although given the complexity of American banking regulation, the scope of its responsibility has sometimes been unclear.

This complexity results to a large extent from the Federal character of the country, which has produced the "dual banking system." Originally, state governments chartered and controlled the banks within their borders. In 1863, with the passage of the National Banking Act, banks could choose to be nationally chartered, but the national banking system proved inadequate to provide a flexible monetary supply, so a new system was superimposed. A series of monetary crises led in 1913 to the establishment of the Federal Reserve System. Now banks could be nationally chartered members, or state-chartered nonmembers or members. Additional crises in the 1930s produced yet another authority in 1933: the Federal Deposit Insurance Corporation.

A complex division of power resulted from this gradual accretion of ruling bodies. National banks remain subject to many state rules while even nonmembers of the Federal Reserve must observe certain federal regulations. In addition, in other areas either the Securities Exchange Commission or the Justice Department has powers over banks. This structure of overlapping and sometimes conflicting authority has produced confusion and frustration. Many serious commentators have suggested revision, and some change appears likely in the future.[1] But for the present, the Fed retains the most power over banks internationally.

The Federal Reserve System concerns itself chiefly with controlling monetary conditions and with assuring the solvency of the banks under its purview. This includes determining whether banks may engage in banking abroad. Under the Federal Reserve Act, all member banks must apply to the Board for permission to establish foreign branches.[2] In considering applications, the Board examines, for each application:

> . . . the conformity of the proposal to the provisions of law and regulation, the condition of the applicant bank or corporation and the capacity of management, and the general appropriateness of the proposal in the light of the broad public purposes the relevant statutes are intended to serve.[3]

In order to lighten the increasingly heavy burden of regulation on the Federal Reserve Board, a Steering Committee on International Banking Regulation for study of means of simplifying and standardizing the regulation of multinational banks has been established.[4]

Federal law places restrictions on the amount of capital necessary to establish foreign branches, but the Bank of England minimum requirements for London entry (which are geared to assets, not capital) impose stricter standards. The Federal Reserve requires annual reports of condition on branches, but does not examine the branches directly. Consolidated monthly reports are also required on total branch assets and liabilities.

Fed policy toward foreign banking activities has been accommodating and has grown more so. Regulation M, which deals with the activities of foreign branches, for many years merely specified action to be taken in the case of disturbed conditions abroad. Given the small number of banks with foreign branches until 1960 (seven), detailed rules were not necessary. But the outward push of the 1960s produced pressure to increase banks' powers abroad and the Federal Reserve obliged. In 1963, after Congress authorized expanded powers abroad, the Federal Reserve clarified and revised Regulation M so that:

1. Banks with a branch in a country abroad no longer needed permission to establish other branches in the same country.
2. Branches could "exercise powers (with certain exceptions) that are usual abroad."
3. Branches could "underwrite and deal in the obligations of the national government of the country."[5]

Rules concerning foreign subsidiaries were similarly liberalized. In 1967, the Federal Reserve again revised Regulation M to permit banks to own stock in foreign banking organizations directly. Formerly, they had to establish special subsidiaries to own foreign bank stock. Here, however, the Fed only made the change unwillingly after the Comptroller of the Currency had given this right to national banks.[6] Regulation M thus facilitated foreign expansion. The power to "exercise powers usual abroad" might allow more freedom abroad than at home, at least in countries with easy banking rules such as Britain. This state of affairs encouraged bankers to expand through foreign operations, or at least placed no barriers before those who wished to do so.

While the powers of branches abroad are governed by Regulation M, the activities of subsidiaries fall under Federal Reserve Regulation Y. The history of Regulation Y is somewhat confusing and the dispute concerning subsidiary powers has been going on for years. Under the law, holding companies owning banks were free to engage in activities prohibited to banks. Since the difference between the holding company and its subsidiary banks might be only one of convenience, banks started to create holding companies through which they could get into other lines of business. The holding company was an artificial arm of the bank. A 1956 law put an end to this, but only for holding companies owning more than one bank. This gave birth to the "one-bank holding company," a device which became popular in the late 1960s. Alarmed at growing bank diversification and freedom, the Federal Reserve called for a new law to limit one-bank holding company activities.[7] Under a 1970 law, the Federal Reserve Board was given the power to determine what activities would be permissible to subsidiaries of one-bank holding companies, including nonmembers of the System. Its list of permissible activities is found in Regulation Y. This list leaves many financial areas open to holding company subsidiaries, although they are still prohibited from domestic investment banking.[8]

Subsidiaries engaged in *purely* foreign banking have long received special treatment. A 1916 amendment to the Federal Reserve Act allowed bank investments in U.S. corporations "principally engaged in international or foreign banking" either directly or through control of foreign institutions, provided they entered into an agreement with the Board to comply with Federal Reserve Regulations.[9] Another amendment in 1919, the Edge Act, provided for federal chartering of these corporations and exempted joint foreign ventures of American banks from antitrust legislation.[10] Federal Reserve Regulation K (Corporations Engaged in Foreign Banking and Financing under the Federal Reserve Act) sets the rules for Edge Act corporations.

Through the Edge Act, American banks can indirectly perform international functions beyond the limits of laws concerning bank subsidiaries with domestic operations. For instance, Edge subsidiaries may hold stock in certain corporations for their own account while under Regulation Y normal holding company subsidiaries could not. Under this rubric, an American bank-owned merchant bank in London is legal; its domestic equivalent would be illegal.[11]

Edge Act subsidiaries for international banking may also be set up outside the state where the bank operates in the United States. Thus, a California bank with a New York Edge Act subsidiary could participate in international financing in New York as long as its New York activities are judged by the Fed to be incidental to foreign or international business.

Originally, there were two kinds of Edge or Agreement corporations: banking corporations and financing corporations, to separate investment from commercial banking activities.[12] In 1963, the Federal Reserve amended Regulation K to eliminate the formal distinction between banking and financing corporations and expanded certain Edge Act powers.[13]

Despite the liberality of the law, few banks expanded through Edge Act corporations after the Second World War—until the 1960s. By the end of 1958, there were only nine such subsidiaries. But as they grew in other ways, American banks began to take interest in the Edge Act, after ignoring it for forty years. California banks first started to use the Edge Act to open New York offices, but others in the late 1960s turned to the Act to expand the powers of their subsidiaries abroad. By the end of 1973, the number of Edge Act and Agreement corporations had grown to 103, and each might in turn own numerous other foreign subsidiaries. Nine have foreign branches. One hybrid form of corporation was devised by Hartford National Bank and James Saxon, the former Comptroller of the Currency, then of American Fletcher National Bank and Trust Company. They brought together seventeen banks to form a jointly owned Edge corporation, Allied Bank International, a New York-based company with a London branch. This enabled smaller banks to participate in the foreign field.

This brief review of Federal Reserve regulation of international activities reveals the friendly attitude of the Fed toward the banks' international expansion. It does not do justice to the frustration the banks felt at home. It was not so much that any individual banking regulation was so onerous in the United States, but rather that competition was impeded by monetary policy, geographical expansion was limited by state laws, and international business was hampered by U.S. balance of payments policy. These considerations will be more fully explored below. In contrast, the freedoms allowed banks abroad convinced many banks that it was time for a move.

THE COMPTROLLER OF THE CURRENCY: NO HOLDS BARRED

The Office of the Comptroller of the Currency, a division of the Treasury Department, regulates certain banking activities of national banks, and over sixty percent of the American banks in Britain are national banks. The Comptroller stands second only to the Federal Reserve Board in controlling the foreign activities of American banks.[14] The Comptroller does not exercise the wide responsibilities of the Federal Reserve in general monetary policy or even in regulating holding companies (since 1970) and Edge Act subsidiaries. He deals strictly with commercial banking activities. Individual Comptrollers have, however, proved influential within this limited area in encouraging both the domestic and international expansion of American banking, particularly before 1970.

The Comptroller's office discharges two main functions: (1) it examines national banks twice every three years and requires annual reports on foreign branches; (2) it executes federal law on the powers of national banks. With the growth of foreign branches, the Comptroller widened his supervision of foreign branches by establishing a Department of International Banking in 1964. Bank examiners for international branches were thus based in Washington and travelled abroad to inspect the branches. By 1972, so many national banks had London branches that the Comptroller opened a special office in the American embassy in London. National bank examinations are standardized and concern themselves chiefly with the solvency of the banks.[15]

In its function as bank examiner, the Comptroller's office can wield considerable power, equal in certain respects to Federal Reserve power. Bank examiners assess the quality of loans outstanding at banks and "classify" these assets according to their soundness. The larger the portion of assets which are "classified," or doubtful, the less sound the bank. If a loan to Company *X* is classified at Bank *Y*, all other banks which have loans outstanding to that company will have to take note. Not only companies, but countries, can lose their ability to borrow as a result of such action. With American banks so important in London, a "classified" foreign country may find markets there difficult to tap. In 1974, the Comptroller labelled all medium- and long-term loans to Italy "problematical." Italy and Italian companies did not get another loan from an American bank until an October 1975 loan managed by Citicorp International Bank.[16]

Recent Comptrollers have often created controversy through their liberal interpretations of the law concerning bank powers and bank mergers. Two Comptrollers, James J. Saxon (a Kennedy appointee) and William B. Camp (a Johnson appointee who continued under the Nixon Administration) dominated the office in the 1960s and early 1970s. They both handled the office as a means of increasing the powers of national banks. Both took a dim view of the American tradition of encouraging small banks.

On frequent occasions, the Comptroller's policy has created conflicts with the more conservative Federal Reserve Board. These disputes affected the ability of banks to operate abroad. For instance, the Comptroller has taken a generous stance on bank mergers, permitting several large banks to become even larger.[17] Both Saxon and Camp wanted to see American banks grow and become important world competitors. The Comptroller revised regulations to facilitate the purchase of banks abroad. Finally, he has lobbied for the extension of bank powers through liberal holding company legislation. Under the 1970 Bank Holding Company Act, however, the Comptroller lost some of his responsibility in approving the activities of bank holding companies and their subsidiaries.

Comptroller Saxon complained that the Federal Reserve's Regulation M restricted the banks too much in their branch business abroad and lobbied in other ways for the extension of bank powers, foreign and domestic. In fact, a number of large banks, including Chase Manhattan, switched to national charters because of Saxon's liberality between 1963 and 1966.[18] If Saxon pleased the big bankers, his successors found no less approbation in the world of high finance. Large banks continued to change over to national charters. Wells Fargo did in 1968. Under William B. Camp, the movement by banks to diversify through one-bank holding companies got under way. Camp approved. In one case involving First National City Bank, he altered the Comptroller's regulations to allow FNCB to operate a mutual fund, an area very close to the securities business. This rule would have extended to foreign operations.[19] The Supreme Court overruled Camp's decision (Investment Company Institute v. Camp) at the same time Congress was also moving to prohibit such diversification through the holding company legislation of 1970. The final legislation put all holding company authority in the Federal

Reserve, assuring stricter rules under Regulation Y than Camp would have written.[20]

Among the regulatory agencies, then, the Comptroller of the Currency represents the most liberal and big-bank-oriented authority. Camp and Saxon both helped nurse the national banks through their prolonged expansion during the 1960s.[21] Camp's successor, James E. Smith, appeared to continue the philosophy of his predecessors. When Franklin National Bank fell into financial difficulties in 1974, Smith showed that he too wanted to see banks expand geographically as much as possible. He favored legislation which would have permitted an out-of-state bank to take over Franklin, even if this meant bending the rule against interstate branch systems. Smith said,

> My interest runs well beyond Franklin. I am of the view that some sort of inter-state access to the major money markets is an inevitable development.[22]

The division of federal authority in regulating banks produces conflicts. The Hunt Commission suggested in 1970 combining the regulatory functions of the Federal Reserve and the Comptroller (and the Federal Deposit Insurance Corporation) to simplify and unify an unsatisfactory situation. Hunt proposed a new office, independent of the Treasury and the Federal Reserve, leaving the Fed its responsibility for monetary policy. There is more to be said, however, for unifying regulation under an expanded Federal Reserve. With its more comprehensive view of the monetary and banking structure, and its greater insulation from political pressure, the Fed is better suited to the task. More today than ever before, the regulation of banking should not be separated from the regulation of the monetary system. In the meantime however, expansion-minded banks are glad to have the Comptroller on their side.

THE STATES: FIFTY-ONE FIEFDOMS

Taken as a whole, the United States market would be the largest banking market in the world. But under American law, banks can operate branches in only one state. The ability to operate certain subsidiaries nationwide under Edge Act and holding company legislation enables some banks to go beyond state limits, but generally, the state branching law separates the United States into fifty-one smaller sovereignties (including the District of Columbia). In most states, banks are not even allowed to operate state-wide. For the banking giants, all of this is most frustrating.

State limitations on branching affect the ability of American banks to go abroad. Size is the single most important factor in international banking, as well as in international business generally. The high start-up and operating costs of a London operation especially demand extensive resources. A bank facing a limited home market could be unable to grow sufficiently to reach international proportions. On the other hand, once large enough, a bank with limited domestic expansion potential might see it as even more important to look for a growth outlet abroad.

Among the largest banks in London,[23] these considerations seem to apply. All are based directly either in New York City, Chicago or California, and directly serve the three most important American banking markets. The banks based in other states do not have access to the resources of these more lucrative areas, so that the home banks in those three areas reap the benefits, protected from outside competition. Banks have pressured various state authorities to liberalize restrictive branching laws. They look with envy on the ability of California banks to branch state-wide, in a state with a population of 20 million. California banks, because of their overwhelming domestic assets, thus figure importantly in international banking. Although the smaller local bankers resist, the large banks have lobbied successfully for changes in many states, arguing that they need wider markets in order to compete both at home and abroad. Action in several states illustrates the competing pressures within and among the states.

New York: While the New York market is undoubtedly the envy of bankers everywhere, New York bankers have themselves felt constrained by state law. Until fairly recently, New York City-based banks could only operate in the city. They were then permitted to move into contiguous counties. Mindful of the California example, they pressured for state-wide banking. Smaller upstate banks fear the incursion, but the big city banks won their case, and state-wide branching became legal in 1976.

New Yorkers also eye other states. One banker said that getting out of New York is the name of the game at present.[24] Former New York state banking supervisor Albright suggested agreements with other states whereby banks would be able to open out-of-state retail branches on a reciprocal basis.[25] New York banks clearly wish to retain their predominance of size among American bankers.

Texas: Texas, of course, represents a banking market of growing importance in the United States, especially because of the oil interests there. Yet, because the state constitution prohibits branch banking, Texas banks have had difficulty competing with banks of international scale. No Texas banks had London branches before

1970. The restrictive branching law has fragmented the Texas market among almost 1300 banks. Since 1970, however, Houston and Dallas banks have turned to multibank holding companies to consolidate the resources of groups of banks. But as *The Banker* said, "The holding company concept was satisfactory only as an interim measure. The new drive was international."[26] Four Texas banks now have London branches. They hope to profit from North Sea oil operations in Britain and to expand in a way they cannot at home.

Even now, small bankers are trying to curb the buildup of large banks through holding company connections. In 1974, a measure narrowly failed in the Texas legislature to restrict holding companies in Texas from controlling more than eight percent of the state's banking and savings and loans deposits. While the law did not pass, the closeness of the vote shows the strength of small-bank forces in Texas.[27]

Illinois: Illinois bankers face the same problems as their Texan counterparts: state law forbids branching. Chicago, however, with its local commodity markets does boast several powerful banks, although only one, Continental Illinois, entered London before 1969. Until 1968, state-chartered banks were not permitted to have foreign branches. Five Chicago banks now have London branches. As in Texas, opposition to expanded branching powers comes from smaller bankers who fear competition. In January, 1973, the Illinois Bankers Association voted 639 to 317 to retain unit branching.[28] The largest banks feel they have been unnecessarily shackled, but any moves in the future to liberalize Illinois law will probably fall short of the freedom found in most other states.

Pennsylvania: Pennsylvania banks, particularly those in Philadelphia, especially resent the powerful New York banks less than one hundred miles away. Pennsylvania's other neighbor, New Jersey, recently approved state-wide branching. Pennsylvania maintains a contiguous county system whereby banks can branch into counties bordering on their head office county.[29] There is now a bill before the Pennsylvania legislature to permit state-wide branching. Once again, the banks are pushing to enlarge their resource bases in order to gain the size they think necessary to compete at the national and international level. Possessing two of the most important American industrial cities, however, Pennsylvania has developed a number of important banks which have moved into international operations, particularly in London. (First Pennsylvania, Mellon Bank, Girard Bank, Philadelphia National, and Fidelity Bank).

As the situation in these states shows, state laws do affect the fortune of the banks. The accidents of state laws determine the potential power and size of local banks which in turn affect their power and size internationally. In addition, the very structure of state regulation sets up artificial barriers to expansion which lead expansion-oriented banks to look overseas for new markets. Meanwhile, the Federal Reserve has consistently approved of foreign expansion even as it remains strict on the question of domestic activities. The Comptroller, as we have seen, generally acts as a lobbyist for expansion, both domestic and foreign. The combination of sticks and carrots has permitted, and sometimes encouraged, the world-wide expansion of American banks. Monetary policy and capital controls provided the final push.

MAKING MONEY

Besides telling the banks what they may or may not do, the Federal Reserve produces their chief raw material: money. The way in which the Fed has managed the money supply was one more inducement to maintain a foreign branch in the 1960s. The quirks of U.S. monetary control played no small part in the development of the Eurodollar market,[30] and that market affected in turn the very mechanism of Federal Reserve money manufacture. The two most important aspects of Federal Reserve policy in this respect are interest rate policy and reserve requirements. Interest rate policy will be examined first.

Interest Rates

Interest rate policy is only one part of monetary policy as a whole, but an optimal interest rate level is usually considered as a policy goal independent of money supply targets. It is particularly important in the international sphere because differences in interest rate levels produce international capital flows. The Fed influences market interest rates by changing the discount rate,[31] by open market operations and by setting maximum rates which banks may offer for deposits (under Regulation Q). It is Regulation Q we are most concerned with here.

Regulation Q and Foreign Branches: The banking collapse of the 1930s had originally convinced legislators that strict controls should regulate American banks in order to prevent excessive competition for deposits. The Banking Act of 1933 gave the Federal Reserve the authority to limit interest payable on deposits. Under this act, no interest could be paid on demand deposits[32] and the Fed would place maximums for all banks on interest payable on time and savings deposits.[33] Eventually, some groups such as savings and loan associations developed a vested interest in the continuation of Regulation Q since they have been allowed to offer a rate on deposits higher than commercial banks. Deposits payable at foreign branches, however, were excluded in order to allow Americans to offer competitive rates abroad. This exemption only proved significant in the 1960s.

Regulation Q limits on interest payable on time deposits have created special problems in the Federal Reserve's regulation of the money supply because they have at times kept the return on time deposits significantly below market rates of interest in the U.S. and abroad. Regulation Q created interest rate differentials between lower controlled rates (bank deposits) and higher uncontrolled rates (such as rates on commercial paper in the U.S. and deposits abroad). It thus produced flows of funds away from domestic banks.[34] London banks could pay higher rates, at least for large dollar deposits for in London there was no interest rate ceiling. Regulation Q became, in fact, a lower limit for the Eurodollar deposit rate.[35] American banks abroad quite naturally tried to capture foreign deposits by paying rates above Regulation Q limits at their foreign branches; others made the decision to set up foreign branches in order to participate in the foreign dollar market. (And as soon as a dollar-owner transferred his account from a U.S. bank to a foreign bank, it was called a Eurodollar.) Figure 5-1 shows the difference between New York and London interest rates on dollars along with the growth of foreign dollar deposits at American banks' British branches before 1970.[36]

Regulation Q encouraged foreign branches in another way in the 1960s. At times of tight money, banks found that they needed more deposits in order to be able to lend to their important customers. But it has already been seen that Regulation Q prohibited banks from increasing their deposits by raising deposit rates. For the banks, it seemed that just when they needed deposits the most they were least able to attract them. But a bank with a foreign branch owned in effect a loophole. The foreign branch *could* raise its deposit rates to attract funds from abroad and then lend the money to its parent in the United States. In other words, the parent which had a foreign branch could get money abroad at times when it was not available at home. This possibility put the large international banks at a potential advantage over their purely domestic competitors until the end of 1969 when the Fed took action to restrict such borrowings.

The Federal Reserve raised Regulation Q ceilings in the course of the 1960s, but kept them below market rates at times. Borrowing

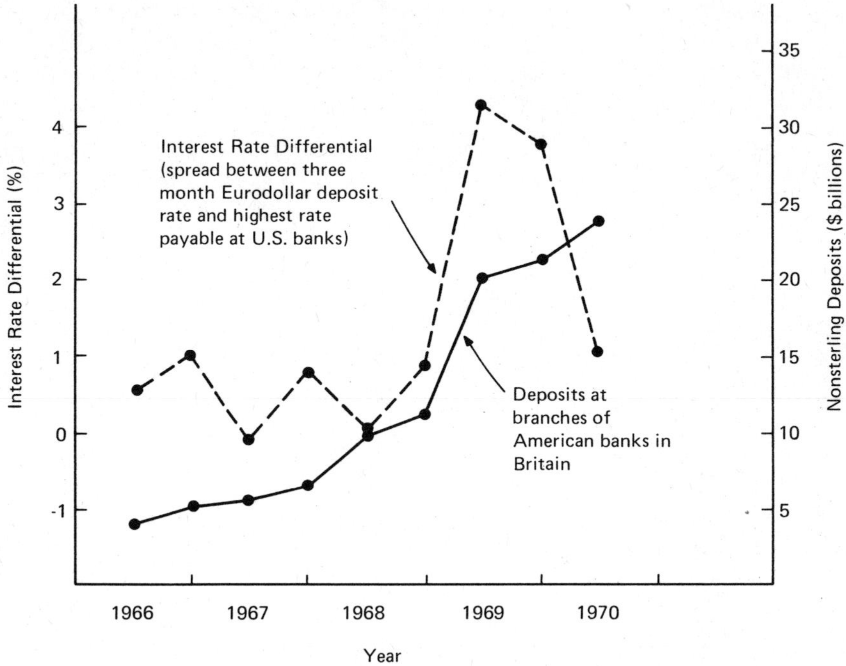

Source: Federal Reserve Bulletin; Bank of England.

Figure 5-1. Branch Deposits, Interest Rate Differentials

from foreign branches grew whenever the ceiling got very much out of line with domestic rates such as those on Treasury bills or commercial paper, a form of direct corporate borrowing. (See Figure 5-2.) The higher the differential between Regulation Q and commercial paper rates, the higher the level of borrowing from foreign branches (called liabilities to foreign branches). In August, 1966, for instance, prime 4-6 month commercial paper in the United States yielded over six percent and the comparable Eurodollar rate was also over six percent. In contrast, Regulation Q set the maximum deposit rate at 5.5 percent—which made bank deposits in the U.S. relatively unattractive when compared to other investments. Not surprisingly, liabilities of U.S. banks to their foreign branches doubled from $2 billion to $4 billion as American banks scrambled for funds.

In late 1969, the differential between the Regulation Q rate and commercial paper rates grew to about three percent. Again, liabilities to foreign branches grew from $6 billion at the end of 1968 to over $14 billion by the end of September 1969.

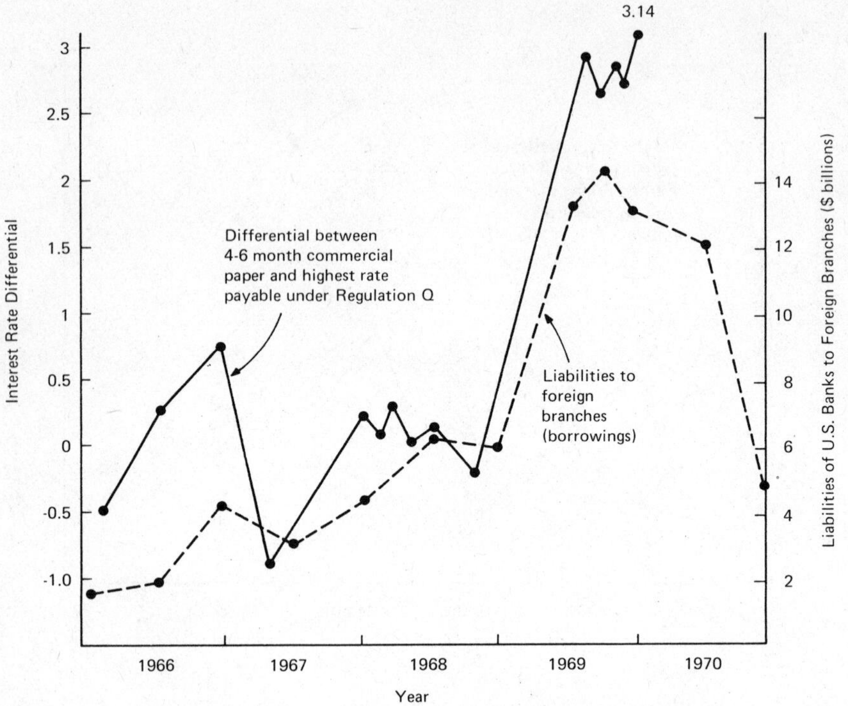

Source: Federal Reserve Bank of St. Louis *Review*, February, 1970 for interest rates; *Federal Reserve Bulletin* borrowings.

Figure 5-2. U.S. Interest Rates and Borrowing from Branches

Figure 5-3 shows the changes between 1966 and mid-1974 in U.S. banks' liabilities to their foreign branches compared with the changes in borrowings from all foreign banks. It can be seen that foreign branches played an important role in supplying funds to parents, particularly before 1970 when money was tight in the United States. In the last half of 1969, the height of the credit crunch, short-term liabilities to foreign banks did not expand to anywhere near the extent of liabilities of parent banks to their branches. It would seem that banks without foreign branches could not or did not have access to Eurodollars so easily as those with foreign branches. Figure 5-3 also shows the dominant position of British branches in supplying parents with funds at times of tight conditions in the United States. In 1969, British branches accounted for one-half of the funds

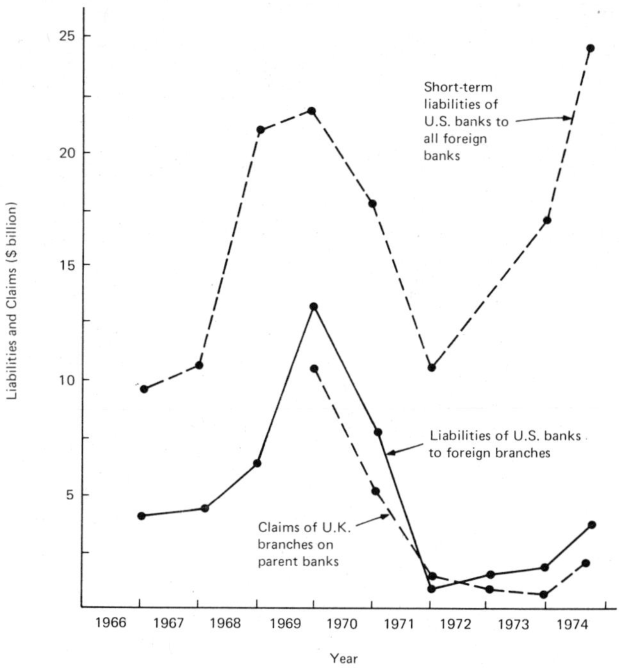

Source: *Federal Reserve Bulletin.*

Note: Data on foreign branch assets are only available starting in December, 1969.

Figure 5-3. U.S. Bank Borrowing from Banks Abroad

supplied by all foreign banks and over 80 percent of the funds supplied by foreign branches.

It should be emphasized that the banks could not tap the Eurodollar market so easily without a controlled institution willing to reallocate funds to the parent under tight money conditions. When money is very tight, banks will ration funds to favored customers. Banks with foreign branches have had what Lees calls "captive" deposits.[37] While one-half of all funds from foreign banks came from branches in 1969, only 26 of 14,000 American banks had British branches. And the big banks probably accounted for a good portion of the borrowing from other foreign banks too. In August, 1969, New York City banks had 70 percent of all the borrowing from foreign branches and 66 percent of the deposits of foreign banks in the U.S. Tight money episodes thus produced new waves of branches in London. Most banks entering London in the late 1960s were clear in their motives. When the Bank of New York came in

1967, *The Banker* said, "The Bank of New York makes no bones about its reasons for wanting to come in. It wants access to the London money market and, in particular, to the Eurodollar market."[38]

The Demise of Regulation Q: The periods of credit restriction in the 1960s thus showed many banks that a foreign branch could be a valuable source of funding. But the concentrated flows of billions of dollars between parent banks and their branches abroad did not please everyone. Smaller banks complained that they took the brunt of tight money while the big banks escaped. In fact, most of the Eurodollar activity *was* concentrated at the big New York banks, notably, Chase, Citibank, and Manufacturers Hanover.[39] Populists in the United States complained that the prime rate in the U.S. was rising as a result of the high cost of funds borrowed abroad. Foreign central banks complained that the demand for Eurodollars and the resultant high Eurodollar interest rates were causing capital outflows and currency crises as arbitrageurs sold foreign currencies in order to profit from high dollar deposit rates in London and elsewhere. The influx of dollars into the U.S. also tended to frustrate the Nixon administration's attempts to control the domestic money supply.

Chairman Martin of the Federal Reserve Board confirmed that the banks were taking action to evade restrictive monetary policy:

> The consensus of the Board is that the devices used by banks to obtain non-depository sources of funds, while they have not made it impossible to achieve the overall objectives on monetary policy, may have delayed the impact of monetary restraint on spending. Furthermore, they have also had undesirable effects in the distribution of monetary restraint among the various sectors of the economy.[40]

He also found that bigger banks with foreign branches had an advantage over smaller domestic banks in an assessment of monetary policy in 1969:

> . . . these sources of funds have been available mainly to the larger banks in the System, and especially to those who have branches abroad or affiliated holding companies. Consequently, the incidence of monetary restraint in the banking system has been unevenly distributed.[41]

Rather than remove Regulation Q in 1969 (which would have been politically difficult) the Federal Reserve solved the problem of capital flows between parent and branch by a new control suggested by Andrew Brimmer, a Reserve Board member. (For a discussion, see the next section on reserve requirements.)

Despite the distortions and inequities resulting from Regulation Q, strong pressures existed for retaining it. Both Presidents Kennedy and Johnson preferred low interest rates and were willing to impose them by means of the Regulation Q ceilings. Members of Congress championed the cause of low interest rates. The savings and loan industry fought for the retention of Regulation Q because it ensured they could compete with commercial banks for deposits.[42] Ceilings are also considered by some to be useful in controlling bank credit by their influence on the supply of loanable funds. But as banks increasingly obtained funds outside of the normal deposit mechanism, some argued that Regulation Q had become less useful as a policy tool.[43]

The Nixon administration did not share the Democrats' preference for low interest rates, nor did it like the idea of administered markets (with some famous exceptions, of course). It faced the worst of all possible worlds in late 1969 when it allowed the difference between other rates and Regulation Q rates to widen. That was the heyday of the Eurodollar. Although the government could not eliminate Q in 1969, it did start down that road at the first opportunity. In 1970 all interest rate ceilings were removed on big short-term deposits, and President Nixon also appointed the Hunt Commission to study the problems of financial institutions that year. In the wake of its recommendations, the Ford administration has joined in the effort to abolish Regulation Q. But because Regulation Q no longer applies to any deposits of over $100,000,[44] interest rate policy no longer affects banks' decisions to open foreign branches. American banks can now offer internationally competitive rates from domestic branches (although other factors still favor foreign branches as will be seen in the following section). But until 1970, Regulation Q did greatly influence the development of the Eurodollar market and the growing participation of American banks in that market.

Reserve Requirements

Reserve requirements are another tool of monetary policy with implications for international banking. By the authority of the Banking Act of 1935, the Federal Reserve Board determines, within certain limits, the reserve requirements on the U.S. deposits of member banks. These were meant to serve two purposes: to contribute to the solvency of banks by ensuring adequate reserves and to assure control of credit by putting a check on the expansion of bank assets. In practice, however, reserve requirement changes are used mainly to influence the supply of credit.[45]

Reserve requirements have the effect of increasing the cost of attracting deposits. So, the higher the reserves required on a certain category of deposit, the more a bank must effectively pay for those funds.[46] Reserve requirements have influenced international developments in two ways: (1) by spurring the growth of the Eurodollar market outside of the United States; (2) by increasing the usefulness of foreign branches to U.S. banks.

Reserves and the Eurodollar Market: Like many other Federal Reserve regulations, reserve requirements do not apply to deposits at foreign branches (Regulation D). American banks in Britain must observe only British regulations in this respect, and the British have not imposed reserve requirements on nonsterling deposits. In the absence of reserve requirements on dollar deposits on Britain, lending dollars from branches there costs less than similar lending from the United States, even when market conditions are the same. A bank can afford to offer higher deposit rates to customers in London than it can in the U.S.; it can also charge lower rates to borrowers. The wholesale nature of the Eurodollar market also contributes to lower costs, thus reinforcing this effect. It is this cost differential which supports the existence of a market for dollars outside of the U.S. It is the crucial factor in the development of the Eurodollar market. Banks with international customers therefore find that to remain competitive they need a foreign branch. In this way, reserve requirement differentials have contributed to the establishment of foreign branches by American banks. And as long as this difference exists there is likely to be a Eurodollar market.

Reserves and Capital Flows: It was seen above that interest rate differentials stimulated huge flows of dollars into and out of the United States. This happened when U.S. banks borrowed from their foreign branches to evade Regulation Q. These capital movements tended to disrupt American monetary policy, as well as monetary policy abroad.

In 1969, the flows of capital into U.S. banks from abroad had become unmanageable. It was thought that the existence of the Eurodollar market made monetary control impossible as the big banks with foreign branches siphoned in foreign funds. But the Fed quickly solved the problem. By imposing a 10 percent special reserve requirement on increases in Eurodollar borrowings above a base level by American banks, the Fed made it more difficult and costly to evade domestic monetary stringency via foreign borrowing. Now, in effect, borrowings from branches were to be treated like deposits in that reserves had to be maintained on them. As Federal Reserve Board member Mitchell said, "As banks extended in scope and magnitude their access to money and credit markets in 1969, apprehension that such techniques were undermining the force of monetary restraint grew . . ."[47] This new reserve requirement enabled the Board to get control over the dollar inflows without altering the whole range of domestic policy.[48] Dollar outflows presented a new problem in 1970 and 1971. Once huge repayments of 1969 borrowings of Eurodollars began in 1970 as monetary conditions eased, the Federal Reserve possessed no comparable tool to stop the outflow.[49]

The use of reserve requirements to cut off the supply of Eurodollars to parent banks is, however, an effective tool which potentially enables the Fed to control movements of funds between parent and branch banks without resorting to changes in general monetary conditions at home. Borrowing from branches (see Figure 5-3) quickly became less significant after imposition of the new reserve requirement. Andrew Brimmer of the Federal Reserve Board estimated that by the end of 1972, the foreign branches in London used only 2.7 percent of their resources for supplying their parents with funds compared to a level of 30 percent in 1969. The change indicates that such borrowing had been discouraged by Fed policy and that the foreign branches no longer existed merely to serve parent banks.[50] The percentage did rise to 4.7 percent in August 1974, but this was still far below the 1969 average.

Marginal reserve requirements on inflows from the Eurodollar market removed therefore for a time one important motive for operating a foreign branch. Now a high price might have to be paid for borrowing from the branch. Some of the smaller banks which came to London only for insurance against tight money may later have regretted the move. Perhaps, however, responding to charges of discrimination, the Fed eventually removed the relatively heavy requirements on Eurodollar borrowing by American banks, bringing the level more in line with the reserves required on comparable domestically acquired funds.

Toward Flexibility: The Federal Reserve Board found these marginal reserve requirements so successful that they decided to use a similar method domestically when the banks began to bid too strongly for deposits. Instead of limiting the growth of deposits by means of Regulation Q, reserve requirements were substituted and Regulation Q removed. In May 1973, the Fed therefore raised the reserve requirement on domestic long-term deposits (CDs) to eight percent at the same time that it lowered the requirement on Eurodollar borrowings to eight percent. Late in 1973, there was even a bias in favor of borrowing Eurodollars, and as Figure 5-3 shows, liabilities to foreign branches did increase in that period. Since May 1975, the reserves required on foreign funds borrowed by American banks have been about the same as those required on domestic time deposits. In effect, the Fed can now regulate the extent to which domestic banks can bid for funds in the U.S. and in the Eurodollar market. It makes borrowing from branches more or less costly just as it pleases.

All of these shifts in reserve requirements indicate that the Federal Reserve has learned to control the banks' access to funds and hence their ability to expand credit. This stands in contrast to 1969 when money seemed to flow uncontrollably into the United States. The change marks an increased level of sophistication in monetary policy and a remarkable flexibility in dealing with new problems. Determined banking authorities can indeed control the banks to the extent they wish. Reserve requirements still play a part in American international banking, of course, even if the Fed has changed the environment. Reserve requirements on deposits in the United States continue to mean that the costs of dollar business are lower abroad. And although parent banks now must pay a higher cost when they borrow from their branches for domestic use, many consider it worthwhile to have that window on the Eurodollar market anyway. It is unlikely, however, that banks will ever again be permitted to distort American monetary policy the way they did in 1969. Reserve requirements have effectively separated the U.S. money market from that huge pool of dollars abroad.

BLOCKING MONEY

Monetary policy stops at the water's edge, but money does not. The Kennedy, Johnson and Nixon administrations all faced the problem of blocking dollar outflows to avoid devaluation. Kennedy moved to tax foreign long-term borrowing from the United States and Johnson went further by limiting outflows for American foreign investment and for bank loans to foreigners. Nixon promised to remove these capital controls, but they, like the war in Vietnam, continued until 1974. These capital controls contributed significantly to the establishment of foreign branches by American banks between 1964 and 1974. The purpose of the capital controls mentioned above was to force international corporations and other big borrowers to obtain their foreign financing outside of the United States. This, of course, meant that banks would need foreign branches if they wished to continue to service their multinational clients effectively.

The Federal Reserve administered the Voluntary Foreign Credit

Restraint Program (VFCRP) between 1965 and 1974. While it limited the amount of foreign loans a bank could make from home offices to foreigners, it did not limit such loans generally from foreign branches. Banks which came to London after 1965 often cited the credit restraint and foreign direct investment programs as reasons for setting up foreign branches—they could continue their foreign lending by substituting the Eurodollar market and foreign currencies obtained abroad for domestic sources.

The Federal Reserve Board expressed somewhat ambivalent attitudes toward the Foreign Credit Restraint Program it administered, although the Board did see the necessity of the program, given American balance of payments accounts. President Johnson announced the program in his balance of payments message of February 10, 1965, as a temporary expedient until the balance of payments could be brought under control. The Board supported the program insofar as it eased a temporary situation, but not as a permanent system of capital control. But the program began to look more permanent than temporary. The Board chose not to impose mandatory controls even when it was authorized to do so in 1968.

As the balance of payments continued to disintegrate the Nixon Administration found itself unable to dismantle Johnson's system of capital controls despite Nixon's promise to do so. Andrew Brimmer, the administrator for the Fed, said the principal impact of the program hit the banks in 1965 and that the limitations had little effect after that in 1966-68.[51] Calling for the end of the controls, the President of Bank of America agreed:

> It is becoming increasingly apparent that the Federal Reserve Program to limit United States bank lending abroad has become largely ineffective, as indicated by the large and consistent leeway available to banks within their guidelines.[52]

Finally, after the American balance of payments did improve after devaluation and other measures, the controls were removed (January 29, 1974).

Although increasingly weakened after 1969, the initially severe restraints did induce American banks to open branches between 1965 and 1974. The 1965 Guidelines asked for a voluntary limitation of foreign credits to 105 percent of the amount outstanding at the end of 1964.[53] After having increased their loans to foreigners by about $200 million per month in early 1965, the banks immediately reduced their foreign loans so that they soon fell below their voluntary quotas.

The 1968 Guidelines imposed more serious restrictions to the extent that they required *a reduction* in the voluntary quotas on foreign lending and requested that banks make *no* new term loans to developed countries in Western Europe, except for the financing of U.S. exports.[54]

By the time the Nixon Administration cancelled the VCFRP, however, it ended without a whimper.[55] As seen in Table 5-1, the banks managed to have a comfortable leeway under the ceilings except in 1965 and 1968. Table 5-2 shows the simultaneous growth of credits granted at foreign branches. Most banks whose foreign lending could have been squeezed by such limits had opened foreign branches, and all banks important in international lending had London branches. Because banks could get around restrictions via foreign branch lending, the Voluntary Foreign Credit Restraint Program encouraged the banks to turn to foreign branch lending.

The Government, in fact, expressed pleasure that the American direct investors abroad could so easily substitute foreign borrowing for the capital exports they had used in the past.[56] The Fed, however, reserved its judgment on the program as a whole, noting that the swell of foreign branches resulting from the VFCR Program might have unknown effects. Governor Brimmer said to the Joint Economic Committee:

Table 5-1. Voluntary Credit Restraints—Foreign Assets of U.S. Banks (£ million)

		Total Foreign Assets Held for Own Account	*Leeway Under Ceilings*
End:			
December,	1964	9,719	–
	1965	9,958	321
	1966	9,844	911
	1967	10,202	1,204
	1968	9,844	476
	1969	10,158	1,942
	1970	10,614	1,942
April,	1971	10,634	1,811

Source: Data from the Federal Reserve as taken from Treasury foreign exchange forms B-2 and B-3 and other sources. Presented by Andrew Brimmer in U.S., Congress, Joint Economic Committee, *The Balance of Payments Mess*, p. 15.

Table 5-2. Foreign Credits of U.S. Banks ($ billion)

	Held by Domestic Offices for Own Account	*Held by Foreign Branches*	
		Amount	*Percent of Total*
1960	4.2	2.4	36.3
1964	9.4	3.9	29.3
1965	9.7	5.5	36.1
1966	9.6	6.0	38.4
1967	9.8	7.7	44.0
1968	9.2	10.2	52.5
1969	9.3	16.1	63.3
1970	9.7	27.6	73.9
1971	12.1	40.2	76.9

Source: As estimated by Andrew Brimmer, "Commercial Bank Lending Abroad and the U.S. Balance of Payments," Speech at the Federal Reserve Bank of Chicago, March 16, 1972.

> One thing that is important and that I would like to stress is that, partly because of the VCFR, the American banks have greatly expanded their network of foreign branches abroad. These are principally concentrated in London. . . . It is hard to estimate the full effect—in either the short run or long run—of this development of the U.S. banking system.[57]

Thus, the Voluntary Foreign Credit Restraint Program, whatever its long-run impact on the balance of payments, may have been most significant in making banks go abroad. The Foreign Direct Investment Program and the Interest Equalization Tax contributed as well.

The Foreign Direct Investment program had a less direct effect on banks. American balance of payments policy increased American business corporations' need for external finance by limiting the amount of capital they could export from home after February, 1965. These became mandatory limits after 1968. The F.D.I.P. increased demands on the Eurodollar market by American investors and by extension, it increased demands on the branches of American banks. A Chase Manhattan study estimated that in 1968 American firms raised 35 percent of their foreign investment funds abroad.[58] A 1969 Commerce Department study showed an even higher proportion of 39 percent raised abroad by majority-owned affiliates.[59] This was up from only 2 percent in 1965. (See Table 5-3.) All of the capital controls seemed to produce the same result: more banks in Britain.

Table 5-3. Corporate Borrowing Abroad Under F.D.I.P.

	1965	*1966*	*1967*	*1968*	*1969*	*1970*
Total Direct Investment Yearly (excluding Canada)	4236	5130	4876	5659	7560	9274
Sources:						
Transfers of Capital	3080	3387	3360	2321	3427	4406
Reinvested Earnings	1058	1109	934	1129	1530	2106
Foreign Borrowing	98	634	582	2209	2603	2762
Foreign Borrowing as % of Direct Investment	2	12	12	39	34	30

Source: U.S. Department of Commerce, *Foreign Direct Investment Program: Selected Statistics, 1972*, p. 5.

The interest equalization tax was the third panel of the capital controls triptych. It was a tax meant to increase the cost of foreign borrowing from the U.S.[60] Originally a tax imposed only on American purchases of long-term foreign securities, the IET was extended to bank loans of more than one year after February 10, 1965. President Johnson noted that bank loans abroad with maturities of over one year had increased by more than one-third in 1964.[61] By adding an extra one percent cost to long-term loans to foreigners, the tax increased the interest cost on such loans by about fifteen percent, although it did not apply to loans of under one year or to export credits. The effect was immediate: the banks' long-term claims on foreigners decreased yearly from 1966 to 1970.[62] At first, the IET on bank loans applied to domestic and foreign branches. Foreign currency loans were untaxed up to a certain level. Of course, the foreign branches could effectively extend longer term credits untaxed by automatically rolling over shorter term loans.

In February, 1967, Johnson exempted all lending activities at foreign branches from the IET. This freed the foreign branches to engage in long-term lending abroad; maturities on dollar loans in London immediately lengthened. The IET was reduced in 1969 and since its removal in 1974, of course, it no longer affects branching decisions by American banks.

The story is clearer now that the American side has been told. Compared to London's, America's banking rules look like Rube Goldberg creations. Not only is the regulatory setup complex, divided among so many authorities, but the substance of the regulations is itself onerous. In the 1960s especially, the gap between domestic constraints and foreign freedoms widened. The regulations reviewed here acted to promote foreign expansion in two ways: (1) positively, by making expansion easy, and (2) negatively, by restricting bank activities at home.

The positive inducements are, in a sense, less important in the 1960s in that they did not undergo great transformations. The Edge Act had been around for a long time—since 1919. Some of the red tape of foreign expansion was cut in the early 1960s, but legal difficulties had rarely been impediments anyway. In addition, mergers served to consolidate the American banking system and to create banks big enough for successful foreign penetration. But all of these positive factors tended to be long-run considerations. They were permissive, but they did not account for the sudden and dramatic increase in international expansion by American banks.

The negative side explains much more; as the domestic rules go tighter, the flow of banks to foreign shores increases. Until 1970, Regulation Q limited the banks' ability to bid for additional deposits. General reserve requirements in the meantime added to parent banks' costs and subtracted from their competitiveness internationally. From 1965 to 1974, capital controls smothered international lending by banks from domestic offices while inflating demand for dollar loans abroad. Less directly, the prohibition against nationwide branching in the United States has acted to force the expansion-minded banks to think of foreign outlets.

Big banks have not lacked reasons for going abroad in the recent past. The smaller the bank, however, the weaker would be the arguments for international branching. Limits on international lending become less important the less international business a bank transacts. Smaller banks typically have less volatile sources of funds than the big, well-known banks whose depositors are sensitive to small interest rate differentials. Small banks therefore felt less threatened by such limits as Regulation Q.[63]

In the last analysis, it is impossible to say which of these factors proved most important in contributing to the bankers' exodus. Table 5-4 shows for the period 1965-1974 the degree to which individual banking regulations influenced the movement abroad. Since 1973, Regulation Q has not been an international factor, and capital controls have played no role since early 1974. The advantage of branch loans to parents has been lessened. No bank has since closed a London branch, but the rush of applications has subsided and some representative offices have been closed in London. It would seem that the restrictions of the American regulatory system did indeed account for the impetus to *open* foreign branches in the 1960s, but that it was not the only reason for *maintaining* such branches. Once

Table 5-4. U.S. Regulations and Foreign Branching

	1965– –66– –67– –68– –69– –70– –71– –72– –73– –74–
Absence of Reserves in Eurodollar Market	XXXXXXXXXXXXXXXXXXXXXXXXXXXXXXXXXXXXXXXXXX
Regulation Q	XXXXXXXXXXXXXXXXXXXXXXXXXXXXXXX////////////////////
Absence of Reserves on Branch Loans to Parent Banks	XXXXXXXXXXXXXXXXX //////
Voluntary Foreign Credit Restraint	XXXXXXXXXXXXXXXXXXXXXXXXXXXXXXXXXXXXXX
Foreign Direct Investment Controls	XXXXXXXXXXXXXXXXXXXXXXXXXXXXXXXXXXXXXX
Interest Equalization Tax	/////////////////XXXXXXXXXXXXXXXXXXXXXXXXXXXX

Strong Impact on Foreign Branching: XXXXXXXXXX
Moderate Impact on Foreign Branching: ////////////////////

having committed one's pride, sunk the costs, developed business, a banker is motivated by different considerations. The Nixon Administration could indeed end the system of capital controls with the confidence that the change would probably help New York without hurting the structure which had developed in London.

It is well to recall here our original argument: government actions crucially determine the economic environment, and hence, the microeconomic decisions by individuals. Certainly the shelf of American policies we have seen above exercised a tremendous impact on the development of international banking. A second point is also worth noting: when a reasonably powerful and imaginative government is unhappy with certain events, it can probably dream up a rule to change their course. In 1969, doomwatchers predicted that the U.S. money supply was being subverted by uncontrollable capital flows. But when marginal reserve requirements were invented that problem (but not others!) virtually disappeared. Of course the choices are not easy for anyone who values freedom and fears bureaucratic encroachment. But there *are* choices, after all: even interdependence has its antidotes.

NOTES TO CHAPTER FIVE

1. The Federal Reserve Board requested that Congress grant it power over the reserves of *all* banks in early 1974. For analysis of the problems of overlapping authority, see for instance, J.L. Robertson, "Federal Banking

Regulation: A Plea for Unification," *Law and Contemporary Problems* 31 (Autumn 1966); Howard Hackley, "Our Baffling Banking System," *Virginia Law Review*, May 1966; U.S. President, *Report of the President's Commission on Financial Structure and Regulation* (The Hunt Report), December 1971 (Published 1972). The Hunt Commission suggested a new banking authority, the Office of the Federal Bank Administrator, which would take over the regulatory duties of both the Federal Reserve Board and the Comptroller of the Currency. Proposals are now pending in Congress largely adopting the Hunt Proposals.

2. Practically all large banks in the United States are members of the Federal Reserve System (although many smaller banks are not), so that the Fed exercises effective control in approving London branches. In 1964, the Comptroller of the Currency, the authority directly over national banks, also demanded prior notification from national banks before establishing foreign branches.

3. U.S. Board of Governors of the Federal Reserve System, unpublished *Report* entitled "Foreign Operations of U.S. Banks and their Supervision," dated June 30, 1967, quoted in Stuart Robinson, *Multinational Banking* (Leiden: Sijthoff, 1971), p. 40. See also Francis A. Lees, *International Banking and Finance* (New York: John Wiley, 1974), pp. 20-21.

4. See George Mitchell (Steering Committee Chairman), "How the Fed Sees Multinational Bank Regulation," *The Banker*, July 1974.

5. Regulation M, August 1, 1963. Under the Banking Act of 1933, (12 U.S.C. par. 24) a national bank may not own for its own account, shares of stock in corporation. Even if the practice is "usual abroad," branches may not act in the capacity of investment bankers. When the change in the law was being considered in Congress, Chairman Martin of the Federal Reserve had stated: ". . . I would not interpret this bill as a *carte blanche* for the full equalization of foreign branch powers except as expressly permitted by Board regulations that would be formulated after consideration of actual conditions and with due regard for the integrity and soundness of the American banking system." Quoted in Ronald E. Covault, "Foreign Branches and Edge Corporations," *National Banking Review*, December 1963.

6. The change in Regulation M (revised 15 March 1967) followed a 1966 amendment to Section 25 of the Federal Reserve Act (12 U.S.C. pars. 601-604a).

7. See L. Mote et al., "One Bank Holding Company," Federal Reserve Bank of Chicago, *Business Conditions*, July 1970. The Federal Reserve had opposed the one-bank holding company loophole in 1956, realizing a potential for abuses. (See Christopher Elias, *The Dollar Barons* (New York: Macmillan, 1973), p. 138). One motive of banks in forming one-bank holding companies was the desire to get access to resources when money was tight, as in 1966 and 1969. Where banks could not attract funds because of interest rate ceilings, the holding companies could offer notes at higher rates.

8. The 1970 Bank Holding Company Act (Section 4(c)(8)) allows one-bank holding companies to engage in activities "so closely related to banking" as to be "a proper incident thereto." (See Jerome W. Shay, "Bank Holding Companies and the Fed: Who's Board?," *Banking Law Journal*, April 1974.) Under the law, a bank had to divest its subsidiaries which did not conform to the Act, although

nonconforming foreign subsidiaries could be kept if they did not engage in domestic U.S. business. For the extent of expansion since the 1970 Act, see F.E. Wrocklage and R.M. McConnell, "How BHC-Act Amendments Changed the Map of Banking in Two Years," *Banking*, December 1972. Diversification includes finance companies, factoring, certain insurance activities, leasing, investment consulting, community development corporations, data processing and other financially related subsidiaries. With the instability of 1974 financial markets, the Federal Reserve showed however, that it wished diversification to slow down. For example, *New York Times*, 12 September 1974.

9. Thus, these subsidiary corporations were termed "Agreement" corporations. The investment in such corporations could not exceed 10 percent of paid-in capital and surplus of the investing bank. (12 U.S.C. par. 601, 603, as amended.) For a review of Edge Act law, see Peter Brunsden, "The Edge Act in U.S. Banking," *The Banker*, February 1973.

10. The Edge Act extended Section 25 of the Federal Reserve Act. Edge Act corporations must have capital of not less than $2 million; all directors must be U.S. citizens and a majority of control must be held by U.S. citizens. For purposes of simplicity, further references to Edge Act corporations are meant to include Agreement corporations as well, even though the rules for each are slightly different. For the origins of the Edge Act, see Joan Hoff Wilson, *American Business and Foreign Policy: 1920-1933* (Boston: Beacon Press, 1971), pp. 16-19; for an overall description: James C. Baker and M. Gerald Bradford, *American Banks Abroad: Edge Act Companies and Multinational Banking* (New York: Praeger, 1974).

11. Edge Act corporations can hold stock in companies "not engaged in the general business of buying or selling goods, wares, merchandise or commodities in the United States, and (only) transacting any business such as . . . may be incidental to its international or foreign business." Federal Reserve Act, Section 25(a)8. Edge corporations with such broad authority must have a financial structure such that demand deposits and acceptance liabilities are less than their own capital and surplus. Investments in the stock of nonfinancial companies cannot exceed $500,000 nor exceed 25 percent of the voting shares in the corporation. Regulation K, par. 211.8, effective January 7, 1969.

12. See J. Herbert Furth, "International Regulations and the Federal Reserve System" in Herbert V. Prochnow, ed., *The Federal Reserve System* (New York: Harper and Bros., 1960), p. 281. The Federal Reserve Board may allow activities abroad which would not be allowed in domestic operations. The purpose is to permit banks to compete on an equal basis abroad. (Regulation K, Sect. 5a.)

13. Regulation K (as revised August 22, 1963). Just as the change in Regulation M permitted additional bank branches in a country, Edge Act subsidiaries could now establish additional branches in countries where they were already operating, with only 30 days notice to the Board. Edge Act corporations could accept time deposits from foreign depositors for safe-keeping or investment. At the same time, they were prohibited from purchasing in the U.S. open market commercial paper and U.S. "investment securities" other than U.S. federal and state government obligations. See Board of Governors of the Federal Reserve System, *Annual Report*, 1963.

14. As mentioned above, all national banks must be members of the Federal

Reserve System. The word "national" must appear in the name of a national bank, although for some, it appears at the end as "N.A." The Federal Deposit Insurance Corporation regulates banks which are neither national nor members of the F.R.S. Because such banks are rare in the international field, the F.D.I.C. is not discussed here.

15. Questions about the efficiency of the Comptroller's oversight of national banks have arisen. The *New York Times* attacked the Comptroller after problems at Franklin National Bank surfaced in 1974 (24 June 1974). The Nader examination of First National City Bank also questions the effectiveness of bank examiners when investigating large banks. See David Leinsdorf and Donald Etra, *Citibank* (with a foreword by Ralph Nader), (New York: Grossman, 1973), pp. 286-303. And after the failure of the U.S. National Bank of San Diego, thirty-two companies brought a joint suit against the Comptroller (and the F.D.I.C.) alleging insufficient supervision by bank examiners. See *Wall Street Journal*, 13 January 1976.

16. The sequence of events at the time Italy was put on the Comptroller's "black list" is confused, but suggestive. The *New York Times* speculated on September 3 that the move was connected with Franklin National Bank's connections with Italian interests. At the same time, however, the Italian government was in trouble, as was its economy. It fell a month later, amid protests over American meddling in political affairs in the Italian press. (For reports in the American press, see Boston *Globe*, 6 October 1974; *New York Times*, 13 November 1974.

17. In approving mergers, advisory opinions are given under the Bank Merger Act of 1960 by the F.D.I.C., the Federal Reserve (if a member bank is involved) and the Comptroller (if a national bank is involved). The final decision is up to the Comptroller if the resultant bank will be a national bank. The Justice Department can challenge any approved merger. In its study of Citibank, the Nader task force found that between 1960 and 1969, the Comptroller's approval rate was 23 percent higher than that of the Justice Department Antitrust Division, while the Federal Reserve Rate was 11 percent lower than the Justice Department rate. (Leinsdorf and Etra, *Citibank*, p. 279). Mergers give banks the most important asset for foreign expansion: size.

18. See for some of Saxon's views, his Congressional testimony: U.S. Congress, House, Committee on Banking & Currency, *Bank Examination and Supervisory Functions, Hearings before the Subcommittee on Bank Supervision and Insurance of the House Committee on Banking and Currency on H.R. 107 and H.R. 6685*, 89th Cong., 1st sess., 1965, p. 388; *New York Times*, 15 September 1963; Hackley, "Our Baffling Banking System," *Virginia Law Review* (June 1966): 771-85. Clark Havighurst in his foreword to *Law and Contemporary Problems* 31 (Autumn 1966): 635, said, "In some respects, Mr. Saxon overtly set out to discredit the regulatory system, particularly with respect to state regulatory power over branch banking."

Saxon took a limited view of his duties as Comptroller. He said in a speech to the American Bankers' Association in 1964:

> It is not the operating policies and practices of the banks, but the total supply of money and credit, which is the proper province of the monetary authority. (i.e. the Federal Reserve).

> In the reforms we have undertaken and advocated, we have one paramount objective: to leave our bank operations to bankers unless restrictions are required to safeguard the solvency and liquidity of the banking system.

(Quoted in "Bankers Step Out: A Survey," *The Economist*, 21 November 1964, p. 863.) His view thus seemed to be: Banking regulation has nothing to do with monetary policy. It is profitable, therefore good. Citibank's Walter Wriston says that David Rockefeller of Chase Manhattan "applied for a national charter—after saying he thought Saxon was crazy," according to Martin Mayer, *The Bankers* (New York: Weybright and Talley, 1974), p. 384.

19. In September, 1962, the authority to grant fiduciary powers to national banks was transferred to the Comptroller from the Federal Reserve. Saxon decided that operating a mutual fund could be interpreted as a fiduciary activity (although the Fed would not have agreed) and gave his approval to FNCB's application to run a mutual fund some time later.

20. For instance, the Federal Reserve decided that holding companies should not own mutual funds because such an association would violate the traditional separation of banking from the securities business. For a good account of the legislation, see Elias, pp. 133-79; Morton Mintz and Jerry S. Cohen, *America, Inc.* (New York: Dell, 1972), pp. 261-67; Etra, *Citibank*, section entitled "Congress Makes a Law." The Comptrollers have encouraged banking "innovation" in other ways. They allowed that Federal Funds borrowed were not deposit liabilities and thus not subject to reserve requirements. A similar ruling was made on subordinated note issues, although since 1970, maturities must exceed seven years.

21. Even in 1974, the First Pennsylvania Bank took a national charter (*Philadelphia Inquirer*, 1 June 1974) adding one more to the list of large banks giving up state charters.

22. Smith also followed his predecessors in other ways. He approved an automatic stock-buying plan for savers offered at Chase Manhattan and some other banks. The Investment Company Institute, representing mutual funds filed suit against the Comptroller, arguing that such activities by banks violate the Glass-Steagall Act separating the banking and investment industries. See *New York Times*, 26 September 1974; 28 October 1974. To some extent, the Federal Reserve showed limited agreement with the Comptroller's view that banks should cross state lines. In 1975, the Fed recommended that when a large bank is in danger of failing, banks from other states should be considered as possible buyers of the endangered bank. See *Federal Reserve Bulletin*, August, 1975, pp. 419-32. Smith announced his resignation in 1976—some argued because of pressure he had undergone in the wake of national bank failures.

23. Those with more than $5 billion in deposits as of June, 1972.

24. Quoted in Mary Campbell, "Commercial Banks Face Fierce Competition," *Financial Times*, 7 February 1974.

25. Jay Palmer, "Major Reform Plan for New York Banking System," *Financial Times*, 5 March 1974. Albright's successor, Eliot Vestner opposes any turn to increased federal regulation, fearing "over-regulation." (Quoted in the *New York Times*, 26 January 1975.)

26. *The Banker*, July 1973, p. 784; Anthony Thomas, "Rivalry Over World Banking Role," *The Times*, 3 July 1973, p. iv.

27. See "Has Republic of Texas Waited Too Long?" *Business Week*, 29 June 1974, p. 82.

28. James L. Rowe, "Solo Bankers," *The Washington Post*, 23 January 1973. In 1973, large numbers of banks broke from the Illinois Association to form the Association for Modern Banking in Illinois (Ambi). It now has over 250 members and accounts for 75 percent of Illinois banking assets. It will pressure the Illinois legislature for liberalization of the branching law. See *The Times*, 23 August 1974.

29. This has led several Philadelphia banks to change their nominal headquarters out of Philadelphia County in order to branch in a wider area.

30. That is, simply the market for dollars deposited in banks outside of the U.S.

31. The rate at which member banks may borrow from Federal Reserve Banks.

32. 12 U.S.C. par. 371(a). There was, for a long time, general agreement that the prohibition on interest payable on demand deposits should be retained. Even the liberal Hunt Commission recommended the retention of interest-free demand deposits (p. 27). It is possible that both commercial and savings banks will be able to pay interest on demand deposits in the future. On 30 September 1975, the Senate Banking Committee approved a bill which would allow this right as of 1 January 1977. *New York Times*, 1 October 1975.

33. 12 U.S.C. par. 371(b).

34. One view of capital flows in response to interest rate differentials stresses the point that a given change in relative interest rates will produce a "stock-shift" in assets, and that continuing flows after the stock adjustment will be small. Long-term improvements in the capital account would thus necessitate a constantly higher interest rate. The implication is that interest rate manipulations such as Kennedy's "Operation Twist" or Johnson's IET would produce in the main a one-time improvement. See William H. Branson, "Monetary Policy and the New View of International Capital Movements," *Brookings Papers on Economic Activity: 2*, 1970, pp. 235-62. On the other hand, an earlier study by Alexander Swoboda ("The Euro-dollar Market: An Interpretation," *Essays in International Finance* (Princeton: February 1968): 64) suggests that institutional changes have produced larger and larger responses to interest rate differentials. The existence of the Eurodollar market has itself *increased* capital mobility if this is so.

35. The secondary market rate on domestic CDs could fall below the Q limit and act as the real floor as in 1967. (See Chart 4.) Jane Sneddon Little, "The Eurodollar Market: Its Nature and Impact," Federal Reserve Bank of Boston, *New England Economic Review*, May/June 1969, pp. 6-7. See also John Atkin, "Eurodollar Interest Rates," *The Banker*, January 1973, p. 25.

36. Frank Mastrapaqua found a significant relationship between the dollar deposits at London branches of U.S. banks (logged) and (1) the value of American direct foreign investment, (2) the differential between eurodollar rates and U.S. deposit rates, (3) the differential between eurodollar rates and Treasury bill rates (negative). His equation explained 99 percent of the variation in levels

of dollar deposits in London between 1962 and 1968. See "U.S. Bank Expansion Via Foreign Branching: Monetary Policy Implications" (New York University Graduate School of Business Administration Institute of Finance *Bulletin* (January 1973) 87-88: 53).

37. Lees, *International Banking*, p. 60.

38. April 1967, p. 351.

39. *The American Banker*, 8 July 1969.

40. Quoted in "International Banking Survey," *The Economist*, 15 November 1967, p. 12.

41. *Federal Reserve Bulletin*, September, 1969, p. 724. Sanford Rose maintains that Citibank is "sensitive" on the question of a competitive advantage gained from its foreign operations. Said Chairman Wriston: "That's just too bad. I know of no rule that requires one to pace oneself to the level of the slowest guy in the room." See Rose, "Why They Call It Fat City," *Fortune*, March, 1975, p. 165. Jane Sneddon Little disputes the argument that multinational banks found a cushion of funds in the Eurodollar market denied smaller banks. Her data however, tend to support Martin's point of view rather than refute it. She shows that big New York banks maintained their share of total bank loans far better in the 1969 credit crunch than they had in previous squeezes. See her *Eurodollars: The Money Market Gypsies* (New York: Harper and Row, 1975), p. 236.

42. Savings and loans would, under free market conditions, have some difficulty competing for deposits because their assets, many of which are in mortgages, produce a lower yield than many commercial bank assets. While the original purpose of Regulation Q was to prevent excessive competition for deposits, it has in practice served to protect the noncommercial banking system. Many argue nevertheless that Regulation Q hurts those it is meant to help. The small saver is doomed to artificially low returns on his savings at the same time that Regulation Q fails to prevent "disintermediation" (withdrawals from savings banks into higher yielding investments) and the drying up of mortgage money when money is tight. Current reform is in the direction of making the savings banks more and more like commercial banks.

43. Mastrapaqua's findings ("U.S. Bank Expansion," p. 62) support this argument. He found that it was possible for Regulation Q effects to be the reverse of intended policy.

44. 30-90 day CDs ($100,000) have been exempt since 24 June 1970; large CDs of longer maturities became exempt 16 May 1973.

45. Board of Governors of the Federal Reserve System, *The Federal Reserve System: Purposes and Functions* (Washington: 1963), p. 53. They vary by the length of time money is on deposit and by the deposit size of the bank. All insured banks in effect face the same limits.

46. The difference to a bank resulting from such reserve requirements can be computed by the formula $\frac{i}{1-r}$, where i is the interest rate on deposits and r is the reserve requirement. Thus, an 8 percent reserve requirement when the borrowing rate is 12 percent raises the real borrowing cost to the bank to 13.04 percent.

47. George W. Mitchell, "A New Look at Monetary Policy Instruments,"

Journal of Money, Credit and Banking, vol. 3, Part 2 (May 1971): 385.

48. Federal Reserve Bulletin, August 1969, announced the changes in Regulations D and M effective October 16, 1969. The requirements also applied to other assets which parent banks acquired from their foreign branches.

49. One effort to stop repayments, oddly enough, was an increase in the requirement to twenty percent from ten. The reserve was based on additions to Eurodollar borrowing above May, 1969, levels. But as borrowings went below the base period figure, the reserve-free base would be decreased by that amount. By raising the requirements to twenty percent, the Fed hoped that banks would stop repayments in order to keep a high reserve-free base. But repayments continued anyway. Another means used to lessen the effect of repayments was the sale of Export-Import Bank securities to the foreign branches.

50. Andrew Brimmer, "Changing Fortunes of U.S. Branch Banks in London," *International Currency Review*, March-April 1973, p. 38.

51. Statement before the Subcommittee on International Exchange and Payments of the Joint Economic Committee, January 15, 1969. Reprinted in *Federal Reserve Bulletin*, January 1969, p. 25. Tighter money conditions after 1965 probably accounted for this; the scarcity of funds in the U.S. would in itself have discouraged capital outflows for foreign loans.

52. Statement of R.A. Peterson, U.S., Congress, House, *Foreign Direct Investment Controls, Hearings before the Subcommittee on Foreign Economic Policy of the Committee on Foreign Affairs*, 91st Cong., 1st sess., p. 315, 1969, Appendix.

53. Issued March 5, 1965. Special priority in lending was to be accorded to export financing, loans to lesser developed countries, and loans to certain countries including Britain (in order not to damage Britain's own balance of payments).

54. See "Developments under the Voluntary Foreign Credit Restraint Program," *Federal Reserve Bulletin*, May 1966, pp. 649-51. In 1966, tight money, as noted above, made the 1965 limits superfluous. For a short account of changes 1965-1969, see *Federal Reserve Bulletin*, January 1969, pp. 28-32. Foreign branches could be very helpful in aiding a bank in reducing its foreign credits. A foreign branch could, with Eurodollar resources, acquire the foreign assets of its head office. The capital inflow from the branch cancels the asset at the office, and might give the parent bank leeway under its quota. The bank as a whole thus avoids contracting foreign credits.

55. The last revisions in the program as of January 1, 1974 (1) raised loan limits by four percent, (2) cancelled restrictions on loans to Western Europe, (3) exempted export credits and other special credits. All banks with $500,000 or more in foreign assets filed monthly reports with the Federal Reserve. See "Revised Guidelines," *Federal Reserve Bulletin*, January 1974, pp. 15-25.

56. The program always geared itself to correcting the balance of payments without crimping foreign investment. As the Department of Commerce said in 1969,

> . . . with regard to foreign business expansion, the aim of the program is not to curtail business expansion abroad. Its purpose is to reduce the use of U.S. funds to finance foreign direct investment, interfering as little as possible in the investment process.

Foreign Direct Investment Controls, Hearings, p. 220. The government went even further when it encouraged American companies to tap the Eurodollar market. James Ling, of Ling-Tempco-Vought said his company was urged to do so, as were others. See *The New York Times*, 23 April 1970. (Quoted by Lees, *International Banking*, p. 398.)

57. U.S. Congress, Joint Economic Committee, *The Balance of Payments Mess, Hearings before the Subcommittee on International Exchange and Payments* (Washington, 1971), pp. 6-7.

58. Cited in Tugendhat, *The Multinationals*, p. 185.

59. U.S. Department of Commerce, Office of Foreign Direct Investment, *Foreign Affiliate Financial Survey: 1966-69*, July, 1971, p. 34.

60. The IET significantly cut the flotation of foreign bonds in the U.S.—except Canada which was exempt. European countries were virtually closed out of New York after they had been increasing borrowing 1960-1963, and had been expected to increase even more, given Administration efforts to keep the domestic rate for long-term borrowers low enough through "Operation Twist."

Bonds Issued in the U.S. by Foreigners ($ million)

Year	*Total*	*Developed Countries (Canada excluded)*
1960	631	60
1961	661	202
1962	1,272	421
1963	1,392	531
1964	1,310	101
1965	1,689	203
1966	1,655	37
1967	2,170	42
1968	2,014	–
1969	1,336	10
1970	1,405	–
1971	1,343	–

Source: International Bank for Reconstruction and Development, unpublished data in Sir Alec Cairncross, *Control of Long-Term International Capital Movements* (Washington: The Brookings Institution, 1973), p. 33.

61. Johnson's speech is printed in the *New York Times*, 11 February 1965, p. 56. It is interesting to note the debate in Congress over whether the President should have been given the stand-by authority to extend IET to bank loans. All had to affirm they had no wish to harm the position of the U.S. as world banker: Senator Gore (Utah): "The question is, shall this country remain the banker of the free world? I hope it can and will." Senator Javits (New York, opposing the Gore amendment extending IET to bank loans):

> . . . it would not in my judgment, and apparently in the judgment of other Senators, operate in a manner conducive to the best outlook for American foreign trade, and for American leadership in the free world in bank credit; there is now a proposal to inhibit further the freedom of action of the banking community.

New York banks, of course, would have been the chief losers from the proposal. (See U.S. Congress, House, Committee on Ways and Means, *Legislative History of H.R. 8000, the Interest Equalization Act PL88-563*, 89th Cong., 2nd sess., 1966, p. 1069.

62. *Survey of Current Business*, June 1972, p. 30.

63. In fact, small banks feel threatened by the removal of Regulation Q since they are less able to compete against big banks by offering more attractive rates to lenders and borrowers.

Chapter Six

Something Happened: The New Banking

For the last three chapters, we have made an extensive tour of government circles. It is time now to return to the microeconomic world of the banks. They were not sitting by idly while the governments in Britain and America manipulated their environment. They reacted, grew, invented and, in most cases, survived. Official regulations presented them with the parameters, but actual responses by the American banks were conditioned by their own drive for profits and expansion.

The bankers facing the world of the 1960s bore little resemblance to their depression forebears. Where the banker image used to call to mind a portly gentleman in homburg and spectacles, the new banker plays tennis, wears contact lenses, and is a graduate of weight-watchers. He is a mover. The underlying difference is that American banking underwent a fundamental change in attitude and technique. Banking became a "go-go" industry, one bent on expansion, performance, and diversification. The case may be overstated, but significant changes cannot be denied. The changes took place concurrently in Britain and the United States. They involved both style and banking technique. They provided, to a great extent, a way to expand *in spite of* the limits the bankers saw in their way. The transformation of American bankers' attitudes at home determined that they would expand abroad if that appeared necessary to their further growth.

For the large-scale exodus of the 1960s and 1970s it was not enough that Britain be attractive or that U.S. regulations be a problem to bankers: the bankers had to view the situation with a combative attitude. In short, they had to be willing to move. Changes within American banking did indeed signal that aggression necessary to the international movement. The new techniques and attitudes of American bankers might have remained a family affair had they saved them for the home market. But of course, part of the process of modernization itself involved an international approach. The combination meant that foreign competitors would have to compete or leave their own field to the invaders. In the case of Britain, American banks brought their innovations to bear on both local sterling business and on the Eurodollar market in London. Banking would never again be the same, either for the British or for the Americans.

CORPORATE HORIZONS ENLARGED

It is difficult to account for the changes in American banking, except to say that every year increased the temporal distance from 1933, the worst Depression year for banks. Every year brought more managers for whom 1929 had about the same significance as 1066. Domestic competition grew increasingly intense among American banks, driving the top ranking banks into continually newer activities. When we observe this on so many competitive fronts, it is not surprising to find the same pattern in international expansion. It makes the international drive comprehensible as a consistent corollary to the domestic rule.

So what was going on? The last chapter has already given us some hints that the banks were diversifying through their holding companies. As Table 6-1 shows, the 1960s saw a proliferation of one-bank holding companies; banks spawned subsidiaries from agri-

Table 6-1. Number of One-Bank Holding Company Formations Registered 31 December 1970

Year	*Number Formed*
Before 1956	83
1956-1960	53
1960-1966	291
1966-June 1968	201
June '68-Dec. '70	690
Total	1,318

Note: Excludes 34 holding companies late in registering.
Source: *Federal Reserve Bulletin*, December 1972.

culture to automobile repair which went against the spirit if not the word of the law. In 1970 the one-bank holding company law limited such subsidiaries to areas "closely related to banking"—a move which finally broke the trend toward nonbank diversification.

Since the capability to diversify through holding companies had always been available, it is interesting to observe the follow the leader aspect of the establishment of holding companies and the subsequent expansion of their lines of business. Where before 1960 the bank holding company hardly existed, now practically all large banks in the U.S. have adopted the holding-company structure. The same follow the leader pattern describes the establishment of Edge Act subsidiaries.

Such refinements of corporate organization may seem arcane, but they signal the phenomenon at the root. Banks began to be extremely growth-conscious as well as profit-conscious. It is not really worthwhile to ask which target dominated, business volume or profit maximization. The evidence is that both goals were of equal weight and both were seen as marking the same coin. Banks tried to maximize their functions, their sources of funds, their deposits and loans, their rates of return. They entered hard competition for customers. They watched (and copied) their rivals' moves.

Holding companies were important in two ways. They allowed the acquisition of nonbank businesses and they gave access to extra funds. The first supported diversification, the second, loan expansion. Holding companies also allowed the possibility of crossing state lines with subsidiaries. Subsidiaries for international banking, of course, are called Edge Act subsidiaries. (Everyone knows that the chief benefit of the Edge Act has come to be that it allows Bank of America to be in New York and Citibank in Texas.)[1]

The holding company movement was motivated by a second desire: to raise funds without observing Regulation Q or reserve requirements on deposits. It was a way to extend loans when additional deposits were unavailable. Holding companies could issue commercial paper and pass the proceeds, reserve-free, to the cash-short bank. The history of the Fed's attempts to control such fund-raising is long: the Board finally began to realize that holding company paper should be treated in the same way as large deposits. Between 1970 and 1974, regulations gradually evolved toward that conclusion.[2] In the meantime, the whole exercise further convinces one that the banks had become almost infinitely inventive in finding ways to secure their growth. No sooner did the Fed cut off one supply of funds than the banks would seek out another. Bank borrowing of Eurodollars was thus only one aspect of the drive for invulnerability, that is, for access to funds regardless of the pressures of monetary policy.

It was, indeed, better to be first with an innovation (as Citibank usually seemed to be) but lacking that, it seemed dangerous not to be second. Martin Mayer summed up the difference which had occurred as well as any:

> Banking has been an industry for a long time, but until the present management of New York's First National City Bank came out of its cocoon in the early 1960's a bank was never really a business.[3]

So when a few banks led the way into new fields and methods, others followed. First it seemed that any self-respecting bank needed the Eurodollar market to cushion the days of tight money at home. Then (when the Fed cut into Eurodollar borrowing in late 1969) it seemed that a self-respecting bank could pick up extra profits abroad by shrewd borrowing and lending to international customers within Eurodollar margins. Then (when this competition became tough with too many interlopers) it seemed that no self respecting bank could admit it was out of its element in competitive London. The big banks, to be sure, had long-established British (and other foreign) branches, but they just as imitatively followed their peers into all forms of diversification. Any self-respecting major bank, for instance, had to set up a merchant bank in London.

Another indicator of the competitive urge was the loan-to-deposit ratio. The more loans a bank made from its deposits, the higher (presumably) would be its earnings.[4] In the late 1940s, the loan to deposit ratio at American banks was about 18 percent while today it has reached about 70 percent. Profits became more and more an indicator of success and bank stocks came to be the high flyers.[5]

The pressures on banks to expand abroad and at home came in the wake of the already impressive multinational spread of U.S. business. It is a truism to say that American banks followed their customers abroad. Rare is the bank which did not talk of the international tentacles of its customers as it proudly opened its London branch. What bank in its right mind would set up foreign branches without *some* customers in mind? Indeed, for a bank in pursuit of its customers, Britain was a likely base abroad. It was the major European trading partner of the U.S. (until Germany overtook it in 1968) and remains the most "popular" European site for American direct foreign investment. American companies account for almost 15 percent of British output in manufacturing.[6] And American firms abroad typically use American banks.[7]

But American investment in Britain had been extensive long before the 1960s, and only the very largest banks had felt it necessary to service their international clients in those earlier years. Somehow, the 1960s brought a spirit of competition which had not existed before. Smaller banks were no longer willing to concede the international field to New York. One banker said, "If an American company over here uses a bank in London to deal with financing of its overseas subsidiaries, the parent company in the States may be tempted to switch to the same bank back there."[8] Albert Miossi of Continental Illinois (Chicago) voiced the same opinion:

> A branch in a foreign center frequently enables a bank to keep an important customer that it might otherwise lose to a competitor. It was through their foreign networks in the 60's that New York banks began to attract customers that Chicago banks were servicing in the Midwest. And whey they began to lose domestic business Chicago banks started to establish branches abroad.[9]

Thus the urge to follow customers seems to be associated not so much with the customer's habits as with the bankers' attitudes toward their fellow bankers.

Many other examples of the extended horizon of American bankers could be added here. But it is already obvious that something had happened, that expansion of any kind came to dominate the talk and actions in banking headquarters across the country by the 1960s. Does this mean that the banks would have moved to Britain regardless of U.S. capital controls, reserve requirements and so on? Surely not so many as actually went. What the competitive atmosphere did was induce banks to seek aggressively ways to avoid domestic stringency and legal barriers. The international growth of U.S. banks was perceived as one way to do it.

AMERICAN INVENTIONS

These changes in bankers' attitudes led to changes in their ways of doing business. They started viewing their balance sheets critically, seeking to lower costs, increase revenues, and add customers and services. Banks began to worry less about the structure of their assets (loans and investments) and more about the structure of their liabilities. They thus changed their style, their lines of business and their liability management.[10] They came up with some rather original financial devices to contribute to the transformations. Their inventiveness helped them in London, since much of British banking had not yet escaped the mentality of earlier days. Let us look at the differences.

Style

Style eludes measurement. It seems to be accessible only to those who spend a long time studying it. Nevertheless, American bankers did develop a new banking style at home—which they exported in large quantities to Britain. The style was, in a sense, an invention because it was calculated and artificial. The new style involves advertising, public relations, modern buildings (or impressively old fashioned ones), and so on. The style developed also extended toward dealing with customers or potential customers. A banker had to dangle inducements to potential customers while making his current clients constantly feel taken care of.

The British style of commercial banking answered to different standards. It was more or less based on the premise that clients did not change bankers, that one did not compete with the fellow down the street, and that old ways of doing business, after all, had worked well for a couple of centuries. Throughout the 1960s, the British mentioned frequently the surprising aggressiveness of the newcomers. The British clearing banks, secure until then within their tight cartel, suddenly came up against the new banking. For instance, one banker had this exchange with the Radcliffe Committee in the good old days of the cartel:

> *Q.* Would you say that there are some clients to whom you refuse credit, but to whom you might be willing to give credit if you were charging them, let us say, twice the rate of interest which you normally charge?
>
> *A.* That is not the way we conduct our affairs. A man is either credit-worthy or not credit-worthy; if he is credit-worthy he gets his accommodation . . . on the terms I have stated.[11]

The Radcliffe Report confirmed the passive nature of the clearers with regard to their overdrafts, saying "... the banks do not ordinarily take any action independently of bank rate to deter or encourage overdrafts by altering the general level of overdraft charges." (Par. 137) This rather passive attitude toward lending paralleled an equally passive attitude about attracting deposits. For instance, some years later, the representative of a large British company testified:

> The company placed sterling deposits with American banks in London but the decision to do this was not taken because of their international coverage, but entirely because of rates offered.[12]

Even by 1968, Alhadeff could still say, "... all but the largest firms in England typically use only one bank, and bank-customer relationships tend to be very stable."[13] The idea that banks should compete for other banks' clients or bid actively for funds was therefore a new one in Britain. Chapter Three already showed that the growth of business by the nonclearing banks increased pressure to end the clearers' cartel—this resulted in part from the incursions on the traditional banks' business.

The Economist criticized British banks in 1966 for falling behind in the adoption of modern techniques. The complaint here was not only that the British bankers failed in aggressiveness, but that they lacked sufficient knowledge. Top managers knew little of up-to-date business administration, there existed no rational methods for choosing branch sites (or for closing branches) and American banks ran far ahead in the use of computers for banking. Another deficiency was in cost accounting: "Many overseas banks, especially American banks, had costed each of their operations. This enables them to calculate exactly what they ought to charge customers."[14] American banks reappeared constantly as the models of the postindustrial revolution.

One British business man tried to get at the root of the difference between British and American banks. He saw it not as a matter of aggressiveness or management, but of flexibility. The American banks in Britain, unencumbered by the huge bureaucracies at the head office, could adapt to a company's needs more readily. The clearers, on the other hand, lacked a good system of customer contacts, having failed to use the American system of assigning account executives.[15] The services provided to business, then, were insufficient, an angle the American banker could play on in his search for customers. A British banker working for an American bank said that he suspected that British companies felt little reluctance to deal with American banks. He added, "I suspect that some of them have been rather poorly treated by their banks on the whole."[16]

A manager of a British bank, who preferred anonymity in dealing with so sensitive a subject, admitted in 1969 that British banks had benefited from the marketing techniques introduced by the Americans. He reviewed the most serious objections to the Americans, however, and implied that there was some justified dislike of their less sophisticated methods. They engaged in staff "poaching"—a "bitter experience." They also "touted" for business, a custom which went beyond "marketing technique." American bankers aroused resentment when they stole away "an old customer of fifty years' standing who "succumbed to the blandishments of the sales pitch of a London-based American banker."[17] But even if British bankers resented the hard sell, they had to think about doing some "touting" themselves.

Certificates of Deposit

In lengthening the maturity of deposits, American banks have probably changed banking in London more significantly than in any other way. As discussed in Chapter Three, the cartel in Britain until 1971 set rates on deposit accounts at seven days' notice and prohibited higher rates on deposits of longer maturities. This system meant that the clearing banks could not easily offer medium or long-term loans; their lending system thus depended heavily on the overdraft, a short-term lending instrument which theoretically complemented the short-term deposits.[18] The cartel rate precluded any significant competition for deposits.

Outside influence began to make British bankers think again about the servicibility of their neat system. Local authorities started to compete aggressively for depositary funds, providing a competitive alternative to bank deposits for large customers.[19] In addition, the accepting houses simultaneously bid for longer term deposits at higher rates.[20] Finally, in 1966, First National City Bank introduced the dollar certificate of deposit, a deposit instrument offering a higher rate on longer deposits. The clearers began slowly to see the advantage in long-term deposits, especially through such a flexible instrument as the CD, which could obviously be used for sterling if the cartel were disbanded. The clearers did in the end set up special subsidiaries so that they, too, could avoid the limits of the cartel. The trend toward acceptance of certificates of deposit had already proved to be a permanent one in the United States and the handwriting thus appeared increasingly clear on the British wall. Over the period 1950-1972 in the United States, the maturity of deposits had revolutionized itself, with time deposits steadily growing in importance.[21] With the growth of certificates of deposit in Britain, the cartel turned into more of a constraint than a convenience. As Alhadeff said, ". . . the clearing banks' policy not to compete flexibly for deposits has had a pronounced effect on their growth."[22]

How did certificates of deposit come to Britain? CDs originated in the United States. They are documents which indicate the deposit of a sum of money with the issuing bank and the promise of the issuer (the bank) to pay the holder the principal amount plus interest at a specified date. They are freely transferable and negotiable. According to the Federal Reserve, certificates of deposit were issued in the United States for many years, but only became important in 1961 when large New York banks started to issue them and when a secondary market for them was created.[23] The existence of a secondary market makes certificates of deposit highly desirable from the point of view of both the issuer and the holder. CDs allow banks to develop a source of long-term deposits, while the negotiability of the instrument allows the depositor to realize at least the discounted value of the certificate at any time. By the end of 1973, large negotiable certificates of deposit amounted to almost 30 percent of the time and savings deposits at large commercial banks in the United States.[24] Until 1973, Regulation Q limited the interest payable on CDs, but the limit did exceed that on regular time deposits.[25] Regulation Q, of course, does not extend to deposits at banks abroad.

Given the freedom of foreign branch deposits from Regulation Q, certificates of deposit issued abroad could be very attractive. The Bank of England recognized the opportunity to further London's attractiveness and therefore took a liberal stance, offering licenses to any authorized bank to issue dollar certificates of deposit in Britain. The first dollar issue was introduced by First National City Bank's London branch in 1966.[26] The field was not entirely free, however, since until 1968, U.K. withholding taxes on certificates of one year or more made medium-term CDs unattractive. The Labour Government adjusted the tax law in that year, abolishing the withholding requirement on interest on certificates of deposit. After 1968, the stock of dollar CDs increased appreciably. Thus, the introduction of the dollar CD and its secondary market enhanced the attractiveness of London as a center for Eurodollars. It also led to changes in the sterling market.

Just as certificates of deposit proved useful in the United States and in the London dollar money markets, so could they perform a function in the sterling market. Legal difficulties prohibited the issue of sterling CDs, however, until the 1968 Finance Act (Section 55) included certificates of deposit within the meaning of "securities" in the Exchange Control Act. Thus, on October 28, 1968, the Bank of England gave permission to a number of authorized banks to issue sterling certificates. At the same time, some members of the London Discount Market Association (several of whom had already been dealing in dollar CDs) formed a secondary market.[27] The clearing banks, of course, found themselves unable to issue sterling CDs in their own names because of the cartel on interest rates. They did get around the cartel by issuing CDs through so-called "backdoor" subsidiaries until the abandonment of the cartel in 1971. In this area, the cartel exerted a purely negative influence on the ability of the clearers to compete. As Einzig said (before September, 1971):

> Unless the clearing banks swim with the tide and suspend their cartel for the benefit of large depositors their relative importance, which has already declined considerably compared with that of non-clearing banks, will decline further.[28]

One oddity of British tax law gave great benefit to those who bought and sold certificates of deposit. Capital gains tax did not apply to the sale of certificates, so that as *The Economist* noted, a one year 11 percent CD costing £50,000 could be sold at a tax-free profit at £55,000 the day before it matured.[29] The authorities felt that this advantage encouraged depositors to place money in bank certificates which might otherwise be invested in Treasury bills. Thus, the 1973 budget included a plan to end the tax loophole. In addition, the Government introduced Inland Revenue deposits to compete with CDs. These are considered as a prepayment of Corporation Tax and yield 2.5 percent above the rate on 3-month Treasury bills.

The certificate of deposit is now a permanent feature of the British banking system. By the end of 1973, about 10 percent of the deposits at the clearing banks were held in CDs. In the market for sterling CDs, the clearing banks tended to hold a greater proportion of certificates of deposit at longer maturities than did other banks.[30] While the clearers do hold a significant proportion of sterling CDs (twice the amount at American banks in Britain), they have not pursued dollar deposits in this way. By 1973, the dollar CD market was divided as shown in Table 6-2.

The Interbank Market

Related to the development of certificates of deposit is the interbank market in Britain, a system under which banks place funds at other banks. Interbank "borrowings" will be in large round denominations, for set periods of time—from overnight to longer periods. The interbank market, while it existed on a very small scale in Britain in the 1950s, grew rapidly in the 1960s based on principles used by American banks at home (in the Federal Funds market) and in Britain (in the Eurodollar market).

Since the 1920s, banks in the United States have borrowed funds from each other, one bank in need of reserves borrowing from another with excess reserves. The so-called Federal Funds market in

Table 6-2. Dollar Certificates of Deposit at Banks in Britain (September, 1973)

	Percent of Total
American Banks	47
Other Foreign Banks	18
Other British Banks	16
Commonwealth Banks	8
Consortium Banks	6
Accepting Banks	3
Clearing Banks	2

Source: "The London Dollar Certificates of Deposit," *Quarterly Bulletin*, December 1973, p. 447.

these reserves refers generally to one-day borrowing. This market fluctuated at a level of about $1 billion until 1964, but grew by 1970 to about $7 billion in the United States. By the end of 1973, the market's volume had reached $15 billion.[31] This growth was aided by Comptroller Saxon's decision in 1963 that Federal Funds borrowed or lent should not be included in the normal limits on lending under the Federal Reserve Act.[32] Beyond the more limited Federal Funds market, banks could also borrow from each other for longer periods. Total interbank borrowings in the United States amounted to $56.5 billion by mid-1975.[33] Interbank borrowing enables a bank with an excess demand for credit to obtain funds from banks with excess reserves.

American banks, then, fell easily into the habit of lending to each other; British banks did not, except through the traditional mechanism of the Discount Houses. When the American banks came to London, however, they imported the idea of the interbank market on an even larger scale and at longer maturities. Without the solid deposit base of the clearing banks and other British banks, the American banks specialized in wholesale deals. They needed to borrow from other banks in order to establish themselves in London.[34] Trading in large lots, they might borrow funds—sterling or dollars—from other banks either to re-lend them to banks or to nonbank customers. The banks, in a sense, became money brokers, dealing for small margins with high volume.

The interbank market in nonsterling currencies is the largest interbank market in London. By October of 1972, the foreign currency liabilities of banks in Britain to other U.K. banks had reached almost $25 billion, most at maturities between 8 days and 6 months.[35] But the sterling interbank market had also assumed significant proportions. While in 1962, interbank borrowing in sterling was only $370 million, by October, 1972, it was valued at about $8.5 billion.

The advent of the interbank market, while it can bring problems because of the unsecured nature of the loans, does contribute to flexibility in the banking system in allowing a fuller use of banking funds and a simple system for allocating excess reserves. But a bank which depends mainly on interbank dealings for its livelihood does lead a somewhat parasitic existence since it no longer fills the basic banking function of taking deposits from the public. It is also more vulnerable to changes in market conditions, especially when the stability of the system is called into question.[36]

Term Loans and Cash Flow Analysis

British bankers traditionally have used an overdraft system for extending credits to their commercial customers. American banks, however, generally use the loan system. The overdraft is a credit line on which the customer can draw, paying interest only on the amount overdrawn. A bank extends a loan, on the other hand, for a specific period of time, for a specific amount, and often for a specific project. While the cartel in Britain set interest rates on advances, in the United States individual banks assessed advances on loans on the merits of the loan itself.[37] American banks have refined the loan system to include term loans, or loans with longer maturities (more than a year). Large term loans are shared among a group of banks in order to spread the risk. In Eurocurrencies, these are called Eurocredits or medium-term syndicated loans.

Term loans, because they absorb funds for longer periods, also require a more intensive credit analysis by the lenders. American banks have thus developed credit analysis as a major part of their term loan business. While British banks are now beginning to develop more term loans, this is a recent development. In his first edition to *Modern Banking*, R.S. Sayers could say:

> English banking notions of abhorring deep interests in particular industrial concerns and preferring short-term loans prevail.[38]

Official encouragement[39] steered the banks toward changing their attitudes in Britain after the publication of the Radcliffe Report, and competition pushed British banks further. In 1969, the *Times* reported that:

> . . . an increasing number of British bankers point to the advantages of the American system which is not only more profitable for the bank but also makes it much easier for them to administer and regulate the level of their lending.[40]

Richard Vokey, then senior vice-president at Citibank in London, said that one of the most important contributions of American banks in Britain has been their method of credit evaluation for term loans. He said:

> Cash flow credit analysis developed a bank term loan which allowed future corporate earning power to replace depreciating fixed assets as security and gave borrowers a more stable capital-base on which to make their investment decision.[41]

In other words, the American asks not what the customer is worth, but whether he will be able to pay. David Ashby, a British economist at Bankers Trust in London, said that the American evaluation method is far more sensible for the banks. While British banks would make advances to Rolls-Royce because of the extensive assets of the company, American banks would assess the company's cash flow to see if the company would be able to service the loan over the necessary period.[42]

The American success with term loans was not lost on the City. British industry had long complained that the choice between short-term overdrafts from clearers and long-term bonds managed by merchant banks did not provide financing alternatives corresponding to the needs of business.[43] While merchant banks in the past supported long-term projects through bond flotations, the increasing need for large investments induced corporations to tap alternate sources of funds, particularly medium and long-term bank loans in sterling and nonsterling currencies. Some London bankers have also learned that necessity of credit analysis from American banks. The head of one large London consortium said in 1973.

> . . . there is now more expertise available for "in-house" project assessment within banks established in the City. This complements the "know-how" normally available from American banks.[44]

The Banker had pleaded for adoption of the newer techniques, saying that "The serene claim that bankers have not 'understood industry' except from a financial point of view now sounds a little hollow."[45]

Even before the ending of the cartel, the clearing banks began to offer medium-term credits through subsidiaries. Now, of course, they may compete more fully without the restraints of the agreement on interest rates.[46] Unfortunately, little information exists on the trend toward longer-term loans in sterling. One estimate put long-term loans at about 10 percent of their total advances, (about $3 billion at the end of 1973), but hard statistics are not yet published. While the Federal Reserve does gather information on term loans in the United States, the Bank of England does not, except for Eurodollars. Such data should be necessary to evaluate the soundness of the banking system in Britain and pressure is now growing to induce the Bank of England to act.[47]

Term lending still dominates far more in the Eurocurrency markets than in sterling markets. Rothschild Intercontinental Bank estimated that in 1973, medium-term public Eurocredits amounted to about $30 billion.[48] The term loan for some years almost supplanted Eurobond borrowings by large corporations. William Brandts, the merchant bankers, estimated that the cost of a Eurobond issue exceeded the cost of medium-term borrowing in London between 1969 and 1973.[49] Although this trend reversed itself around November 1974, thus giving a new lease on life to the Eurobond market, the relatively small amounts which can be raised by bond-issuing means that many organizations still must turn to shorter term Eurocurrency instruments.[50]

In recent years there has been a trend to even longer terms for Euromarket credits—which will tend to affect the length of domestic credits as well. Originally, medium-term credits predominated—those between three and seven years. In 1973, maturities of over 10 years became common.[51] Unfortunately, the quality of credit analysis which is needed for term loans may have declined in the Eurocurrency markets. First of all, syndicated loans tend to shift the responsibility away from participating banks which assume that the managers of the credit have allowed for risk. Secondly, competition in London (60 new banks entered in 1972 and 1973) led banks to extend credits to borrowers which would have been shunned in previous years.[52] But it is the largest American banks which account for most of the term lending at foreign branches. One paper done at the Federal Reserve concluded that a source of reassurance was the fact that term lending (loans of over one year) is concentrated in these large banks with "an established record in term-lending to foreign borrowers." In mid-1972, only nine banks extended 76 percent of all term-credits from American branches abroad. Almost half of all term loans from foreign branches came from Britain.[53]

To the extent that the biggest banks are considered "failsafe," it is well that they hold the bulk of the long-term business. With the onset of harder times after 1973, defaults became more likely and banks began to retrench and to shorten the terms on some loans. But defaults could still mean serious problems, particularly for smaller banks with fewer resources.

While British bankers have begun to adopt the term loan system in some instances, American bankers have begun to offer overdraft facilities in the United States. Customers tend to favor overdrafts over loans because they pay only for the amount of money actually used; corporations need not plan so tightly for full use of their advances, nor maintain compensating balances. Overdrafts are more automatic than normal lines of credit; revolving credits also involve a fee paid on the unused portion of the credit line. Thus, the customer will usually prefer the flexibility of an overdraft while the bank prefers the predictability of the loan system. Most sizeable American banks have now installed overdraft facilities, available at least for their larger personal depositors. Others offer special accounts with overdraft facilities, charging a flat monthly fee for the privilege. The bank credit card is really just a variation on the overdraft theme, common now in both the United States and Britain. Given the cross-fertilization between British and American banks, it is not surprising that each has adopted the methods of the other. The development of more varied forms of credit has generally resulted from the efforts of banks to respond to their customers' needs. The American banks quickly saw the unmet demand for medium-term bank credit in Britain and moved to fill the gap.

Variable Rates

One feature pioneered in the Eurodollar market has influenced banking technique in the United States. This is the use of variable interest rates on bank loans. The use of variable interest rates follows from the other developments in money markets, particularly the rising trend in interest rates and lengthening terms on loans.

In the Eurodollar market, terms for loans lengthened gradually over the course of the 1960s. Until 1965, Eurodollars could be borrowed for periods of up to six months, and sometimes up to a year.[54] The demand for longer-term loans grew, however, so that now Eurocurrency credits have extended beyond ten years. The banks could not have made the transition to longer-term credits under a system of fixed rates on the loans, however, because the costs of raising funds would have outstripped the return over the last several years. For instance, when American banks called heavily on the Eurodollar market in 1966, rates climbed steeply. Banks financing longer-term commitments by short-term borrowings found themselves caught in a profits squeeze. They began to negotiate loan agreements with the interest adjustable every six months according to market conditions. This variable rate loan is now the most popular instrument in the Eurodollar market.[55]

Banks do try to lengthen the maturities of their deposits to match the lengthening maturities on loans, but there is never a match between the two—maturities on loans have lengthened more than the maturities of deposits.[56] Eurodollar deposit rates are now publicly quoted for five year maturities, but the terms of loans tend to go even longer. The uncertainties attached to loans of longer duration thus necessitate the variable rate, rising in relation to prevailing market rates, usually the Eurodollar rate. The lending bank (or more properly, the lending banks, since most large credits are syndicated among a number of banks) thus attracts short-term funds at the going market rate, assured that the loan will generate a sufficient return over its life. One problem is that the seeming diminution of risk represents only a lesser risk for the bank in its initial calculations. The burden of uncertainty actually shifts to the borrower who may be facing higher debt servicing costs in the future. Some borrowers may overestimate their ability to pay should interest rates go very high. The bank, of course, must also assess the ability of the borrower to pay—variable rates add to everyone's uncertainty invariably. In addition, with the wide syndication of loans, less care may be taken by individual lenders to analyze the credit-worthiness of the borrower.

The evolution of the term loan business in the United States is similar to that in the Eurocurrency markets. In recent years rising interest rates made term lending activities hazardous for the banks. For instance, the prime rate in the United States fell as low as 5¼ percent in 1971 but went above 11 percent in 1974. A term commitment made in 1971 at a fixed rate would have been unprofitable. The banks accordingly changed their methods, borrowing the techniques of the Eurodollar market. In 1969, when American banks borrowed heavily in Europe, they started to extend credit lines to companies at a fixed percentage above the variable Eurodollar loan rate. In so doing, the American borrower submitted to the same floating rate system which he would have met had he tried to borrow directly in the Eurodollar market.[57] When credit conditions eased temporarily in the United States, the technique was dropped, but not forgotten.

Now in the United States, most term loans at large banks are tied to the prime rate, varying in cost as the prime varies. In 1972, "cap loans" put a maximum on the rate a company would have to pay.[58]

The development of variable rate loans has changed loan agreements in other ways in the United States. Unlike British banks, American banks traditionally demanded that borrowers maintain a certain portion of the loan in deposits at the bank—these deposits are called compensating balances. With the new flexibility, however, so-called "all in the rate" loans without compensating balances began to occur.[59]

THE NEW BANKING AND COMPETITION

Vast alterations in corporate expansion patterns inevitably set off competitive reactions. Both the smaller American banks and the British banks found themselves somewhat behind the times with the "new banking" movement. They have answered sometimes by fighting, sometimes by joining and sometimes by losing out entirely.

Most trends seem to run against the interests of small, purely domestic, American bankers. Those who could afford it often set up "shell" branches in the Bahamas and other banking havens. (A shell branch is one which exists more as a legal fiction than as an architectural reality.) This was one way they could participate in Eurodollar activities free from U.S. capital controls and reserve requirements—without the huge startup and overhead costs of a London outlet. Yet the world-wide coverage and resultant flexibility of the international banks based in the United States remains as a threat to small American banks.

While small banks have increasingly copied the management methods of the leaders, they have relied heavily on the protection of state laws which prohibit unlimited branching. Antitrust laws theoretically prohibit overweaning market control but have, in reality, done little to stop takeovers and mergers. It has been the policy in many areas to promote the consolidation of the local banking system. Competition among the big banks thus results in a decline in the competitive viability of the small.

British banks, unlike the local American banks, have held onto a few secret weapons against the incoming multinationals. The clearing banks, which perform the normal commercial banking functions in Britain, have a natural advantage in their extensive systems of local branches. The American banks have not been able to nullify this advantage to any great extent, and most in fact discourage the pursuit of small depositors who want sterling checking accounts and the like. Some would say that American efforts to open small low-key money shops and finance companies were designed to crack the home market in Britain, but success has been limited. On the other hand, the British merchant banks, similar to American investment banks, are at least safe from takeovers by Americans because of a long-standing British policy against foreign control of these institutions (now modified somewhat to a more liberal stance toward European Community investors).

The British banks have adapted to the new competition and have proved dynamic in many ways. The clearing banks did give up the cartel, if slowly, and they have borrowed many American techniques. Old cartel-lie patterns persist, of course, but with the Americans in London (and, increasingly, elsewhere in Britain) the British cannot remain oblivious to the newcomers. Smaller British "banks," called near-banks or fringe banks, did not fare so well. Many overexpanded during the early 1970s and fell into difficulties with the downturn of 1974 and 1975. Such reverses prompted the Bank of England to propose closer supervision, particularly of fringe banks, in Britain.

Although the real effect of competition from American banks is difficult to assess, the figures do show that they have at least gained a share of London's business which the clearers lost. In mid-1960, American bank deposits amounted to 5 percent of clearing banks' deposits. By mid-1973, American deposits actually exceeded those at clearing banks. While the American edge is for the most part attributable to dollar deposits, the clearing banks showed less growth generally as they left the newer money markets to other institutions. In sterling markets, they depended on the natural advantage of their vast branch networks and on the legal protection of the Bank of England's credit ceilings. Even by 1976, the pundits were still calling attention to the difference between the Americans and the British. Early in that year, three American banks lowered their base rates on sterling loans and quickly experienced a surge in demand. The British banks lost another piece of business to Citibank in mid-1976 when the American bank offered a more favorable rate to the British computer company, ICL. This sort of pressure at least keeps the clearers and other British banks on their competitive toes.

May the competitive effects of American banks in Britain be compared to competitive effects in other industries? Bankers are similar to other foreign investors in a number of ways. Certain theories of foreign direct investment apply equally well to both. Relative size, market characteristics, diversification needs, and so on seem to be concepts of general applicability. This chapter's review of American "inventions" might also lead one to believe that the product life cycle theory of foreign investment, which has been applied to manufacturing, might be applied to banking as well. That theory[60] argues that foreign investors tend to be those who develop new products in their home markets, and then develop foreign markets on the basis of the experience gained at home and an oligopolistic or monopolistic position which comes from their innovation. While this theory is suggestive in light of the innovations which have been transferred from American domestic banks to their foreign branches, it only applies peripherally to the banks.

In a few cases, an American banking technique is comparable to an invention which is exploited in the foreign market. Foreigners, inexperienced in the new field, may take some time before they copy the innovation and eat into the market position gained by the Americans. This pattern, however, is not typical. One salient case where such an innovation was tested in Britain brought little return to its progenitor. Citibank thought that it would capitalize in Britain on its knowledge of the "little man" and his banking habits. This move, through the establishment of money shops, seemed after its initial fanfare to have the immediate benefits once ascribed to lighting all of the lamps in China: high promise but low fulfillment.

The main areas of American success in Britain depart from the product life cycle model. Most banks have not even attempted to penetrate local financial markets. Most have pursued London business not with the object of exploiting an innovation but more with the idea of domestic survival in mind. And to the extent that the motive for British branching is avoidance of U.S. controls, follow the leader psychology, prestige, diversification, or customer demands (and these can be counted as the most significant) then the product cycle hypothesis must be assigned a marginal position. It would seem too that the tendency in banking is toward relatively short imitation periods. Service innovations cannot be patented and any big profit maker is likely to be copied by other banks. Thus, while we may speak in terms of American inventions in banking, it must be realized that such innovations find quick diffusion throughout the banking system.

One competitive phenomenon which has been observed outside of banking is what Edward M. Graham has described as the "exchange of threat."[61] Fellow oligopolists usually try to maintain their market shares. A typical response to a foreign investor by a host country competitor, therefore, might be to return the favor by investing in the country of the interloper. In fact, British banks have begun to expand in the United States in recent years. Takeovers have given branch systems to Lloyd's Bank in California and to Barclay's and Midland Bank (through its participation in the European-American Banking Company) in New York State. Other British banks have various outlets—mainly for international business—in the United

States. This "exchange of threat" model has also been called exchange of hostage because cross investment gives each side a mutual hold over the other country's firms. To the extent that the exchange of threat model describes a real phenomenon, the product life cycle model loses some validity. The product life cycle model demands that the foreign investor have an advantage over the host country competitor which arises from superior products or techniques. If British banks can come into the United States almost as easily as American can enter Britain, it can hardly be said that the British are irretrievably backward. In fact, it seems that the Americans have an advantage in the London market which arises not from their modernity so much as from the fact that they represent the dollar. American bank branches have a link to the U.S. money market and to the Federal Reserve as lender of last resort which gives them a natural advantage. They are more like rich kids who also have brains rather than like poor kids who have made their mark by dint of brains alone.

Many bankers must indeed have felt like Joseph Heller's hero who knew that at some point his life had veered off the predicted course, but could not figure out exactly when or why. In banking, certificates of deposit, interbank operations, cash flow analysis, variable rate loans and other forms of financial virtuosity are what happened. The changes in style and technique which American banks brought to Britain all signalled a banking revolution in which the commercial bank, as known in the U.S. and Britain, became a new species. Rather than sit back passively taking in deposits at short term and lending them safely at short-term, the new banker saw ways to aggrandize himself by adding new aspects to his business. He performed ancillary financial services through new subsidiaries. He extended his long-term operations by adding new money market techniques. He increased his geographical coverage domestically and internationally. With such attitudes, he was unlikely to take new government regulations lying down. The new banker was very likely to go to Britain.

NOTES TO CHAPTER SIX

1. At the end of 1972, 21 out-of-state banks had New York Edge Act subsidiaries. In other states, the principle out-of-state operators were Citibank, Chase and Bank of America.

2. Commercial paper of holding companies was subjected to reserve requirements if used by the bank in 1970; in 1973 when the Fed established marginal reserve requirements on increases of bank-issued certificates of deposit, it also applied the marginal requirements to funds obtained by banks from holding

company-issued obligations. Bank-issued obligations of less than seven years maturity had been subject to Regulation Q ceilings on interest rates; in 1974, a bill was passed to give the Federal Reserve and other banking authorities the power to regulate holding company issues redeemable before seven years from issue. This action was in response to an offer by Citicorp and other holding companies of $1,000 denomination floating rate notes which were redeemable. See *The Washington Post*, 28 June, 9 July, 13 August 1974; *New York Times*, 12 September 1974. In effect, reserve requirements generally apply now to most sources of banks' funds and interest rate ceilings apply to smaller denomination deposits and other liabilities, that is, deposits of under $100,000. U.S. banks had raised over $2 billion by issuing notes and debentures in both 1973 and 1974. 1974 issues of the floating rate notes amounted to more than $1.1 billion (*New York Times*, 30 January 1975).

3. *The Bankers* (New York: Weybright and Talley, 1974), p. 16. One example of the usefulness of a holding company is found in the case of FNCB. Citibank transferred its travellers check business to FNCB Services Corporation, a subsidiary corporation. Under Federal Reserve regulations, the bank would have had to keep reserves of 17.5 percent, as on demand deposits. But as a subsidiary of the holding company, the travellers check business would be free of reserve requirements.

4. There are large caveats to that statement, but given traditional alternatives to loans such as government bonds, it did tend to be true within limits.

5. It will be further discussed below how banks "took off" in the 60s and 70s. Any historian of banking would have expected banks under the circumstances to have turned to riskier investments in order to earn high returns. They did in fact do so, and the result was predictable: bank failures, falling profits and huge loan losses in 1975.

6. U.S., Congress, Joint Economic Committee, *The Multinational Corporation and International Investment, Hearings before the Subcommittee on Foreign Economic Policy*, 91st Cong., 2d sess., pt. 4, 1970.

7. U.S. Congress, Senate, Committee on Finance, *Implications of Multinational Firms for World Trade and Investment and for U.S. Trade and Labor*, 93rd Cong., 1st sess., 1973, p. 521. A study of multinationals at Harvard showed that a majority of the companies reviewed used both local banks and branches of American banks. Sometimes better rates can be obtained because of the parent company's association with the banks at home. See Sidney M. Robbins and Robert B. Stobaugh, *Money in the Multinational Enterprise* (New York: Basic Books, 1973), pp. 66-67. The bank may even serve as a conduit of information to the parent company, keeping it informed of activities by the subsidiary.

8. "Why the Fast Spread of U.S. Banks Overseas," *U.S. News and World Report*, 4 December 1972, p. 65.

9. Alfred F. Miossi, "Chicago as an International Financial Center," *The Banker* (December 1971): 1508.

10. G. Walter Woodworth, *The Management of Cyclical Liquidity of Commercial Banks* (Boston: Bankers Publishing Company, 1967).

11. Quoted in Alhadeff, *Competition and Controls*, p. 302.

12. Monopolies Commission, *Report on the Proposed Merger of Barclays,*

etc., par. 107. While it was reported that American banks generally kept their rates on advances in line with cartel rates at that time, (par. 178) the cartel rates fell increasingly behind rates in other London markets in later years.

13. Alhadeff, *Competition and Controls*, p. 312. Of course, the differences tend to be differences of degree rather than of kind.

14. "Through Foreign Eyes," in "Supplement," 26 November 1966, p. xxxviii.

15. Interview with Michael Julien in *Euromoney*, August, 1973, pp. 50-52.

16. Interview at Morgan Guaranty Bank, London, 27 June 1973.

17. "A British Banker's View," *The Banker*, October, 1969, pp. 1063-71.

18. In Britain, the overdraft is technically repayable on the demand of the lender, although many individuals and companies treat overdrafts as advances of a much longer term since repayment demands are rare.

19. Sayers, *Modern Banking*, 7th ed., pp. 328-9.

20. *The Economist*, 6 June 1964, p. 1133.

21. The time deposit component of deposits in the United States had grown from 26 percent in 1950 to 34 percent in 1960 to 51 percent in 1970 and 65 percent in December, 1973 (*Federal Reserve Bulletins*). Part of the impetus for the change came from more aggressive corporate treasurers seeking to maximize the noninterest bearing component of their cash assets.

22. Alhadeff, *Competition and Controls*, p. 285.

23. See "Negotiable Time Certificates of Deposit," *Federal Reserve Bulletin*, April 1963, p. 458.

24. Large negotiable CDs issued to individuals, partnerships and corporations at large commercial banks, December 26, 1973. (*Federal Reserve Bulletin.*)

25. Effective May 16, 1973, certificates of deposit of $100,000 or more were exempt from a maximum rate of interest. (*Federal Reserve Bulletin*, June 1973, p. 447.) On July 16, 1973, time deposits of at least $1,000 with a maturity of four years or more became exempt as well. (*Federal Reserve Bulletin*, August 1973, p. 582.) These smaller CDs only remained exempt until November 1973.

26. Dollar CDs are issued for standard maturities from 30 days to five years. The minimum deposit is $25,000 (and higher, depending on the bank and the maturity) and they are issued in multiples of $1,000. Units of $1 million can occur. (See Einzig, *Parallel Money Markets*, vol. 1, p. 161.) They are therefore similar in most respects to Treasury bills except that they lack the backing of the U.S. Government. A newer kind of CD, the "tranche" CD, has appeared recently. It is issued and placed much the same way bond issues are, each issue being at the same maturity, interest rate, etc. See J.B. Clark, "Tranche CD's: An Appraisal," *Euromoney*, April 1973, pp. 33-35.

27. The minimum deposit was initially set at £50,000, the maximum at £250,000. They could be issued at maturities from three months to five years. See *Quarterly Bulletin*, September 1968, p. 239. Fifty banks entered the market at the start. (*The Economist*, 26 October 1968, pp. 86-87.) Now the maximum is at £500,000 and by September, 1972, 144 banks were licensed to issue sterling CDs, (see "Sterling Certificates of Deposit," 12 *Quarterly Bulletin*, December, 1972, pp. 489-90.)

28. Einzig, *Parallel Money Markets*, vol. 1, p. 103.

29. March 10, 1973, p. 95.

30. As of April 18, 1973. See "Sterling Certificates of Deposit and the Inter-Bank Market," *Quarterly Bulletin*, March 1973, p. 309.

31. See James M. Boughton, *Monetary Policy and the Federal Funds Market* (Durham: Duke University Press, 1972), pp. 74-75; also *Federal Reserve Bulletins.* Interbank deposits may even be said to have become an American habit in the nineteenth century before the establishment of a central bank. Lacking a central reserve, banks naturally began to place reserve deposits at banks larger than themselves.

32. Boughton, *Monetary Policy*, p. 9.

33. Charles N. Stabler, "Obscure Billion-Dollar Business Emerges as a Key to Money Supply, Interest Rates," *Wall Street Journal*, 17 May 1976.

34. As Einzig described the process, "Most new foreign bank branches operate in inter-bank sterling deposits, especially the American banks. Even though they came to London mainly for the purpose of having direct access to the Eurodollar market, they are anxious to supplement and diversify their activities and increase their earnings by taking a hand in other markets. If their parent institutions are of high standing, their names are taken for considerable amounts for inter-bank sterling deposits." (*Parallel Money Markets*, vol. 1, p. 41.)

35. I.B.R.O., *The Future of London*, pp. 2-3.

36. That such banks are more vulnerable was proved dangerously true in 1974. When the fall of the German Bankhaus Herstatt produced a lack of confidence in the world banking system, an *ad hoc* solution by depositors was to place funds with the biggest banks. The banks themselves limited the "names" of banks they would deal with in the interbank market. A three or four tiered market developed in which smaller banks below the likes of Chase Manhattan, Bank of America, and other huge banks, had to pay higher rates than the giants in London. (Lewis Beman, "How It All Came Apart in the Eurodollar Market," *Fortune*, February 1975, p. 191.)

37. As Hayes said of American banking: "Highly rigid policy criteria are therefore the exception and not the rule, particularly on credits extended major corporate customers." (Douglas Hayes, *Bank Lending Policies: Domestic and International*, Michigan Business Studies, vol. XVIII, No. 4 (University of Michigan, 1971), p. 21.) American banks, of course, also extend lines of credit to credit-worthy customers, which are similar to, but not the same as, overdrafts. In the United States, term loans have generally represented about one third of all business loans since the war. (See Hayes, p. 109; also Paul B. Trescott, *Financing American Enterprise*, (New York: Harper and Row, 1963), p. 224.) At the end of 1973, term loans at 160 reporting banks represented 37 percent of commercial and industrial loans. (*Federal Reserve Bulletin.*)

38. First edition, corrected. (London: Oxford University Press, 1939, p. 231.)

39. Radcliffe Report, par. 942; J.S.G. Wilson, *Monetary Policy and the Development of Money Markets* (London: George Allen and Unwin, 1966), p. 86.

40. Anthony Harris, "Banks Look at U.S. Fixed Loans Schemes," *The Times*, 30 June 1969. Of course, American banks must offer overdraft facilities in

Britain in order to be competitive there, but as a banker at Morgan Guaranty said, "We prefer to keep as low a profile as possible in this area." Quoted in William Hall, "Money from the American Banks," *The Financial Times*, 21 January 1974.

41. "Impact of the U.S. Banks on British Banking," *The Banker*, October 1969, p. 1055.

42. Interview, London, September 5, 1973. Quinn calls the British approach (as described here) "backward-looking," and the American cash flow approach "forward-looking." Brian Scott Quinn, *The New Euromarkets* (London: Macmillan, 1975), p. 225.

43. See, for instance, the *Radcliffe Report*, par. 932-52.

44. Alberto A. Weissmuller, "Big Project Financing—A Look Ahead," *The Banker*, May 1973, p. 466.

45. "Commentary," March 1971, p. 236.

46. See Richard Fry, "Banks Explore New Loan Horizons," *The Times*, 5 May 1969.

47. See, for example, E.C. Wade, "Do We Know What We Are Doing?" *The Banker*, February 1974, pp. 179-80.

48. *The Financial Times*, 4 March 1974, p. 15.

49. Anthony Greayer, "An Introduction to Lending in the Eurocurrency Market," (Brandt's, 1973); Mary Campbell, "Bank Loans Cheaper than Eurobonds," *The Financial Times*, 20 September 1973.

50. *The Economist*, 10 May 1975.

51. 18.2 percent of all 1973 Eurocredits were for over 10 years. In March, 1973, a 17 year credit was extended to Sonatrach. See Dr. Yoon S. Park, "Structure of the Eurocredit Market," *Euromoney*, April 1974, p. 75. For the effects on banks' stability, see Chapter 9.

52. Lewis Beman, "How It All Came Apart in the Eurodollar Market," *Fortune*, February 1975, p. 87.

53. See Henry S. Terrell, "The Foreign Term Lending Activities of U.S. Banks," International Finance Discussion Paper no. 23, Federal Reserve Bank, 2 February 1973. (Mimeographed.)

54. See Paul Einzig, *The Euro-Dollar System*, 1st ed., (New York: Macmillan, 1964), p. 20.

55. See Bell, *The Eurodollar Market*, p. 35. For a review of the technical aspects of variable rates, see Paul Einzig, *Roll-Over Credits: The System of Adaptable Interest Rates* (New York: St. Martin's Press, 1973).

56. See Chapter Nine for a statistical review of the maturity structure at banks in the U.K.

57. The individual, of course, would still need a bank as intermediary in order to borrow in the Eurodollar market.

58. Continental-Illinois originated a seven-year term loan in 1972 designed to give the borrower "an outside fix on what it will cost." *The New York Times*, 25 May 1972.

59. See John D. Wilson, "Latest Developments in U.S. Bank Loan Pricing," *Euromoney*, May 1974, p. 63; H. Erich Heinemann, "Largest U.S. Banks Ease Lending Terms," *The New York Times*, 14 August 1972. The assurance that

banks could bid for the needed deposits was only assured after Regulation Q was removed from large CDs in 1973. See also Richard B. Miller, "Everybody's Floating the Loan Rate," *Banker's Magazine* 158 (Spring 1975): 2.

60. This model is mainly associated with Raymond Vernon, *Sovereignty at Bay* (New York: Basic Books, 1971), p. 65ff.

61. Edward M. Graham, "Oligopolistic Imitation and European Direct Investment in the United States" (Ph.D. dissertation, Harvard Business School, 1974).

Chapter Seven

The Establishment and Other Bankers: What the American Do

More than one manager of an American bank branch, the morning after the big champagne opening, must have sat down at his desk, looked out onto the dull London scene and said, "What now?" What did the likes of forty American banks do, once having made the move to the City? With both changing financial conditions and changing government regulations, the decision to set up a branch might have been based on a situation which no longer even existed. The biggest banks, that is to say the "establishment," faced problems different from the smaller banks trying to break into the London markets. But all shared one goal: to grow as much as possible. The activities of American banks in Britain will be described here, first, by a look at one of the smallest and one of the largest banks. Then, the aggregate business of all American banks in Britain will be examined. We will see that the American banks, particularly the biggest among them, are important indeed. In the next chapter, the implications of this fact will be assessed.

LONDON SMALLFRY: FIDELITY

Fidelity Bank of Philadelphia's parent holding company is the 43rd largest in the United States. It is a $3 billion (assets) bank, so it is comfortably within the size range of American banks in Britain. Like many comparable banks, Fidelity opened a Bahamas branch before moving to London, but it made plans to test the ground in London as well. Fidelity had a minority holding in the London firm of Henry Ansbacher; it opened a representative office at the Ansbacher address in 1971.

Fidelity, as the fourth largest Philadelphia bank, surely held the mouse's share of the local international banking business. The bank had, however, made a fair number of investments in foreign financial institutions through its New York Edge Act subsidiary, Fidelity International Bank (New York). Twenty-one foreign affiliates (including Ansbacher's) were listed by 1972. Fidelity had even tried the experiment of setting up a joint Edge Act subsidiary with several other American banks in 1968, but bought out its partners in 1971. Fidelity, therefore, was no stranger to international ambitions.

Unlike most banks, Fidelity lacked secretiveness. It allowed its financial prognostications to be published in *The Banker* in July, 1973, six months after opening its branch in London. Its planned expenses for the first year were:

230,000	office costs (leasing 12,000 ft.^{2}, subletting 7,000 ft.^{2} at a profit.
120,000	staff costs (excluding salaries of three Americans!)
160,000	other expenses
$510,000[1]	Total expected operating costs

To break even, Fidelity assumed a need for:

$ 40 million	in commercial loans, earning 1 percent average return
$110 million	in interbank placements, earning 1/8 percent average return
$537,500	Income on the above (average return of 1/2 percent)

Fidelity admitted that it had not achieved the above mix in its business; rather than having one-quarter of its book in commercial (as opposed to interbank) loans, it only had one-tenth of its business in commercial loans. Despite this high dependence on interbank dealings, Fidelity claimed its return was higher than expected, and that when the commercial end of the business had been improved, they might build up a $200 million volume and earn $1,500,000—producing a neat profit![2]

Regardless of Fidelity's success or failure, the story reveals how little nonbank business smaller banks engage in in London. They borrow money from banks, relend it to other banks and hope to make money on high volume and low margins. And mostly they stick with dollars. In mid-1973 (when Fidelity was viewing its future) British branches of American banks together did 75 percent of their lending to banks. In December, 1974, the figure was still at a similar level. The bigger banks naturally do more lending for final use by commercial customers. The practice of syndicating huge commercial and government borrowings gives all of the smaller banks a chance to lend to customers they would otherwise be unable to service, but the relationship is indirect. All in all, it can be seen that the average American bank joining the flock across the Atlantic was simply a money-market middleman, and probably not a terribly profitable one at that.[3] But it should be remembered that the branch is not alone. It brings intangible benefits, particularly in terms of prestige. Smaller banks with expanding international arms can also attract better recruits who see a chance to make a mark more easily than at Chase or Morgan. Thus, even though the branch fails to generate a high return, a bank may still feel that the benefits outweigh the costs.

THE ESTABLISHMENT

Fidelity was a late arrival in London, typical of the banks which followed the lead of others. But these smaller banks wield little of the power in London. They may participate in syndicated Eurodollar loans—but it is the "establishment" which manages the big deals and earns the fees. This establishment displays a pattern of activity in London very different from that of the lesser competitors. With far greater resources abroad, the big banks addressed much of their effort toward developing business away from dependence on inter-bank Eurodollar activities.

Which banks belong to the establishment? In Chapter Two (Figure 2-2) six banks seemed to stand out from the rest, with large assets (over $20 billion) and big London operations (over 500 staff).[4] A few others also seem to have fairly extended ambitions—Chemical Bank, Continental Illinois, First Chicago, Marine Midland, and First National Bank of Boston. The dominance of these banks parallels the concentration of power in the United States, where the dozen largest (among 13,000 banks) control over 20 percent of all domestic banking assets. Not surprisingly, concentration of international assets is higher: the twelve largest international banks control over 70 percent of foreign branch assets.[5]

Those same banks surely dominate in London as well, but it is difficult to determine by exactly how much. A study by Andrew

Brimmer showed that at the end of 1972, fifteen large banks in London held 43 percent of American bank deposits there, or $19 billion. He excluded three large banks however: which we can assume to be Citibank, Chase, and Bank of America.[6] Given the share of these three banks in total American foreign branch deposits (about 43 percent), it is reasonable to assume that together they control almost as great a proportion of deposits at London branches, perhaps 35 percent. This would mean British deposits of between $4 and $6 billion each for the three or four largest banks there in 1972, and perhaps somewhat more. For the biggest banks, overall foreign deposits generally doubled between mid-1972 and mid-1974. Citibank, for instance, had total foreign deposits in June, 1974 of $21.5 billion. If Citibank conformed to the industry average of attracting over half of all foreign deposits in Britain, then it would hold perhaps $10 billion in Britain alone, although the real figure, given Citibank's broader distribution, is probably closer to $6 billion.[7] Such estimates are necessarily crude because figures on branch assets are a tightly guarded secret. Hints such as Brimmer's do exist: the *Financial Times* offered the information that Banker's Trust's London 1973 assets had reached about $2 billion.[8] With total foreign deposits in mid-1974 at $6.9 billion, British branch deposits are probably now considerably over $2 billion. (Banker's Trust ranks sixth among American banks and fifth in terms of foreign deposits.) Thus, the top five international banks certainly each exceed $3-4 billion in London assets while most of the top dozen must possess resources in London alone which would surpass the total resources of most American banks.

First National City cannot be described as a "typical" establishment bank because it is almost too important. As the *Wall Street Journal* said, "A cynic might say that the banks of the United States are divided into two classes. The first class is composed of First National City Bank of New York and the second is composed of all the others."[9] But its history in London does provide an ideal type to contrast with the story of Fidelity. The contrast is astounding; Citicorp can hardly describe itself. It must, in effect, generalize about its activities given the fact that it has 1,095 offices of itself, its subsidiaries and affiliates in 95 countries (1973). The second largest U.S. bank with 1974 assets of $57.8 billion, it will probably soon be the largest. It already is largest in terms of employees, foreign assets, and foreign income.[10] It proudly proclaims that it earns the majority of its profits outside of the United States (25 percent of its foreign income arises in Europe).

Citibank, naturally, has huge interests in Britain, but many of its activities there are of recent vintage. Its original branch in London predates World War I, yet Citibank did not really pursue expansion there until the 1960s. In 1964, Citibank placed first among U.S. banks in deposits at all foreign offices ($1.8 billion), but at that time, total deposits at all American banks in Britain were only $2.6 billion.

Much of the bank's international push has come from its last chairman, George Moore, and its present one, Walter Wriston. One of its first changes of policy in Britain was to buy a minority share in the merchant bank, Hill, Samuel. This was sold in 1968. Citibank has since generally followed a "go-it-alone" philosophy avoiding joint enterprises, with a few exceptions.[11] Most of its joint operations have now been sold. But the first moves at expansion in the sixties were joint: Hill Samuel; Midland-Citibank factors; International Commercial Bank; National and Grindlay's Bank (1969). (Citibank, to its chagrin, had to increase its share in National and Grindlay's to 49 percent when a Grindlay's subsidiary got into serious trouble in 1975.)

Feeling more adventuresome, Citibank then began to build new businesses, particularly in Britain. It created Citicorp International Capital, Ltd., Citicorp International Bank Ltd., (1972), and Citibank Financial Trust Ltd. (1967). It opened London offices of Citicorp Venture Capital, Citicorp Leasing International, etc. The establishment of such subsidiaries marks the significant difference between the establishment and the crowd: business goes far beyond the interbank deals of the minor league.

Citibank sought to penetrate domestic U.K. money markets by pioneering the "money shop" concept (through Citibank Financial Trust). American banks find it difficult to get into local sterling business because they face in this area the competition of the huge clearing banks which seem to have offices on every block in the entire island. So, discovering that half the adult population in Britain was without a bank account, Citibank decided to lure these potential customers out of their fears by opening friendly "stores" for consumer loans. (Typically, the rest of the establishment soon laid similar plans.) By 1973, there were 43 money shops, although expansion of these was slowed in 1974-75.

A second big move by Citibank was the establishment of Citicorp International Bank Ltd., in 1972. (Again, by 1975, ten American banks had followed suit.) This "merchant bank" was to become more than just a commercial bank—under the Edge Act, it could underwrite and distribute securities overseas. According to the bank itself, it would do that, as well as "engage in development and industrial term lending, syndicate loans, extend and arrange convertible currency credits and offer financial advisory services."[12]

It is impossible to know to what extent Citibank's British business is conducted in sterling, a mark of local penetration. It was estimated by the *Financial Times*[13] that the big American banks carry about 25 percent of their loans in sterling, which for Citibank might amount to over $1 billion. Of course, Citibank's sterling business could be largely with the subsidiaries of American corporations in Britain, but the bank claims to do better than most in attracting local British customers at the corporate level.

How does the parent manage its many legs, arms and fingers? (Citibank's fingers even seem to have fingers.) The answer may be, "with difficulty." In 1974, Citibank inaugurated a new organizational system to rationalize its world business. The idea was that the traditional dichotomy between the international and national divisions had become a problem because Citibank's biggest and best customers were being treated simultaneously by two different groups. The problem was to coordinate the two. The bank created the World Corporation Group while keeping the old setup (with some realignment of accounts). The outcome of this system of creative tension is yet to be judged. The complexity of the corporation constantly demands new responses anyway. Change seems to be the rule at Citibank.

Like all big international banks, Citibank has a large portion of its personnel and effort in London. This results not only from Eurodollar activities there, but also from the British concentration of its global customers. After the United States, the greatest number of Citibank's multinational customers are based in Britain: 72 against 42 in Japan, 23 in Germany and even fewer elsewhere. Citibank is so important in Britain that it can afford certain luxuries. The bank broke a long tradition by basing its headquarters outside of the high-rent City in 1975. The Bank of England had long insisted that the institutions under its purview should be close at hand, clustered around Threadneedle Street so that quick visits could (theoretically) be made in person.

Citibank was chosen to illustrate the qualities of the typical establishment American bank in Britain, yet it seems that there is little that is typical about it. But if Citibank retains a unique position as an innovator, its innovations quickly become typical as others follow. The follow the leader phenomenon which has been commonly observed often finds Citibank as the leader. (Of course Citibank does not have the last word in every case. Morgan Guaranty retains some of the cachet of a banker's banker and a millionaire's financier; the Rockefeller's still stand behind Chase; Bank of America is still number one. Whatever its ambitions, Citibank may be unable to overcome these facts.)

Between Fidelity and Citibank lies the main spectrum of American branches in London. The only other American banks which do not fit somewhere between the two are the smaller banks which belong to consortia and have no other London operations. Their problems are very different, resulting mainly from the fact that such joint operations often lack heads. Some smaller banks expected to derive the benefits of a London branch by limited investments in such consortia—but that is not usually what they received. And, being small for the most part, these consortia found it difficult to attract business when the Euromarkets got shaky in 1974. That episode will reappear in the next chapter. In the meantime, the banks taken in the aggregate are as interesting as they are individually.

THE AMERICAN BANKS: EURODOLLARS ARE OUR DOLLARS

Whatever their individual peculiarities, as a group the American banks in Britain transact most of their business in dollars. They are the single most important group in the London Eurodollar market. Although other banks have expanded their Eurodollar operations, the American banks have, in general, maintained their share of the market, despite some fluctuations. A few statistics show the trend since the mid-1960s.[14]

The figures of the Bank for International Settlements (BIS) provide a starting point for assessing the share of American banks in London in Eurodollars, since the BIS collects the most comprehensive data on this subject. By most measures, American branches in London held their largest share of the Eurodollar market in 1969, when demand for dollars in the United States intensified. Table 7-1 shows the growth of the Eurodollar market according to the BIS between 1965 and 1974 (although the net figures from 1969 on include all Eurocurrencies). The second column shows the growth of the Eurodollar and Eurocurrency business of American banks in Britain but by a somewhat different measure. By this measure, American banks would average about 25 to 30 percent of the total market, but that share would be less if more exact figures could be obtained.

These figures confirm that the American banks in Britain compete vigorously in the Eurocurrency market, at least in the dollar end of it. Other London banks, of course, also participate in Eurocurrency trading, making London the unquestioned leader in the field. Like the American banks, or perhaps because of them, London reached the peak of its influence in 1969. A better measure of London's dominance is its share of the world's holdings of dollars as seen in the figures on short-term liabilities to foreigners denominated in dollars.

Table 7-1. American Banks in Britain in the Eurocurrency Market (1965-1974) ($ million)

	All Reporting Banks (BIS)		*American Banks*
Year	*Eurodollar*	*Eurocurrency*	*Eurocurrency*
1965	11,500		2,495
1966,	14,500		4,222
1967	17,500		5,453
1968,	25,000		9,413
1969	37,500	44,000	16,452
1970		57,000	19,274
1971		71,000	21,518
1972		92,000	28,356
1973		132,000	39,259
1974		177,000	47,409

Note: The BIS figures are one interpretation of the Eurodollar and Eurocurrency markets, that is, all foreign currency (or dollar) liabilities of banks net of interbank deposits in nine reporting European countries. The figures for American banks in Britain are from the Bank of England and are thus not strictly comparable. They are the nonsterling liabilities of U.S. banks in Britain less nonsterling liabilities to other U.K. banks. The American bank figures include therefore Eurocurrency liabilities to banks not resident in the U.K. while the BIS figures theoretically include only liabilities to banks outside of the reporting area. This difference inflates my figures on American banks.

There is reason to believe that inclusion of the liabilities of American banks to non-U.K. banks may not, on the other hand be too out of line. Interbank deposits are excluded by the BIS because they mean that the same deposit would be counted twice otherwise. But many banks which do not themselves operate on any scale in the Eurocurrency markets probably place their dollar deposits at the American banks in London because they lack the facilities to on-lend them profitably elsewhere. Thus these bank deposits with American banks in London are more like primary deposits than like interbank deposits. Since the data do not distinguish between American banks' nonsterling liabilities to banks outside of the reporting area from those to banks within the reporting area, it was decided to include all liabilities to non-U.K. banks rather than to exclude all of them.

Source: BIS *Annual Reports*; Bank of England *Quarterly Bulletins.*

For the most part, these liabilities represent the deposits of dollars made in a given country by a nonresident of that country. (Thus, it excludes dollar deposits at a British bank made by a British resident or dollar deposits at a French bank by a resident of France.) Table 7-2 establishes the position of London in the Eurodollar market in terms of these external liabilities. London's share is indicated in column three, while column five shows the relative importance of American banks in London. Column six shows the American bank share of the "world" total. The table shows the growing share of the American banks until about 1969 and then their declining share after that year as competition from other banks increased.

Table 7-2. The Eurodollar Market: Short-Term Dollar External Liabilities ($ million)

	(1) Short-term $ Liabilities of Reporting European Countries Plus Canada and Japan to Nonresidents (BIS)	(2) External $ Liabilities of U.K. Banks (BIS)	(3) U.K. Share of $ Liabilities (%) (2/1)	(4) External $ Liabilities at American Branches in U.K. (estimated)	(5) American Share of U.K. Liabilities (%) (4/2)	American Share of Total Market (4/1) (%)
1964	14,610	4,380	30	1,994	46	14
1965	16,270	5,260	32	2,377	45	15
1966	19,420	7,590	39	3,917	52	21
1967	23,870	9,560	40	4,990	52	21
1968	33,490	15,370	46	8,721	57	26
1969	54,250	23,700	40	14,471	56	27
1970	68,740	31,400	46	16,013	51	23
1971	83,150	36,930	44	17,664	48	21
1972	111,760	48,230	43	21,699	45	19
1973	153,660	69,170	45	25,751	37	17

Note: Table 7-2 uses another BIS proxy for the size of the Eurodollar market: short-term liabilities to non-U.K. residents. This measure therefore includes deposits from banks outside of each reporting country, and therefore demonstrates London's capability for drawing dollar deposits from all external sources. This measure of the "total market" still excludes centers in the Bahamas, Singapore and elsewhere. The estimate for American bank dollar liabilities to non-U.K. residents was obtained from several sources.

1) 1964-65: American branches in London nonsterling liabilities to non-U.K. residents (from Bank of England).

2) 1966-68: Same as above plus an estimate of dollar certificates of deposit issued to non-U.K. residents.

3) 1969-73: Federal Reserve data for dollar liabilities of U.K. branches minus Bank of England data for (a) nonsterling liabilities to U.K. residents (most of which are probably in dollars), and (b) an estimate of dollar certificates of deposit issued to U.K. residents. Here, American bank liabilities are once again understated by the exclusion of American consortia banks, which accounted for about two percent of U.K. short-term liabilities to non-U.K. residents in nonsterling currencies at the end of 1972.

Source: *BIS Annual Reports*; Bank of England *Quarterly Bulletins; Federal Reserve Bulletins.*

Most analysis of the Eurocurrency markets concerns itself with the potential credit-creating power which results from the re-depositing of the proceeds of loans in the system. For that purpose, interbank deposits only put "noise" in the figures. Interbank deposits inflate the totals—without necessarily adding to the real amount of Eurocurrency credit available. The BIS, for instance, tries to present figures which exclude this "double counting" by netting out interbank deposits when it estimates the size of the markets. Yet, in measuring the relative power of different classes of banks in the Eurocurrency market, gross liabilities (that is, liabilities to banks as well as nonbanks) provide a picture of which banks involve themselves most heavily in Eurodollar business.[15] Interbank deposits may not directly increase total Eurodollar credit availability, but they are important for individual banks. The trends in interbank deposits also reflect the general availability of credit and interest rate levels. The strongest banks in the interbank market will exert a powerful influence over the cost of funds and the interbank rate is the base used to determine Eurocurrency loan rates.

By the measure of *gross* deposits, the branches of American banks appear to be as strong in their hold over the Eurocurrency market as the net deposit figure indicated.[16] Table 7-3 compares the relative position of the American banks with that of the British banks (including some Commonwealth banks). It shows the gross nonsterling deposits of British banks (Column 1), of American branch

Table 7-3. Gross Nonsterling Deposits at Banks in Britain ($ million)

	British Banks (Clearing, Accepting, Overseas and Commonwealth)		*American Banks in Britain*		*British % of American Gross Deposits*
	Amount (1)	*Rate of Growth*	*Amount (2)*	*Rate of Growth*	*(3)*
1965	1,013		2,594		39
1966	3,404	36%	4,368	68%	78
1967	5,055	49	6,734	54	75
1968	5,942	18	11,431	70	52
1969	9,729	64	21,741	90	45
1970	13,814	42	25,452	17	54
1971	16,322	18	27,696	9	59
1972	23,736	45	35,950	30	66
1973	34,932	47	52,022	45	67

Source: Bank of England, *Quarterly Bulletin.*

banks (Column 2) and the relations between the two (Column 3).[17] As the last column indicates, British banks have gained somewhat in the foreign currency business since 1969, but the American banks still lead the field by far with almost 50 percent more in nonsterling deposits than all of the above British banks together. Even as the ownership of dollars switched increasingly to the oil producing countries after 1973, American banks in London were reported to be the chief recipients of those surplus dollars.[18] Care should be taken of course, to distinguish between the American banks which carry large Eurodollar books and those of lesser significance. As the cases of Fidelity and Citibank illustrated, the branches in London vary enormously in size. The tremendous influence ascribed to the American banks resides in a limited number of banks.

What kinds of people do the British branches lend to? Who would want dollars outside of the United States? And who are the depositors in the market? Many have answered these questions elsewhere, although usually in rather general terms.[19] One problem is that as economic conditions change, so does the cast of characters in the Eurocurrency markets. For instance, central banks in countries with large balance of payments surpluses have often been depositors (both openly and covertly) while deficit countries borrow (avoiding thereby the clutches of the I.M.F.). Parent U.S. banks clearly borrowed huge chunks in 1969; U.S. corporations borrowed to avoid capital controls on dollar outflows from the United States from 1965 to 1974; foreign corporations borrowed for the same reason, and perhaps to obtain cheaper funds; speculators borrowed hoping to repay at a profit after a dollar devaluation or revaluation of marks, Swiss francs or whatever; public corporations borrowed to finance huge investments. There have long been people willing to hold dollars because dollars remain the most-used international asset. So the Eurodollar market did not lack for participants. With accumulated U.S. deficits, it did not lack for dollars either. The BIS provides a view of the sources (depositors) and uses (borrowers) as seen in Table 7-4 on the next page.

Loans in London's Eurodollar market run from small and safe to huge and questionable. Some examples in which American banks have participated show the range and flavor of the market.

1976: Indonesia, $425 million
1976: Hong Kong Mass Transit Railway Corporation, $400 million
1976: Credit Commercial de France, $25 million in floating rate notes, due 1981.
1975: Central Bank of Uruguay, $130 million

1975: Nippon Seiko K.K. (guaranteed by Fuji Bank), $15 million, 9¼% notes due 1980.
1974: U.K. Electricity Council, $500 million, with variable spread over London Interbank Offer Rate (LIBO).
1974: France, $1.5 billion.
1974: United Kingdom, $2.5 billion, for ten years at variable spread.
1973: Ekofisk Consortium, $150 million.
1973: Yugoslavian banking group, $64 million, for 10 years at 1 percent spread.
1973: Bank of Greece, $200 million, 12 years.
1973: British Gas Corporation, $250 million, 7 years.
1973: ENEL (the official Italian energy agency, government guaranteed), $1 billion, 10 years.

Table 7-4. Sources and Uses of Funds in the Eurocurrency Market (1974)

	Sources	*Uses*	*Net Position*
Reporting European Area	68.5	61.9	−6.6
Banks	31.6	20.9	−10.7
Non-Banks	36.9	41.0	+4.1
United States	11.9	18.2	+6.3
Rest of world	95.3	94.6	−0.7
Unallocated	1.3	2.3	+1.0
Total	177.0	177.0	–

Source: B.I.S.

Smaller loans tend to go to corporations, but in the past few years, especially since the 1973 jump in oil prices, governments have been the biggest individual takers. The other side of the same story made the large oil-producing countries into depositors in the Eurodollar market. Thus, for American banks holding the bulk of foreign dollar deposits, trade has been brisk. And even if for many banks their share of a loan is small, the total stakes are huge. Fidelity, Citibank, and those in the middle are deeply involved in the international economy.

Although the Eurodollar market is an international one, it has special significance for Britain. Eurodollars can be borrowed by the U.K. public and private sector. Then, the British borrower can either spend the dollars abroad or convert them into sterling for use at home. For the private sector, exchange control permission is necessary and, as of January 1971, foreign currency borrowing was only permitted for periods of over five years. The government, however, can also be a user of Eurodollars. When the Treasury or a local government authority or a nationalized industry borrows Eurodollars, foreign exchange reserves are increased. The government has encouraged such borrowings, particularly since March, 1973.[20]

The American banks, as the largest suppliers of Eurodollars, have lent dollars in both the public and private sector. They participated in the big official loans of 1973-74. In 1973, Bankers Trust, among others, managed a $250 million loan to the British Gas Corporation.[21] Bank of America, Chase, Citibank, Manufacturers Hanover, and Morgan Guaranty all negotiated with the British Post Office for a $500 million loan at about the same time.[22] The energy crisis at the end of the year gave birth to even bigger public borrowings. The Electricity Council took $500 million. The British Government loan of $2.5 billion in 1974, although managed by British banks, included Bank of America and Chase Manhattan as participants.[23] A January 1975 list of U.K. Treasury-guaranteed loans listed a total of $8.4 billion,[24] to which the Americans contributed, directly or indirectly, a large share. By mid-1975, they were lending $1.7 billion to the British public sector[25] and $3.3 billion to the private sector. While the Eurodollar market is international, therefore, it still exists as a source of domestic credit in Britain.

WE ALSO BUY STERLING

The power of the American branches in the Eurodollar market overshadows their activities in the British sterling markets. Their interests there are relatively small, but growing. Until 1971, British authorities maintained strict ceilings on growth in sterling lending, virtually freezing such credits at American banks at low levels. In addition, most banks in the 1960s and early 1970s concentrated on channelling dollars from Europe into the United States and on supplying the needs of their American multinational customers squeezed by U.S. capital controls. Then several changes forced the U.K. branches into trying to decrease their dependence on dollar business.

1. The Federal Reserve made lending of Eurodollars to parent banks less profitable by special reserve requirements in late 1969.[26]
2. The Bank of England liberalized its policy on sterling credits in late 1971 (although it became less liberal again in December, 1973).
3. Increased competition in Eurodollar lending narrowed profit

margins considerably as market conditions eased after 1970 in the United States.
4. Capital controls were phased out under the Nixon Administration—a change which had been announced earlier and thus affected expectations for some time before the announcement of the new policy in early 1974.

All of these changes induced the American banks to reassess their London operations. As dollar banking became less profitable, they turned to sterling business—or at least the larger banks moved in this direction. 1972 and 1973 saw a great deal of growth in sterling business after the September 1971 changes, although aggressive bidding for deposits became more difficult again after December, 1973. The big banks, as we have seen, also opened specialized subsidiaries for local U.K. financial operations.

American banks still transact much of their sterling business with American clients in Britain—these clients, mostly multinational corporations, need the normal day-to-day financial services for their British business. Those banks which have been in Britain longest, of course, maintain more customer relationships with British companies, but these remain relatively limited. A survey of thirteen American banks in 1967 showed that only 16 percent of sterling advances from those banks were extended to British-owned companies while 78 percent went to subsidiaries and branches of American companies. At that time, the Americans seemed to find more success in drawing deposits from British companies, while lending more to American companies. Forty-eight percent of their sterling deposits came from British owned companies,[27] four times the advances to British companies. This indicates at least a small scale rechannelling of funds from British sources to American companies.

Today, British companies may account for a greater share than the 16 percent of sterling advances made by American banks in 1967. But American banks still shy away from developing relationships with smaller U.K. firms. They prefer British companies in need of world-wide finance—an area in which American banks feel they possess the greatest expertise. Few sources indicate that American banks have made great inroads with British companies. This is not to say, however, that their involvement in the British economy is equally small: American-owned companies themselves account for a significant portion of the British business sector. The American banks may also play a role in directing funds toward American customers in Britain. This changes the allocation of credits within the U.K. away from British companies and toward Americans.

Table 7-5. Sterling Deposits of American Banks in Britain ($ million)

				American Banks' Sterling Deposits as % of:	
	Deposits at American Banks	*Deposits at Clearing Banks*	*Deposits at All U.K. Banks*	*All U.K. Banks*	*Clearing Banks*
End					
1971	3,646	28,164	52,913	6.9	12.9
1972	6,086	35,815	73,853	8.2	17.0
1973	9,468	47,071	98,700	9.6	20.1
June,					
1974	9,643	50,350	101,784	9.5	19.2
1975	9,200	49,113	98,171	9.4	18.7

Source: Bank of England, *Quarterly Bulletin.*

The pressure to increase sterling business shows up in the figures, at least for the "liberal" period between September, 1971 and December, 1973. Table 7-5 shows that the American banks began to make gains in drawing sterling deposits. Their share of total U.K. sterling deposits grew to almost 10 percent, and their position in relation to the clearers improved even more. Sterling deposits at American banks in Britain reached 20 percent of the level at the clearing banks in 1973. When the Bank of England imposed new limits on growth in interest-bearing deposits, the Americans once again fell back.

The American banks' sterling advances to U.K. residents have not grown commensurately with their interbank sterling business. (See Table 7-6.) The proceeds of increased sterling deposits contributed to over a doubling of sterling advances to U.K. residents in 1972 and 1973, compared to tripling of holdings of sterling certificates of deposit and almost a quadrupling of sterling balances held at other U.K. banks. Thus, even in their sterling business, the American banks specialize in the wholesale money markets. In addition, some of these funds placed with "other U.K. banks" (under the Bank of England classification) went to the new subsidiaries and affiliates of the big American banks. Actual sterling assets are heavily concentrated at the very largest U.S. banks with longer London histories. The ninth largest of American banks with U.K. branches was reported to hold a sterling book of $400 million.[28] The banks larger than that, particularly Citibank, Morgan, Chase will tend to hold the bulk of the American banks' $9 billion in sterling assets.

Table 7-6. Sterling Advances to U.K. Residents ($ million)

	From American Banks	From Clearing Banks	From All U.K. Banks	American Banks' Sterling Advances as % from: All U.K. Banks	Clearing Banks
End					
1971	1,279	13,267	20,460	6.3	9.6
1972	2,112	20,585	37,750	6.1	10.3
1973	3,490	27,310	48,137	7.2	12.8
June					
1974	3,328	30,024	51,842	6.4	11.1
1975	4,239	26,415	48,404	8.8	16.0

Note: 1975 figures are distorted by two factors: depreciation of sterling and a new statistical series of the Bank of England. Under the old series, the American banks' share would be 1-2 percent less in 1975.

Source: Bank of England, *Quarterly Bulletin.*

The renewed credit restriction program of December, 1973, once again limited the growth of the American banks' sterling business, but not so harshly as the old credit ceilings once did. By restraining increases in interest-bearing liabilities, the Bank of England plan did curb the ambitions of the wholesale banks more than, for instance, the clearers. Lacking the wide branch system of the clearers (and thus lacking interest-free deposit accounts generally) the American banks depend on their ability to bid for deposits by using the money market instruments discussed in the last chapter. Yet the restriction program aimed principally at limiting growth in high-interest certificates of deposit, since the scramble for such funds put upward pressure on interest rates and on the supply of credit. Thus, the American banks again faced a period of limited growth in their sterling business. But their expansion during the two years of relative freedom shows that they would have both the power and the will to gain an even greater share of the market when such controls were removed in early 1975.

This chapter brings to an end, in one sense, the history of American banks in Britain. The reasons for the development and concentration of American banks in London should be clear now, even if the medley of government actions described here is intricate, and even if the range of banking activities is wide. Three broad factors coalesced to produce this concentration: (1) the internal drive to expansion by the American banks; (2) the limits to expansion imposed by the American federal and local governments; and (3) the British government policy of making Britain a banking haven. But this explanation leaves out an important dimension of the phenomenon in ignoring its impact on the international system. When the stakes are so large, when so many have involved themselves, when governments enter the game, surely the outcomes take on new significance. It is to these areas that the last chapters turn.

NOTES TO CHAPTER SEVEN

1. This was probably somewhat low as an estimate, but does correspond to potential minimum costs cited elsewhere. See for instance, *Banking in London: An Introduction for Foreign Banks* (London: Veritatem Nominees, 1976), p. 12-1.

2. Fidelity's projected operating costs may have grown quickly, although the bank then claimed they were operating below the cost projection. Higher estimates of minimum costs have been made. But Fidelity reportedly did manage to generate $280 million in loans in 1973, and thus may not have come out so badly. (The $280m figure comes from Lewis Beman, "How It All Came Apart on the Eurodollar Market," *Fortune* (February 1975), p. 87.)

3. Profit margins narrowed considerably on Eurodollar business, in fact, and undoubtedly brought problems in 1974-75. *Euromoney* told the story of an anonymous U.S. branch. (See G. Richard Thoman and William T. Kerr, Jr., "International business, what strategy for U.S. regional banks?" *Euromoney*, June 1974, pp. 33-36.) This branch had a staff of 15, a size so small that services had to be limited. The branch therefore (like Fidelity) relied on money market operations and participations. But with spreads increasingly low, the branch was questioning its own viability. It was not even gaining customer relationships since its loans through syndicates only produced relationships with the syndicate itself.

4. Bank of America, Citibank, Chase, Morgan Guaranty, Manufacturers Hanover, Bankers Trust. American Express, while not a commercial bank in the U.S., might be added to the list.

5. The ten largest American international banks (as of mid-1972) were: ($ million)

Year	*Foreign Deposits (June, 1972)*	*Foreign Deposits as Percentage of all Foreign Deposits*
FNCB	11,564	17
Bank of America	10,726	15
Chase Manhattan	7,838	11
Morgan Guaranty	4,071	6
Bankers Trust	2,971	4
Manufacturers Hanover	2,941	4
Marine Midland	2,352	3
Chemical Bank	2,267	3

(note 5 continued)

Year	*Foreign Deposits (June, 1972)*	*Foreign Deposits as Percentage of all Foreign Deposits*
First National Bank of Chicago	2,206	3
Continental Illinois	2,199	3
All banks' foreign branches	69,865	

Source: Andrew Brimmer, "Changing Fortunes of U.S. Branch Banks in London," *International Currency Review* (March/April 1973): 40; *Federal Reserve Bulletin.*

6. Brimmer, "Changing Fortunes," p. 40. Brimmer did not specifically say that he excluded these three. His total sample of 20 banks, however, included two banks without London branches. He took a subsample from the eighteen remaining, saying he excluded "several of the largest."

7. For confirmation, see Sanford Rose, "Why They Call It Fat City," *Fortune*, March, 1975, p. 110.

8. 21 January 1974, p. 20.

9. 6 May 1975.

10. In 1974, Citicorp's international earnings were $194 million against Bank of America's poor second, $100.1 million (*The Banker*, May 1975, p. 537).

11. Among the establishment, Morgan Guaranty, Chase and Bank of America tend more to join forces with other large banks from industrialized countries.

12. *Annual Report* (1972).

13. 21 January 1974.

14. For a picture of the overall assets and liabilities of American branches in Britain, see Appendix A.

15. David Ashby ("The $300 Billion Super-Dollar Market," *The Banker*, May, 1974, p. 440), an economist at Bankers Trust in London, put forward the idea that the Eurocurrency market should be measured by the gross assets of all banks in the Eurocurrency market, including claims on other banks. His estimate of the "super-dollar market," for instance, was $314 billion in 1973 compared with the net BIS figure of $132 billion. The BIS was moved in 1974 to calculate a *world net* figure. It arrived at the same conclusion as Ashby did for 1973: $155 billion.

16. Interestingly, the American banks in London seem to hold about the same share of the Eurocurrency market no matter what measure is used. For instance, by the BIS measure of the Eurocurrency market in Europe, they hold from 15 to 20 percent of the market as indicated in Table 7-1, above. By the BIS measure of short-term external dollar liabilities, they hold 17 percent of a slightly larger market (Europe plus Japan and Canada). Using gross nonsterling deposits against David Ashby's "super-dollar market" the banks still hold about 17 percent.

17. Other foreign banks, particularly the Japanese banks in Britain, also play an important part in the Eurocurrency market there. But the business of "Other Foreign banks" and "Consortium Banks" under the Bank of England classification includes many kinds of banks, even some subsidiaries of American banks.

Since the most interesting aspect here is the competition between American and British banks, and since the other data give unclear results, this analysis excluded the other foreign banks in Britain.

18. See "Survey of World Finance," *The Economist*, 14 December 1974. Bank for International Settlements, 45th *Annual Report* (Basle: June 1975), p. 134.

19. The first important descriptions of the Eurodollar market I have found are: "Market in 'Eurodollars,'" *The Economist*, 9 April 1960, p. 190; Alan R. Holmes and Fred H. Klopstock, "The Market for Dollar Deposits in Europe," Federal Reserve Bank of New York *Monthly Review* (November 1960). Paul Einzig wrote the first authoritative book on Eurodollars: *The Eurodollar System: Practice and Theory of International Interest Rates* (London: Macmillan, 1967). For the most recent effort, see Jane Sneddon Little, *Euro-dollars: The Money Market Gypsies* (New York: Harper and Row, 1975). Little provides information on the technical questions of the kinds of financial instruments used in the market. See also Chapter Six of this book.

20. One dissenter was the peppery *Financial Times* journalist, C. Gordon Tether. In his bogus "Oscar Awards" for 1973, he gave the Treasury the grand prize for "Most Wanton Behaviour," citing "its desperate efforts to get public bodies of all descriptions to raise money on the Euro-markets so as to help it paper over the massive British payments gap." *Financial Times*, 4 February 1974.

21. *The Times*, 3 November 1973.

22. Ibid., 26 September 1973.

23. Ibid., 30 March 1974.

24. Quinn, *The New Euromarkets*, p. 261.

25. Not including $557 million in loans to local authorities.

26. For instance, in 1969, U.K. branches used over 40 percent of their resources to meet the needs of parent banks. (Brimmer, "Changing Fortunes," p. 37.) By 1972, they were using less than three percent for this purpose. The decline in demand from U.S. sources made competition for business in London much stiffer. Brimmer found that the rate of return on assets at London branches for 1972 was far below the standard for American bank assets generally.

27. Great Britain, Monopolies Commission, *Report on the Proposed Merger of Barclay's, etc.*, Appendix 9, "Aggregated replies to a questionnaire sent to the American banks operating in London," p. 75.

28. *The Economist*, 6 March 1976, p. 90.

Chapter Eight

Reverberations I: Three Questions About American Banks

The wave of American banks hit Britain with greatest impact in the late 1960s and early 1970s, but its ripples are still spreading. As the American banks have changed, they have altered the character of the international financial system. The movement took power from the efforts of both the American and British governments to preserve the value of their currencies and the health of their respective banking communities. Today, however, both shores look very different. Currencies were washed from their moorings and money flows faster than ever before. Many claim that the governments have proved their impotence in the face of the multinationals—especially the banks. Barnet and Müller, among the most recent critics of world-wide corporations, contend that "this global economic process is producing a new concentration of political power in what are, in legal and political terms, private hands."[1] Or, as the AFL-CIO's chief lobbyist complained, "corporations and banks put profits ahead of patriotism."[2]

In fact, someone somewhere has probably accused the banks of causing virtually every financial ill of the modern world. They have drained money away from corporate investment or they have poured too much into the corporations; they have retained too much profit abroad or sent too much home; they have set off monetary crises; they have rejected traditional prudence; they have overexpanded, speculated, lobbied—even cheated. Meanwhile, defenders claim that the banks promote efficiency, channel investment to capital-scarce areas, improve the balance of payments (for somebody), increase competition, promote world unity—or whatever. Often what one man sees as desirable, another judges reprehensible. What one calls world integration, another calls loss of national autonomy.

We have seen thus far how government policies in both Britain and the United States have promoted the movement of American banks to London. But we have not judged this movement or its effects. It is clear why the governments chose the policies they did and it is clear why the banks responded by moving to Britain, but it may still be possible that the critics are right—that the system has gone out of control. Have the governments spawned a financial monster?

Financial monster arguments against multinational corporations generally take four forms. The first assumes that government policy promotes the general welfare, but that multinationals can insulate themselves from government control by crossing national borders. Thus, the government is too *limited* to regulate them. The second argument charges that government is "*captive*"—that it promotes the multinational (private interests) at the expense of society as a whole (public interests). The third argument states that the government is *mistaken* in its policies—that it carries out a policy without knowledge of the negative consequences which follow. The fourth assigns no particular guilt, but simply says that the multinationals are so much bigger than governments that the regulators are too *weak* to control them.

From the start, I have argued that the British and American governments do not fail in their purposes out of weakness. While some governments may be too limited to control multinationals, this does not apply to a country like Britain attempting to control banks within its territory. Both governments have to some extent been captive: the British captive to an historical position and to financial interests; the Americans to big banks seeking wider powers. There is occasional evidence of mistakes in policy—usually it seems that the negative consequences of a policy are recognized, but taken as acceptable risks. A final argument, of course, is that the governments have been *rational*, that is to say, they have acted in the public interest in promoting the international expansion of banks. To the extent that rationality is found in this sense, and to the extent that government power is sufficient, financial monster arguments lose validity.

This chapter and the following will review the most significant effects flowing from the internationalization of American banks in Britain, specifically:

1. Whether the movement of American banks to Britain has worsened inflation in the United States or Britain.

If governments have succeeded with the best possible policy, they are rational. If the presumed inflationary effects were geographically beyond their control, they were limited. If technically beyond their control, weak. If unexpected, mistaken. Finally, if there was a solution to the problem in the public interest and against the private interests, and within the ability of the government to carry out, we must judge the government captive to private interests in the event of failure to act for the public good.[3]

2. Whether the banks have contributed to the difficulties of maintaining currency values at reasonable and stable levels.
3. Whether the banks have contributed to Britain's international income.

   This question involves charges that the British government has in fact been captive to interests in the City. Some argue that the government has been rational in promoting the influx of foreign banks because of the increment to Britain's reserves, while others argue that the whole effort is not worth it in terms of the monetary return.
4. Whether the international banking system has become less stable. (Chapter Nine.)

   Some have claimed in this area that the governments involved have allowed bankers to be unnecessarily careless. Others argue again for rationality on the grounds that modern banking promotes efficiency and growth, values which justify any additional risks.

The areas to be examined here and in the next chapter include the problems most frequently mentioned by critics of American banks. If it seems that I cast blame on the governments rather than on the banks below, it is not because the banks are to be absolved of responsibility for their action. But I am convinced by the argument that corporations do not by their very nature act as agents of the General Will, and we waste time in expecting them to act spontaneously against their own interests.[4] Perhaps instead, in Rousseau's words, we should "force them to be free."

DO BANKS CAUSE INFLATION?

Since no two experts agree about who or what causes inflation, it is unlikely that we will prove the banks guilty here. But given the frequency of the charge, the available evidence should be examined. George Meany's simple faith that the cause of inflation is higher prices does not take us very far and neither does a facile assertion of bank malfeasance.

The belief that banks "cause" inflation assumes first of all a demand-pull theory of inflation where the demand for goods exceeds their supply. Thus, in a fully employed economy, an increase in credit would stimulate increased demands for goods and hence higher prices. Or, the phenomenon could be viewed from a monetarist perspective to say that an increase in the money supply under fully employed conditions would produce the same result. Certain aspects of the banks' international activities do raise suspicions in Britain and the United States that monetary authorities now have less control over credit creation than they once had. The two most likely trouble spots are: (1) the banks' new and sophisticated operating techniques (the "new banking") and (2) the banks' Eurodollar activities. The connection with inflation is complex and somewhat speculative, but important nevertheless.

New Techniques

Economics states that an increase in the demand for goods will produce higher prices in a free market with full employment. Since bank credit allows borrowers to demand goods, it follows that the way in which banks manage their assets and liabilities affects the credit supply of a country. The whole movement toward the "new banking" described in Chapter Six is a movement toward more active bidding for funds with the purpose of increasing a bank's earning assets. In other words, banks have indeed been trying to expand their ability to grant credit. On the other side, governments try to control the credit creating activities of banks in order to restrain potential inflation.

The new aggressiveness of British and American banks tends to weaken the influence of central banks over the process of credit creation to the extent that the regulators fail to respond to the banks' new methods. In fact, banks today do not even feel they have the option to submit to monetary controls. While the banking authorities may wish to see a speedy contraction of credit, the bankers say they can only lessen their volume of loans gradually.[5] As one banker said, "Sure we could turn down a loan to a good corporate client who had maintained good balances with us over the years, but not until after we had sold our building and all of the furniture."[6] The banking system has changed so substantially from a "passive" to an "active" system that monetary controls must substantially change if central banks are to maintain their hold over national money supplies. Faced with a determined effort by monetary authorities to restrict credit, banks have learned to invent ever-newer techniques; the authorities must, then, be equally inventive. Simplified, the change is illustrated below.

The Passive System: In Britain under the old cartel system, the Bank of England fixed Bank Rate, knowing the clearing banks would in turn set their interest rates accordingly by an agreed-upon formula. The banks would draw deposits passively, taking in whatever funds the rate attracted, and lending whatever was available. They might draw down investments to accommodate higher demand for advances, but basically, their latitude was restricted.

In the United States for many years, Regulation Q similarly restricted the extent to which banks could increase deposits and similarly restricted their ability to increase loans.

The Active System: (In somewhat exaggerated form.) As seen in Chapter Six, American banks abandoned the passive approach and contributed to similar changes in Britain where the cartel was scrapped in 1971. Now a banker may meet a potential client willing to pay more than the going rate in order to borrow funds. Lacking available resources, the banker may now be able to satisfy the demand if he is willing to:

1. Raise the rate he offers on certificates of deposit to increase his loanable funds.
2. Borrow dollars from a foreign branch (or from a foreign bank) to meet the demand at home.
3. Have the bank holding company issue securities.
4. Borrow in the domestic interbank market.

A British banker can similarly offer certificates of deposit, or borrow from other banks, branches, or subsidiaries.

Under passive conditions, bank credit would have been restricted. The implication is that the changing techniques decrease the ability of the authorities to restrict credit. The so-called "unsatisfied fringe" of borrowers need no longer go unsatisfied. New techniques permit, then, active bidding for funds with which the banks can increase their loan portfolios.

The banks have learned to live in an inflationary world, but probably contribute a fair part to the inflation themselves. Another example shows how variable rate loans work in this direction:

Passive System: Assuming an outlook of restrictive central bank policy and higher interest rates in the future, a bank (in Britain or

America) refuses a five-year loan at the prime rate because the return on the loan will be less than the bank's future costs of raising money. Expectations about future rate changes thus affect present policies.

Active System: Facing the same outlook as the bank above, the active bank is no longer constrained by a fixed return on a loan it grants. By extending a revolving credit or any type of variable rate loan, the bank can be more generous, knowing that (barring default) its income from the credit will increase if the cost of funds increases. In the first instance, the outlook of tight money causes the bank to restrict credit—in the second, funds are pumped into the economy.[7]

The above examples provide an oversimplified picture of the transformation, but show nevertheless that the opportunities for inflationary credit expansion have increased. At some point, naturally, loan demand should slacken as borrowers face interest costs higher than they will be able to repay. (Then again, the borrower may think that *his* income will increase too if prices for goods rise along with interest rates.)

Both the Bank of England and the Federal Reserve can counter such tendencies toward credit expansion with appropriate credit control, but they sometimes fear frustrating legitimate needs for credit when they restrain the credit base. Many believe that selective credit controls would channel funds in the right directions since general credit restriction affects all classes of borrowers, productive and nonproductive. Selective controls would therefore only limit certain kinds of credit which authorities view as nonessential or harmful.[8]

The Bank of England uses a form of selective credit control when it notifies banks that certain classes of borrowers are to be favored (e.g. exporters) while others are to be discouraged (property speculators).

Both the Bank of England and the Federal Reserve, as seen in previous chapters, have used reserve requirements (or special deposits) to cut off unwarranted growth of interest-bearing liabilities such as certificates of deposit. Both only developed this tool in 1973. The Fed, of course, had used a similar method to restrict Eurodollar borrowing since 1969. But each method has its drawbacks. Selective credit controls can be cumbersome. They are also anathema at least to America laissez-faire advocates. Limits on growth in either liabilities or assets tend to kill off competition since no bank can grow faster than another. Interest rate ceilings produce distortions in the flows of funds. But to the extent that central banks wish to counter the new credit-creating banking techniques (which also distort the allocation of credit and favor big banks) they will have to use these tools nevertheless. Because of the problems associated with some of these methods of control, some now advocate fewer controls. It would be better to improve controls and to look for ways to diminish undesirable side effects rather than give up in the face of difficulties.[9]

Eurodollars

The entry of American banks into the Eurodollar market is, in a sense, just one aspect of the new banking—but a most important one. Borrowing Eurodollars from foreign branches to supply credit needs in the United States was itself one method of bidding for funds, particularly until late 1969. There is good evidence that those operations of the 1960s *were* inflationary in the United States. In Britain, the use of Eurodollars switched into sterling could have similar inflationary effects. The role of the respective governments in each case is instructive: both have at their command the ability to stop inflation if they choose.

The U.S. Case: The use of Eurodollars and foreign branches by American banks can expand U.S. credit in a somewhat complex fashion: through its impact on the reserve base of the American banking system as a whole.

Theoretically, reserve requirements influence the degree to which a banking system can increase earning assets, or the supply of credit nationally. As every introductory economics textbook shows, the banking system can expand credit to a maximum of $\frac{1}{\text{reserve requirement}}$. Thus, a reserve of 20 percent potentially supports a total credit expansion of five times an initial deposit excluding possible leakages from the system.[10] If, therefore, reserve requirements differ according to the kind of deposit, then different kinds of deposits will produce different levels of credit expansion. Lower reserves required on time deposits, for instance, mean that shifts from time deposits to demand deposits may produce contractions in credit as required reserves increase. A simple shift from domestic time deposits to deposits in foreign branches can therefore produce a contraction in domestic credit since the U.S. banking system must maintain higher reserves on its liabilities to foreign branches or banks than it had to maintain on the simple time deposit domestically.

But what happens when domestic banks borrow from foreign

branches? A variety of outcomes is possible, depending on how the foreign branch funds that borrowing. In most cases, the reserve base of the U.S. banking system increases, thus permitting expansion in the U.S. credit supply. This credit expansion is greater when:

1. The foreign branch funds the loan by attracting dollars from other banks in the Eurodollar market.
2. There are no marginal reserve requirements on such borrowings (i.e., until September 1969).

Credit expansion is less when the foreign branch has to attract funds *from* the United States in order to lend *to* its parent. In this case, lending power is simply transferred from one bank in the U.S. to another.[11]

On the whole, the inflationary impact would appear to be somewhat limited if the only real shifts involve switches between time and demand deposits in the U.S. But the actual effect *within* a short time span could be significant, as in 1969. At that time borrowings from Eurodollar market branches quickly ran up to about $15 billion without commensurate capital outflows.

The United States did worry about resulting credit expansion in 1969, but devised a fairly simple solution: to penalize Eurodollar borrowing by parent banks by putting reserve requirements on such borrowing. The success of the new policy was almost instantaneous. It was an interference with the free market, of course, but then that is what banking regulation is all about. By raising or lowering these marginal requirements, the Federal Reserve can increase or decrease these expansionary effects at will.

The British Case: American banks also account for a considerable portion of the credit extended to U.K. residents. At times, their activities have given the Bank of England concern that too many sterling credits have gone into the British economy. This contributed to the 1971 decision to bring all foreign banks into the new credit control system, and to the 1973 Bank effort to restrict aggressive bidding for sterling funds.

The American banks' Eurodollar business affects the British economy to the extent that it can also widen the availability of loanable funds. Eurodollar advances to U.K. residents (switched into sterling) clearly increase the U.K. money supply. Aside from lending to individuals or corporations, American banks can also switch dollars into sterling for loans to finance houses or local authorities—with the same expansionary effect on the supply of money. The

Bank of England has on occasion faced a dilemma with respect to the inflationary impact of such loans. At the same time that the Bank wished to dampen inflation, it also wished to protect the value of sterling. Eurodollars switched into sterling may expand credit, but they also strengthen official British reserves. Thus, policy has changed over time, depending on the current priorities.

Most of the disagreement over the expansionary effect of Eurodollars outside of the United States centers on whether or not there is a multiplication of Eurodollar deposits through the classic banking mechanism. A battle has raged for some years over whether Eurodollars lent out find their way back into the system, thus multiplying deposits. This question is somewhat irrelevant in the case of credit creation in an individual country such as Britain.[12] The stock of Eurodollars has assumed such proportions that the potential credit creation within Britain is not limited by the supply of Eurodollar funds or by whether dollar credits are redeposited within the system. The only limits come from regulations restricting access to that supply.

The Bank of England and the Treasury acknowledged the significance of the foreign currency switched into sterling for domestic use in Britain. They said in 1969: "... the possibility of switching in and out of foreign currency has had implications for the balance of payments, interest rate policy, and exchange control."[13] Eric Chalmers also saw the Eurodollar market as a factor undermining monetary control in Britain, saying:

> The acceptance of euro-dollar deposits and the swapping of them into sterling by merchant and foreign banks in London can make possible a sudden and significant increase in the volume of credit, notably by the proceeds of such swaps being placed on deposit with hire purchase finance companies (consumer credit). They may also be placed on a short-term basis with ... local authorities, thereby increasing either current or capital expenditure in the public sector.[14]

The Bank of England, meanwhile, sometimes preferred the increase in international reserves such operations created in Britain. This was true before the 1967 devaluation when the Bank of England supported the forward exchange rate for the pound. This reduced the cost of forward cover and thus encouraged the swapping of dollars into sterling.[15] The 1967 devaluation only corrected Britain's accounts for a limited period and the Bank continued to be divided between its concern for the balance of payments and its desire to control the domestic money supply. Wilson's government made tax changes to encourage capital inflows further. The 1968 and 1969

Finance Acts made foreign borrowing easier by British corporations first, (1968) by making interest payments deductible on borrowings for domestic use and second, (1969) by abolishing a duty on foreign loan capital financing.

Although the Labour Government approved of maneuvers to draw dollars into the reserves, they did come under some criticism for doing so. A Fabian essay, for instance, commented in 1971:

> In periods of balance of payments strain the Bank of England has encouraged short-term capital inflows despite their counter-productive effects in increasing domestic liquidity, at a time when government policy normally is concerned to restrain it. . . .[16]

Warren McClam suggests that foreign currency loans for domestic use amounted to about $660 million in 1970.[17] In 1971, access to the Eurodollar market by British corporations was restricted to long-term borrowing, but since then, the government has itself entered the market by storm. The U.K. has had one of the worst inflation records of all time in the 1970s. It is clear, however, that the Eurodollar market would have no direct impact in this area if the government determined to restrict access to it or to counteract its effects by open market operations. The banks cannot in this sense take the blame for the government's lack of monetary control.

Arguing from the above, it would seem that governments rather than banks must take the responsibility for the inflation of the last decade. Banks, like the rest of us, hold as much money as their governments see fit to allow. Without today's active banking techniques, governments might pursue an even *more* expansionary course. It seems to be a universal law that officials will spend as much as they possibly can.

There is, in this case, however, a difference between the British and the Americans. If the Americans face an "excess" supply of dollars, they are themselves responsible for that outcome. The years of American balance of payments deficits and domestic monetary ease contributed in turn to the pool of Eurodollars abroad. The huge dimensions of the Eurodollar market became a potential credit supply in countries like Britain, and those countries were forced to deal with a problem they did not themselves create. From this perspective, the blame for world inflation shifts away from the banks, and toward the source of excess liquidity, the United States. As Paul Volcker, former U.S. Undersecretary for Monetary Affairs said in 1971,

> . . . the Eurodollar market may facilitate large flows, but it is not that market which gives rise to the differences in national economic conditions and interest rates from which the basic incentives arise.[18]

American banks may be faulted in one serious respect in their British operations (as well as in the United States). Riding the inflationary boom of the 1970s, they financed real estate ventures which were eventually to go sour.[19] Joining British financial houses, they made funds available in the property market and thus fueled an even greater price explosion. These financial booms are always bound to dissolve. In this case, the banks hurt not only the economy, but also themselves. But the American banks were hardly the leaders of this game—they seemed to follow the lead of the British themselves.

A caveat. Although in the last analysis, governments determine inflation, banks are aware that they too play a role. Citing the excessive credit extensions by the banks in recent years, the chairman of First National Bank of Chicago said,

> If inflation heats up again, First National of Chicago is going to be much more conservative in making loans. We can tighten the money supply ourselves by being more particular.[20]

But to return to our earlier skepticism about the nature of corporate motivation, we should not expect such manifestations of "social responsibility" unless the likes of First Chicago finds that responsibility accords with its particular interest.

DO AMERICAN BANKS ATTACK CURRENCIES?

As one banker in London archly points out, no one speculates against a strong currency. And as others have added, currency attacks existed long before the Eurodollar market was dreamed of, and long before there were any American banks abroad. And banks need not be in London in order to speculate; they can buy and sell currencies in their own backyards. Finally, one must distinguish between multinational banks and multinational corporations: much bank activity in foreign exchange markets may simply be for the accounts of customers. Yet the suspicion persists that the internationalization of American banking is associated with the currency instability of the late sixties and the seventies. Three issues are involved. (1) Are the banks more likely to speculate in foreign currencies when they have foreign branches and operate in the Eurodollar market? (2) Have they indeed increased foreign exchange operations for their own account? (3) Are these activities beyond the reach of government control?

Is Speculation More Likely?

A logical case can be made that operations abroad increase a bank's foreign exchange activities. Limited to domestic branches, a bank will be less likely to hold foreign currencies. For instance, at the end of 1975, the foreign branches of American banks had claims payable in foreign currencies worth $43,053 million; the foreign currency claims of all banks in the United States amounted to only $1,403 million. Since the banks count their profits in dollars, they will doubtless get into the business of protecting—or even increasing—the dollar value of their income. And once the bank gets into the habit of foreign exchange operations, it may even begin to look for profits in that market.

As for the Eurodollar market (and presumably the banks' operations in it), it is more difficult to say that it makes speculation more likely in itself. Some argue that the presence of over $100 billion in relatively liquid form in the Eurodollar market oils the wheels of the speculators. No *logical* case supports this argument since the location of a deposit (say, in London instead of New York) does not *a priori* mean that the depositor is more likely to speculate. Yet there may be institutional or psychological reasons to believe that such huge markets promote an atmosphere or an ethic conducive to speculative capital movements—but such issues will be argued indefinitely and without conclusions.

Has Speculation Increased?

Unfortunately, banks do not publish the facts of their foreign exchange activities. When asked, bankers invariably claim that their business is not to speculate—although they admit other bankers may do so. Even if we can detect shifts in the banks' positions during a currency upheaval (which we can),[21] there is no way to know whether the banks or their customers initiated the shifts. And a further consideration should be weighed: the currency instability of the 1970s probably necessitates increased foreign exchange transactions as the need for hedging increases. In the foreign exchange market, there is no visible difference between hedging and speculation. Like a liberal's view of sin, it is a matter of conscience.

All of these conceptual difficulties make it impossible to estimate actual currency flows initiated by American banks for their own account. But some bits of information do indicate vastly increased foreign exchange activity, particularly between 1971 and the 1974 failures of the German Bankhaus Herstatt and Franklin National Bank. This increase was probably, among banks, speculative in character—that is to say, it was carried out purely for profit. But it also appears that American banks were not the heaviest speculators in this period. What is the evidence?

1. Exchange rates have fluctuated erratically and with large swings—particularly in 1973 when the dollar was allowed to float freely.
2. Some banks have reported large foreign exchange losses.
3. Some banks have reported large increases in income from foreign exchange business since 1971.
4. Rumors exist to the extent that banks have speculated heavily.

While these facts may be taken as indicators of bank speculation, they are not conclusive as such.

1. Exchange rate swings may be associated with a very real lack of knowledge in the market of where rates *should* be.

2. Known examples of bank speculation seem often to involve fraud, or unauthorized activities by lower level employees.[22]

3. Banks with weak management controls seem to have increased their exposure without being aware of it.[23]

4. Reported American bank losses in foreign exchange have occurred in important cases as a result of failures by banks they were dealing with, rather than by miscalculation of the direction of rate changes. (Morgan Guaranty and Seattle First National Bank together lost over $35 million in undelivered marks when Bankhaus Herstatt fell in 1974.)

5. Reported foreign exchange losses by banks have been concentrated at continental banks. The biggest examples are: Herstatt, Union Bank of Switzerland, Banque de Bruxelles, Lloyd's Bank in Lugano. *The Times* of London suggested that increased foreign exchange activities by German banks in 1973 and 1974 were a result of *decreased* foreign exchange business by American and British banks.[24]

6. Increased income from foreign exchange dealing may arise from fees obtained for services for the account of others in which the bank itself takes no risk. During the 1973-75 periods of instability, the margins banks demanded grew higher.

7. Movements of intracorporation funds (leads and lags) by non-bank multinational corporations could account for recent rate fluctuations. This need not entail large speculative movements by any particular actors. A statement to the J.E.C. by Alan Teck of Chemical Bank describes this process.

Senator Percy. Can you cite a case that in your judgment went beyond the normal business operations of an industrial corporation, of a case where the financial officer manipulated the money markets in order to speculate and make a quick profit? [The implication here seems to be that "quick profits" are somehow evil.] Can you give us a specific case? You don't have to name names, but give us the dimension, the size of it and the circumstances.

Mr. Teck. I can answer you in one word: "No." It may be that the reason people are having difficulty finding a scapegoat if you will, for the so-called massive monetary flows, is that in one sense there may not be massive monetary flows. Let me explain. And I am going to overgeneralize to make a point.

A recent study by the U.S. Tariff Commission estimated that approximately \$267 billion was held in foreign liquid funds by multinational corporations and banks. That study was done some time ago, so let's round the amount to \$300 billion. That means that if there is a 1-percent movement, \$3 billion will flow from one asset to another. Even in today's market \$3 billion represents a massive flow in absolute terms. Why can a 1 percent shift move the markets so significantly? Often it is because market activity is relatively thin as a result of the other 99 percent being held constant. In other words, because of the persistent annual deficit in the U.S. balance of payments, there has been a huge accumulation of funds abroad, and in absolute terms the funds' movements may be considered massive while in percentage terms they may be no greater than they were in previous decades. Perhaps the reason why no one has been able to pinpoint a culprit for these large movements might be because in percentage terms the movements are really relatively small and may not represent any noticeable change in anyone's behavioral patterns.[25]

8. Outflows from American banks may result from foreigners drawing down existing credit lines at the banks for personal speculative activities.

9. U.S. government policy and objective economic conditions may themselves account for much instability in the dollar rate. 1973 and 1974 were, after all, unsettled times. Watergate weakened confidence in 1973, the removal of price controls spurred fears of U.S. inflation, and until July, the U.S. steadfastly refused to intervene in exchange markets, perhaps even desiring dollar depreciation. The Mideast War of October left no one knowing what would be the long term implications for the dollar and other currencies. Early 1974 saw the removal of American capital controls, again raising doubts. The losses of Franklin, Herstatt, and smaller banks led to large shifts of business away from second-ranking banks and further unsettled dealing conditions; the increasingly deep American recession also spread gloom. In 1975, by contrast, the Federal Reserve showed much

greater willingness to intervene to steady markets, the U.S. balance of trade had turned favorable, inflation appeared to ease, as did the recession. Mid-1975 thus saw a quick reversal of the dollar's earlier decline. Given these facts, the role of banks as *initiators* or currency crises must be strongly discounted.

Still, it is probably true that some American banks in Britain, hurt by the narrowing of profits on Eurocurrency business in 1973 particularly, turned to foreign exchange operations in an effort to profit from the volatility. It is almost a truism that more American banks now engage in foreign exchange than did before the great international movement of the 1960s. It does not follow, however that they should, as a class, be accused of irresponsibility—although individual banks such as the now-defunct Franklin National Bank must deserve the punishment the market dealt them. Under a system of floating exchange rates, it is even possible to say that when major dealers withdraw from the markets, the thin volume resulting may promote instability and volatility. The best defense for a currency is still a sound economic policy.[26]

Have Governments Lost Control?

Exchange controls are notoriously ineffective. There always seems to be a Kuwait gap somewhere and governments do not have thumbs big enough to fill the holes. But if governments cannot maintain "unrealistic" exchange rates, they nevertheless can exercise a good deal of control over excessive exchange manipulation by banks. The degree of control, however, must be weighed against competing values: freedom of international capital movements is sacrificed to the extent that control increases.

In discussing the problem of controlling speculative capital movements, I shall distinguish between those pressures against currencies reflecting "fundamental disequilibria" and those which reflect short-term runs which are likely to reverse themselves. While these two types of capital flight are at times difficult to separate, any sensible conclusions depend on the distinction. Governments' attempts to control speculation in the former case necessarily doom themselves; policies designed to maintain currency values in the face of short-term flows, on the other hand, should be construed as legitimate and desirable.

The American Case: The pressure against the dollar until August, 1971, resulted from the long-term deterioration of the American balance of payments. The most significant lesson from that experience is that a determined government can maintain its currency's value under very adverse circumstances. Eschewing controls over individuals, the U.S. government did install a capital control program (the I.E.T., F.D.I.P. and V.F.C.R.) which appeared to be ineffective (1) as a long-term program or (2) as a program directed against short-term speculation.[27] Large movements out of dollars in 1971 seemed at the time to bear a speculative character—but in retrospect, a decade of neglect followed by a policy of "benign neglect" invited the attack. 1971 was hardly a failure of the government to control its banks or corporations.

The speculative period of 1973 seems to offer a better example of government impotence in the face of the money managers and banks. Activity in the foreign exchanges multiplied, the dollar fell below its apparent long-term value and capital flows grew. But was the government impotent? Treasury protests at the low dollar value resemble somewhat those of Queen Gertrude. In fact, the New York Federal Reserve failed to intervene in the markets until July, 1973. In addition, data were woefully inadequate. Until very recently, neither the Federal Reserve nor the Treasury collected systematic information on foreign exchange exposure by corporations or banks.[28] We should not interpret U.S. indolence as impotence. Public disclosure of foreign exchange data by the banks might instead be a worthwhile display of virility.

A final charge remains. Some argue that even a determined government lacks the resources to counter speculative flows. In late March, 1975, the Federal Reserve's indebtedness from foreign exchange operations was at a peak of $1.1 billion—and the dollar had still fallen by 15 percent against the D-mark since the preceding September. Would stronger intervention have staunched the decline? *Should* the dollar have been propped up in the face of growing recession in the U.S.? What level of rate variation is tolerable? These questions actually ask for the author's definition of the public interest. I believe the United States could have exercised more control in the last five years. The government convinced of the reversibility of a sudden flight into or out of its currency based on transitory conditions should incur low costs by an active stabilization policy. If long-term underlying conditions are adverse, on the other hand, it can hardly blame the "gnomes."

The British Case: The British offer both a parallel and a contrast to the Americans in dealing with banker-speculators. Both countries demonstrated the long-run futility of defending a misvalued parity. (And like the Americans, the British still managed to hold the line much longer than anyone could expect.) British exchange control techniques contrast strongly with the American system in that the

British Exchange Control places quantitative limits on open positions taken by banks, as seen in Chapter Four. Although banks in Britain can speculate in nonsterling currencies by matching positions taken in one foreign currency against positions in another, the presence of a reporting system tends to modulate speculation. The chairman of Continental Illinois bank said for instance,

> One of the few regulations I can think of in this respect is the one put out by the Bank of England for years and years. . . . The Bank of England is probably the best equipped of any central bank in this respect.[29]

The conclusion which follows is that—whatever the problems of establishing a stable monetary system—the difficulties of speculation do not arise in the independent powers of the American banks, at least those operating in London. But whatever the facts of the case, blaming speculators will continue to be a popular game for politicians. Surely we will hear many times again words like those of President Nixon in his August 1971 address:

> In the past seven years, there has been an average of one international monetary crisis every year. Who gains from these crises? Not the working man; not the investors; and not the real producers of wealth. The gainers are international money speculators. Because they thrive on crises, they help to create them.
>
> In recent weeks, the speculators have been waging an all-out war on the American dollar. . . . Accordingly I have directed the Secretary of the Treasury to take the action necessary to defend the dollar against the speculators.

DO AMERICAN BANKS HELP THE POUND?

Whatever the negative effects ascribed to American banks in Britain, they nevertheless win almost uncritical approval there. The prevailing axiom has it that the balance of payments needs all the help it can get; the City gains needed foreign exchange in its international business; the American banks contribute to the City's stature and income. Ergo the British strategy of welcome. Although the direct contribution of American banks to invisible (service) earnings is potentially calculable, their contribution to London's position and prestige is not. Yet many in Britain resist any moves to limit foreign banks for fear that the City's stature, and thus its invisible earnings, would be diminished.

The Committee on Invisible Exports defends the foreign activities of the City from this point of view. One of its main purposes seems to be to publicize the contribution which invisible earnings add to the balance of payments. Given the acceptance of its principle axiom by *both* parties, the Committee has had no small success. William M. Clarke, the Chairman of the Committee, says that the role of invisibles is crucial to Britain and stresses the bi-partisan support for his committee. He admits that, given their remittances in the form of repatriated profits, the American banks probably add very little directly to invisibles. The Americans however, are, in his terms, the "cement" in the City of London, linking together its various parts.[30]

A closer look at invisible earnings casts some doubt on this reasoning that foreign banks are crucial to the City's position or to invisibles. Table 8-1 displays the record in Britain's current account balance between 1966 and 1972 (the balance for goods and services, excluding capital flows). The table clearly puts the contribution of invisibles to the balance of payments into perspective. Invisibles in most years have accounted for all or part of a current account surplus or have lessened the deficit. But the current account is only a part of the total balance of payments, and while invisibles do play a crucial part, banking income is only a small portion of invisible income. The banking proportion has even declined since 1966. Total invisible income actually depends most importantly on returns on foreign investment and on the foreign income of the insurance industry in London. The 1971 figures, which are representative of the normal proportions, show the relatively minimal contribution of banking. (See Table 8-2.) Even the more optimistic figures published

Table 8-1. United Kingdom: Current Account Balance (£ million)

	Current Account (+ Surplus; – Deficit)	*Net Invisibles*	*Net Banking Earnings*
1966	+64	+157	+22
1967	–312	+242	+29
1968	–288	+377	+67
1969	+444	+587	+116
1970	+707	+716	+127
1971	+1,093	+808	+98
1972	+114	+791	+134
1973	–1,115	+1,185	+111
1974	–3,830	+1,430	n.a.

Source: "The United Kingdom's Invisible Account 1962-1972," Bank of England, *Quarterly Bulletin*, June 1973. Figures are updated where possible with revised Bank of England figures. Banking earnings are from the Committee on Invisible Exports.

Table 8-2. Net Invisible Income in the United Kingdom: 1971 (£ million)

Sector	*Amount Earned*
Private Sector interest, dividends and profits	+669
Insurance	+381
Banking	+53
Other, including government	–362
Total invisible balance	+741

Source: Great Britain, Central Office of Information, *Britain's Invisible Exports*, Reference Pamphlet no. 93 (London: H.M.S.O., 1973).

by the Committee on Invisible exports assign banking earnings a small part in the City contribution to the balance of payments. Where the government data ascribe about 7 percent of 1971 invisibles to banking income, the Committee finds about 12 percent of invisibles due to banking income. The difference between the two figures results from different methods of accounting for bank income from foreign sources.[31] But whatever method is used, several areas of agreement can be found. First, banking contributes relatively little to the British balance of payments overall or to invisibles in particular. Second, foreign banks' net contribution to the British balance of payments becomes insignificant after allowance for repatriation is made. It seems that any defense of foreign banks in Britain on balance of payments terms must in the end rely on William Clarke's argument about their being "cement." But the argument has certain crucial flaws.

The largest components of U.K. invisible income do not depend on the foreign financial community in London at all. Most invisible income comes from the insurance industry and income from foreign investments. Some interesting data compiled by W.A.P. Manser suggests that invisible earnings of Britain between 1885 and 1938 (at 1968 values) were three times greater than they were by 1968.[32]

Thus while the City of London's success turned out to be the comeback story of the postwar financial world, the contribution of foreign banks to its success should be differentiated carefully. American banks do provide employment and generate income. They do not, however, do much for the British reserves outside of lending the government dollars when it gets into trouble. Any arguments in favor of furthering the international banking business in London should exclude the benefits of such a policy to the balance of payments.

Limited, mistaken, captive, weak? Or rational? Have the reverberations from the changing banking system proved to be beyond the powers of government? Or have governments dealt with problems in light of rational priorities? The evidence of this chapter indicates that both the British and the American governments have the power, if not the will, to control dislocations in the world of international finance. The game still takes place within the rules written by officialdom. Yet problems do remain.

In the case of *inflation* through credit expansion, plenty of tools exist to bring about cutbacks and to counter new banking techniques. Therefore, the governments have been neither too weak nor too limited to handle the banks. They can use reserve requirements, capital controls and general and selective credit controls if they choose. Reserve requirements alone seem sufficient, at least under most circumstances. The British may be characterized as limited in the sense that incoming Eurodollars are the result of U.S. policy and hence beyond home control—but in fact, the British do regulate money supply increases resulting from dollar inflows so choice still exists.

When it comes to inflation, it should be remembered that banks have traditionally been an important *anti*inflationist group. Monetary authorities have generally dealt strictly with inflationary actions by banks—and without too much in the way of opposition. One could argue that the interests of the banks and of the authorities converge on this issue. Others argue in both Britain and the U.S. (but more often in Britain) that the authorities are captives of the banks because of a bias *against* monetary expansion. When arguments exist on both sides of an issue in this way, it is a sign that underlying values are in conflict. It can be concluded that governments can and do control credit creation by the banks. That those same governments nevertheless allow excessive inflation seems to have more to do with broad questions of domestic politics than it has to do with any particular relationship between the banks and the monetary authorities.

While overall credit policy tends to be relatively rational, it does seem to contain a certain bias in favor of larger banks in the United States. American tradition and local regulation favored the small banks for most of our history, but the way in which the new banking and the Eurodollar market have been allowed to grow works to the advantage of the large banks with international arms. Is the American government then captive to big bank interests on this ground? Or is such a policy rational? The questions boil down to asking whether American policy toward internationalization of banking is good or bad, and that is perhaps the wrong way to approach the reality of the thing. Policy-makers always see their own decisions as rational. For this reason, we can say rather that there exists a convergence of interests between the big banks anxious to expand and the policy-makers who wish to maximize the world-wide spread of American banks and the dollar.

The second question of this chapter, *speculation*, raises the same issues as inflation. At a technical level, speculation is more difficult to control with respect to banks outside of domestic borders. Speculation can bring down a currency value without any domestic transactions taking place at all. But it seems once again that the stumbling block lies at home in an unwillingness to manipulate domestic economies to keep currencies stable. It is not so much that speculators lie outside our control; we ourselves have increasingly resisted self-control. Speculation is the predictable cost of unilateralism in national economic policy. Some have insinuated that because banks can profit from speculation that they favor systems which allow it, for instance, floating. While individual banks have supported floating systems, notably Citibank, that position is the exception rather than the rule.

Governments should nevertheless fear the power of banks to speculate against or for currencies whose value can be expected to change. This has happened and will continue to happen as long as countries trade openly with one another. Large fluctuations in values in response to short-term reversible trends are, of course, undesirable. Experience under the fixed rate Bretton Woods system shows that governments can counter such variations, through a combination of intervention in the markets and capital controls. Experience also shows that these solutions will be useless to deal with long-term irreversible trends. This band-aid approach was the real doom of Bretton Woods.

To make intelligent assessments in the realm of foreign exchange policy, governments do need data. The British government has indeed long collected information on currency dealing; the United States has not. The banks resist it and seem for no good reason to have successfully avoided public disclosure. In this particular area, the banks do seem to have captured the U.S. policy apparatus. In Britain, on the other hand, the shared concern of both banks and government that support of sterling was paramount may have enabled the authorities to impose the strict British standard. A convergence theory may also explain the acceptance by American banks of the capital control program of the 1960s. It turned out, of course, that they were not much hurt by it anyway.

A final argument in defense of government rationality might be that the governments now tolerate speculation as a bearable cost they pay for independence in economic policy making. There is no evidence that this is so. The United States has always enjoyed remarkable independence as the dominant country anyway; Britain now has found that currency fluctuations constrict policy freedom as much as did the rules of Bretton Woods. Britain's problem has never been the speculators anyway; it has been the inability to grow and inflate at the same general rate as the rest of her trading partners. The attacks on both the dollar and sterling, even if carried out by banks alone (and we have no proof of this) originated instead in the domestic economic policies in the two countries.

We are still left with the third question on *the British pound.* It affects, naturally, only judgments on the British government. The claim of rationality looks very weak in light of the data presented here. The American banks do not contribute in any significant way to British reserves—although they do contribute to the importance of London as an international financial center. But if the policy of running an international banking center is not particularly rational from the balance of payments point of view, how can it be described? It might be rational as a policy giving psychic benefits to the country—an illusion of greatness not yet entirely dissipated. If nothing were lost in the process, there would be no problem with even this weak argument. The charge that the promotion of the City drains off talent and resources from the rest of the country must, however, be set against the pursuit of grandeur. The choice in these terms cannot be judged coldly rational.

It has been said that the development of the City and of foreign banking there, while not exactly rational, was not the result of private promotion either; the historical base of financial life in the City had simply created a world which habit commanded be preserved. If no one had ever argued otherwise, this might be tenable. But the contrary is true. Numerous critics of the City have demonstrated its failures with respect to the domestic economy. The Labour Party has accepted this position as a sort of doctrine of faith. History does seem to have had its impact, but is insufficient alone as an explanation of British encouragement of the international banking community in London. That American banks went to London is not simply a mistake of history.

Are the British guilty as charged? Has the government given in to private interests? Which private interests? It can be said at once that the American banks did not promote their own ends against the wishes of the domestic banking community in Britain. Because of the identity of views, we cannot separate the foreign from the home interests in favor of encouraging foreign banks. In fact, the presence of non-American, non-British banks in London broadens the banking constituency even further. In the absence of convincing arguments to the contrary, we must conclude that these banking interests have indeed won concessions which benefit themselves and for the most part only themselves.

A final note. The path the British government chose might not have maximized the welfare of that country. But now that it has built up London the way it has, a sudden retreat could be worse. Actions against the interests of foreign banks could set off waves of indignation in America and elsewhere; the support of an important interest group internally would be jeopardized (the financial bureaucracy within government, the financial community itself); capital flight could follow. Any change would have to be slow and imperceptible.

It is both disappointing and predictable that the conclusions here are not simple. But easy answers tend not to be very good ones. We started out with some questions about American banks but were really looking for some answers about governments in their relations with multinational companies. The multinational banks do, as claimed, create problems for governments in their attempts to regulate economic life—but not, as often claimed, because they are more powerful than the governments or because the multinationals live in a jurisdiction larger than the nation state. When governments have failed to act for the collective good, it has been most often a case of political captivity based on domestic struggles for power and support rather than on either ignorance or impotence.

NOTES TO CHAPTER EIGHT

1. Richard J. Barnet and Ronald E. Müller, *Global Reach: The Power of the Multinational Corporations* (New York: Simon and Schuster, 1974), p. 214.

2. Andrew Biemiller, quoted in Gurney Breckenfeld, "Coping with the Nation State," *Saturday Review*, 24 January, 1976.

3. To argue that a government is captive, one must make the case that a policy serves only a private interest, and not the public interest. An assessment of the public interest, unfortunately, will always reflect the priorities of the judge.

4. This line of thought is followed by social critic Michael Harrington in *Toward a Democratic Left* (Baltimore: Penguin Books, 1969).

5. Of course, the banking mechanism also multiplies this effect as the loans made by one bank are redeposited in another.

6. Quoted by Guy E. Noyes (of Morgan Guaranty Trust) in Noyes, "Bank

Competition and Monetary Policy," Federal Reserve Bank of Philadelphia *Business Review*, April 1970, p. 22. Noyes argued that the pressures of competition force banks to continue to extend credits even when money tightens and even if such credits do not maximize profits.

7. A similar distinction between old-style and new-style banking is made by Martin Mayer, *The Bankers*.

8. Under the Nixon Administration's price control system a form of selective control was instituted by the Committee on Interest and Dividends. Between April, 1973 and April, 1974 banks were asked to offer a lower rate on small business loans. Since compliance was not mandatory, the system did not have much effect and was viewed as a way for banks to dampen pressures in opposition to their high rates. See John H. Allen, "Two-Tier Prime Appears to Fade," *The New York Times*, 6 November 1974. Representative Henry Reuss, Chairman of the House Banking and Currency Committee, tends to favor efforts to influence the allocation of credit. In 1974, he introduced a bill designed to place heavier reserve requirements on funds for "non-priority uses," like "Bahamian gambling casinos," "conglomerate takeovers" or "inflation-inducing over-expenditures." See *The Washington Post*, 29 June 1974.

9. For instance, the U.S. Congress and Administration are now moving to end ceilings on interest payable on deposits. (There are now no ceilings on deposits over $100,000.) The phasing out of such ceilings tends to promote the practice of actively bidding for depository funds. The flexible use of reserve requirements, however, does seem to be a useful alternative for controlling credit expansion without some of the undesirable effects of interest ceilings or quantitative controls.

10. The leakages may in fact reduce the multiplier considerably. One estimate for the M1 (demand deposits only) multiplier was as low as 1.25. See Ronald L. Teigen, "The Demand For and Supply of Money," in Warren L. Smith, R.L. Teigen, (eds.), *Readings in Money National Income and Stabilization Policy* (Homewood: Richard D. Irwin, 1974), pp. 68-103.

11. For a complete analysis of the impact of dollar shifts into and out of the Eurodollar market on U.S. credit, see Mastrapaqua, *U.S. Bank Expansion*.

12. This question is no doubt highly significant, but will not be discussed here. Some analysts say that the deposit-creating potential in the Eurodollar market is infinite because of the lack of reserve requirements. Others contend that deposits can be multiplied several times; others say not at all. See, for discussions of this question: Fred H. Klopstock, *The Eurodollar Market: Some Unresolved Issues*, Princeton Essays in International Finance, no. 65, (Princeton: 1968); Milton Friedman, "The Eurodollar Market: Some First Principles," *Morgan Guaranty Survey*, October, 1969; Helmut W. Mayer, *Some Theoretical Problems Relating to the Euro-dollar Market*, Princeton Essays, no. 79 (1970); Fritz Machlup, "The Magicians and their Rabbits," *Morgan Guaranty Survey*, May 1971. See also a running series of articles on the subject by Machlup, Mayer and others in the Banca Nazionale del Lavoro *Quarterly Review* between 1970 and 1972, and two articles in *Euromoney*; Jacques Rueff, "How the Euromarkets Contribute to World Inflation," (April 1975); Jacques Riboud, "Why Rueff is Wrong over Euromarkets," (September 1975). A sensible view was put

forward by Andrew D. Crockett, "The Eurodollar Market: An Attempt to Clarify Some Basic Issues," *International Monetary Fund Staff Papers* 23 (July 1976) 2: 375-86.

13. See "The Operation of Monetary Policy Since Radcliffe," by the Bank of England in consultation with the Treasury in David R. Croome and Harry G. Johnson, eds., *Money in Britain* (London: Oxford University, 24 November 1970), p. 215.

14. Eric Chalmers, *U.K. Monetary Policy* (London: W.P. Griffith and Sons, 1968), p. 11.

15. *Ibid.*, pp. 105-107; Sir Eric Roll, "The Impact of Economic Policy on the Financial System of the United Kingdom," Lecture given at Reading University 24 November 1970.

16. W. Kennett; L. Whitty; S. Holland, "Sovereignty and Multinational Corporations," Fabian Tract No. 409 (London: 1971).

17. "Credit Substitution and the Eurocurrency Market" Banca Nazionale del Lavoro *Quarterly Review*, December 1972, p. 340.

18. U.S., Congress, Joint Economic Committee, *The Balance of Payments Mess, Hearings*, Subcommittee on International Exchange and Payments, 92d. Cong., 1st sess., 1971, pp. 84-85.

19. By the end of 1974, total bank lending to the British property and construction industry totalled $10 billion, or one-half of all lending to manufacturing. See *The Economist*, "Survey of British Banking," 9 August 1975. *The Economist* estimated that at least seven American banks lent from $2 million to $20 million each to the failed Stern property group, for instance: Continental Illinois, Marine Midland, Chemical, Citibank, First International Bancshares, Bank of America, First Chicago.

Eurodollar loans have also been made available to American real estate investment trusts (REITS), but American banks overextended themselves in lending to REITS from domestic branches much more than from abroad.

20. Seth King, "Chicago's Ebullient Banker," *New York Times*, 22 February 1976.

21. See, for instance, U.S., Senate, Committee on Foreign Relations, *Multinational Corporations in the Dollar Devaluation Crisis: Report on a Questionnaire*, Staff Report for the Subcommittee on Multinational Corporations, 94th Cong., 1st Sess., June 1975, pp. 87-93.

22. See Richard A. Debs, "International Banking: An Address," Federal Reserve Bank of New York, 57 *Monthly Review* 6 (June 1975), p. 126. Of course, it is not unusual for upper level managers to practice the technique of "deniability" that is, to remain technically innocent but perhaps informally guilty.

23. See comment by E. Holloway of Bankers Trust (London) in *New York Times*, 13 October 1974; also "Observer," "Imprudence and Over-prudence in Foreign Exchange," *International Currency Review* July/August 1974.

24. *The Times* 20 August 1974.

25. U.S. Congress, Joint Economic Committee, *How Well Are Fluctuating Exchange Rates Working? Hearings*, Subcommittee on International Economics, 93rd Cong., 1st Sess., 1973, p. 91.

26. An interesting study by Robert Russell analyzes twenty exchange crises from 1960 to 1973. He finds no crisis in which actual economic conditions or reports were unimportant. Although the size of movements into and away from currencies increased during crises over the period, governments' willingness to finance deficits or alter internal policies declined. Russell concludes that avoiding such crises may not be "a particularly salient objective for the governments." I conclude that it is this very attitude which encourages speculators who only stand to gain when governments back down. See Russell's paper "Crisis Management in the International Monetary System: 1960-1973." Paper presented at the meeting of the International Studies Association, 1973.

27. For evidence, see John Hewson and Eisaku Sakabibara, "The Impact of U.S. Controls on Capital Outflows on the U.S. Balance of Payments—An Exploratory Study," 14 June 1974. (I.M.F. mimeographed); U.S., Congress, Joint Economic Committee, *The Balance of Payments Mess, Hearings*, Subcommittee on International Exchange and Payments, 92d Cong., 1st Sess., 1971, pp. 1-48; Sir Alec Cairncross, *Control of Long Term International Capital Movements* (Washington: The Brookings Institution, 1973); U.S., Congress, Senate, *The International Financial Crisis*, Subcommittee on International Finance and Resources, 93d. Cong., 1st Sess., 1973, p. 133. See also Chapter Five in this book.

28. The Federal Reserve now checks on major international banks by survey; the Treasury, under the Par Value Modification Act, issued regulations for monthly reports of activities in nine currencies on 24 February 1975.

29. Quoted by Roger Anderson, *The Economist*, 14 December 1974, Survey, p. 44.

30. Interview, London, 6 September 1973. Support for the preservation of invisible earnings is, in fact, a generally accepted axiom with the Bank of England, the Treasury and both major parties.

31. Committee on Invisible Exports, *Annual Report 1974-75* (London: July 1975), p. 25; Benjamin J. Cohen, *The Future of Sterling as an International Currency* (London: Macmillan, 1971), p. 12.

32. W.A.P. Manser, *Britain in Balance* (Harmondsworth: Penguin, 1973), p. 174.

Chapter Nine

Reverberations II: Has the International Banking System Become Unstable?

Item: On January 23, 1976, the Federal Deposit Insurance Corporation lists 350 banks on its "problem" list.

Item: In early 1976, a Federal Reserve official expresses concern over American banks' exposure to possible bad loans to developing countries.

Item: In September 1974, the Bank of England asks for assurances that London's international consortia banks will be supported in the event of a crash.

Item: In 1974, the Eurodollar market fragments so that only a few of the world's largest banks can attract funds at normal rates.

Item: In December 1973 the Bank of England is forced to set up a "lifeboat" to support the weak links in the British banking system.

Few would argue that the international banking system has become more stable in the past decade. There are many reasons for the rash of banking losses and failures—not least of all, world-wide recession. To what extent can this growing weakness be associated with American banks' international activities? And what does this mean in terms of policy?

Two issues can be separated here. At a somewhat technical level, American banks may weaken the U.S., British, (and world) banking systems by overexpansion or by imprudence in their international business. But more generally, we may consider that the very spread of American banks itself increases potential instability—regardless of the prudence or imprudence of individual banks. In other words, the increased interdependence of the world financial system carries costs not obvious from observation of individual banks' behavior and perhaps greater than the presumed benefits of efficiency and free market wealth maximization. These costs may fall asymmetrically: one government can become sensitive to them (but able to deal with problems); another can become vulnerable, or unable to counteract the negative results.[1]

The argument here is that governments can usually deal with specifically harmful banking actions. It has already been seen that the British and American authorities possess at least potential power to curb speculation or excess credit creation. Whether or not they activate that power turns on questions of domestic politics and domestic value priorities. Decreasing sensitivity, or even vulnerability, to the various parts of an interdependent system, however, is a more general goal with no corresponding tool outside of the rather blunt mercantilist solution of withdrawal. It may be that some pullback would provide at least a partial answer—but an answer which should be kept on the shelf until the alternative of asserting national sovereignty and control has been exhausted. While mercantilists profess to admire the nation state, they too often underestimate its potential.[2]

WHAT HAS HAPPENED TO QUALITY?

According to legal phraseology, a prudent man is a trustee for someone else's money who invests the funds according to commonly accepted standards of financial wisdom. Bankers are expected to conform to a standard of prudence—one not easy to define. Such a standard must apply to their international activities as well. Does it? Should there be concern over the American banks in Britain? If so, can governments act? Even though lesser banks see them as a sort of upper class, elites (the international banks) have their special vices too. Most commonly mentioned are:

1. Dangerous reliance on "new banking" techniques;
2. Expansion into areas outside traditional commercial banking;
3. Extensions of shaky loans to foreign countries;
4. Overcompetition leading to unwise credit decisions;
5. Worsening maturity structures for assets and liabilities (lending longer and longer while borrowing shorter and shorter).

New Banking Again

Certain aspects of recently developed banking techniques increase risks to the banks. Simply put, their sources of funds—nationally and internationally—have become less reliable. American banks, and, increasingly their competitors abroad, bid actively for dollars and other currencies in certificates of deposit, federal funds (in the U.S.) and interbank funds (abroad). The reason risk increases is that most of these are noninsured deposits: any question marks over a bank may produce violent withdrawals from that bank. A second problem is that banks also increase risks by putting their own funds at other banks which may be insecure. These are the sources of disquiet in theory, but the fears expressed have already been confirmed in a few cases.

1. When U.S. National Bank of San Diego collapsed in October, 1973, some $90 million in inter-bank loans outstanding were ignored by the F.D.I.C. *The Financial Times* (of London) noted:

> That event produced a major shock for a considerable number of European banks including in London National Westminster and Barclays. The details of this situation threatened to undermine the trust on which the international money markets must operate.[3]

2. After the fall of Franklin National Bank and of Herstatt, depositors in the Eurodollar market demanded higher rates from smaller banks. In addition, most banks reduced the number of banks they would even deal with.[4] Consortia suffered the most from the loss of depositors, Western American Bank being among the seriously wounded.

3. The New York City fiscal crisis had some repercussions in international interbank dealings. Since many of the large New York banks had invested in city securities (and 234 U.S. banks had invested over 50 percent of their capital)[5] foreign depositors began to prefer non-New York banks. Banks like Bank of America, Mellon (Pittsburgh), Girard (Philadelphia) and Northern Trust (Chicago) were said to have received some of the switched funds.[6]

4. Similar deposit transfers occurred in the wake of 1975-76 press disclosures that major banks appeared on the Federal Reserve, Comptroller of the Currency and F.D.I.C. lists of problem banks. Yet because of underlying confidence in official willingness to back the biggest banks to the hilt, smaller banks were probably the biggest losers.

While some may scoff at the notion that "modern" banking methods pose unnecessary dangers to solvency, there have been indications that even the banks themselves believe they have gone too far. *The Economist* said at the end of 1974,

> . . . some old-fashioned parlance is now heard in smart streamlined banking parlours. The accent has changed from turning money at high volumes on slim margins, and pivoting a fast-expanding balance sheet on a minimum of capital resources and reserves, to cutting one's cloth to more traditional canons of banking prudence.[7]

Such sentiment led to the proposals for stricter bank regulation in Britain which were set out in the August 1976 White Paper. Robert C. Holland, a member of the Board of Governors of the Federal Reserve expressed the Fed's concern at American banks' "heavy reliance on liability management,"—their dependence on bidding for CD's and other sources of funds saying:

> Such instruments have proved not only highly interest-sensitive, but also highly confidence-sensitive in times of stress.[8]

Or as Arthur Burns commented:

> Clearly the far flung changes . . . have served the public in many ways. There is, however, another side of the ledger. The very forces that have produced innovative, highly competitive banking have also led to some trends that go far to explain the uneasiness that so concerns us in 1974.[9]

Thus the new banking does increase risks within the system; and as bankers increase their dealings with foreign banks, they increase their sensitivity to events abroad. (Naturally, this sensitivity works in both directions.) Without implying that the risk is commensurate, we can compare the situation to the 1920s. Then, bankers blindly made what were considered to be liquid and safe loans to brokers. Today, bankers similarly feel that interbank dealings enjoy the virtues of safety and liquidity. But the virtues of the system can also be its downfall: liquidity for depositors must in turn mean more potential volatility in bank liabilities. And, like the brokers of the 1920s, unsound banks make poor credit risks.

Functional Diversification

Chapter Five showed how both the Edge Act (governing the activities of subsidiaries for international finance) and Federal Reserve Regulation Y (governing all holding company subsidiaries) permit American banks to enter into a wide range of activities. The Edge Act allows broader scope abroad than does Regulation Y domestically.

In theory, affiliation with companies which are not commercial banks may increase risks to banks. These subsidiaries or affiliates are usually engaged in financial activities considered more subject to uncertainty—long-term financing, underwriting, real estate, etc. By association, a bank holding company may be suspected of assuming some of these added risks, even when the necessity to do so is not a legal one. Chase Manhattan Corporation could therefore look relatively troubled because of its association with the Chase Manhattan Mortgage and Realty Trust. And when the bank reported an earnings decline and assumption of over $85 million in nonearning property, the problems inherent in risky association became clear.[10]

While there is a growing concern about diversification within the U.S., it should be noted that risks can be even higher in London. There, the merchant bank subsidiaries of American banks have even greater freedoms. Since the Edge Act (1919) preceded the Banking Act of 1933, it is not surprising that broad powers were granted the banks abroad—all commercial banks enjoyed wider investment privileges before 1933. It is somewhat odd that today, when the financial world has become so interdependent, the authorities should consider that American banks' higher risks abroad are of low relevance to the banks' positions at home. Why, if an activity is considered "dangerous" at home is it not so dangerous elsewhere? The industry and official argument states that banks must have powers equal to their competitors abroad. That argument follows if one believes an American corporation must have an equal right to compete with domestic operators within any foreign market.

The fear about foreign diversification of American banks does not base itself on theory only. The Banking Act of 1933 responded to very real abuses and a very real banking crash. While the insurance of bank deposits has gone a long way to guarantee against runs, the increasing turn to noninsured funds and untraditional activities abroad does explain some recent nervousness about the system. And some banks have been embarrassed in London.

The example of Marine Midland's British merchant bank, Intermarine, Ltd., illustrates the worst possibilities. Eager to expand, Marine Midland opened its fully-owned subsidiary in 1970. By 1973, it listed assets of $1.1 billion. Unfortunately, a good portion of these assets was in the British property market and in tankers. While the bank's problems went beyond difficulties abroad,[11] the parent did absorb substantial losses from Intermarine, reducing the merchant bank's assets to less than $200 million by the end of September 1975. In the fourth quarter of 1975, the parent bank reported losses itself. The authorities should realize that banks consider it possible to take higher risks through affiliated companies—they should also realize that the risks taken in this way can be just as important as those taken directly.

Country Loans

It is common knowledge that Eurocurrency banks have lent fairly heavily to countries in the Third, Fourth (and Second) Worlds.[12] How far individual banks have gone is more of a secret. Each bank sets its own limits (within Federal Reserve standards on loans per borrower) for how much it will lend in any one country. These limits are set at the head office, so that a branch can only make decisions within the preset parameters. Martin Mayer estimated in late 1975 that potential American bank losses from exposure to country defaults might be on the order to $3 billion, with loans to Argentina, Zambia, Chad, Sri Lanka, and the Philippines most suspect.[13]

Bankers often answer the questions about country credits the way one American banker in London responded:

> Of course, it's true that some of our clients will not be able to service their debt if a slump deprives them of their markets for export commodities while their import bill mounts. So what? So the creditor banks meet. They can't seize the country's embassy or the Ambassador's Rolls Royce but then no one will be coarse enough to use a swear-word like "default." They will discuss rescheduling the debt. And why not? Countries do not disappear. Even Indonesia or Chile or Ghana didn't go down the drain. We rescheduled their debts and we fully expect to have to do the same in 1975 for Brazil or Gabon or Greece. Everyone will get repaid in the end and there will be no apocalypse. Of course, if we have to reschedule a debt for 30 years without interest, that will be rough on the smaller banks in the Eurodollar market. But then, they should never have got in with the Big League lenders.[14]

But while countries do not disappear, they do sometimes default and two problems must be faced here. First, in a time of low confidence in the financial system and of pressures on earnings, loss of interest under a rescheduling agreement can be serious. Secondly, the use of new loans to cover repayment of old ones can clearly mean that involvement in shaky propositions increases. There has as yet been little in the way of outright defaults, but loans to pay off loans have become more common. Indonesia (which did actually miss payments in 1975) secured such a backup loan through Morgan Guaranty and nine others for $300 million. Argentina, whose political position was precarious even to an optimist, got a renewal of $33 million from Chase and $100 from Bank of America, Chemical and First National Bank of Boston.[15] South Korea seems increasingly to be in a weak position. At least eight American banks have over 1 percent of all their loans in South Korea—a total of over $2 billion. Meanwhile, the American embassy reported that Korea would get no more long-term loans.[16] And even as Brazil's external deficit for 1975 approached $5.5 billion, it had $2.5 billion in Eurocurrency credits. The list of countries getting deeper and deeper in debt to the banks could be extended, and many U.S. bank regulators have shown concern. There remains the historical rule that international loans show a lower default rate than domestic loans and this record may continue to hold. Generally, however, American bank involvement in the Eurocurrency market has increased involvement in the fate of other countries, and added exposure to foreign risks.

The whole issue can be viewed from another standpoint. With the rise in oil prices and increased deficits of non-oil developing countries, the need for financing these countries became urgent. OPEC countries and the developed countries have contributed somewhat to easing the burdens, but the private financial institutions can be held largely responsible for ensuring that the "recycling" task could be achieved. If the deficits continue without abatement and the recession deepens, further solutions must be found. But the private sector has performed a service in at least buying time for devising new solutions. The U.S. and other authorities should recognize that the whole world has a stake in assuring the soundness of these foreign loans.

Overcompetition?

In an age where oligopoly is the usual charge, it may seem strange to fear the effects of overcompetition. The optimistic tones of classical economics would have it that market entrants keep prices at the "correct" competitive level, perhaps driving out the inefficient producers. Beneficent as this outcome may seem, it is not a process which should be allowed to work freely in the banking industry. As previous sections have illustrated, banking possesses a certain fragility; the loss of an "inefficient producer" may turn into a loss to all. The classical model assumes that none of the market entrants holds so much market power that it can manipulate prices—that is to say, take an operating loss temporarily until competitors are driven away. The real world of banking does not conform exactly to the classical form. And since our tolerance for banking failures must remain limited, some worry is not misplaced.

London has attracted a large number of banks, most of whom aim for a slice of the same business. Some thirty new American banks entered London in the last decade—and at the same time, banks from other countries joined the rush to the Eurocurrency center. By the end of 1974, there were 244 foreign banks from 53 countries in London. Big entrants from Germany and Japan particularly expanded there. All of this meant a squeeze on the London "take," particularly in 1973, and a feeling of nervousness about the possibilities for future earnings in the Eurodollar market. As prime borrowers became less available, lower quality borrowers demanded lower rates ("spreads") and received them. Japanese banks took some of the blame for reduced earnings. They reportedly held substantial dollar deposits resulting from the Japanese balance of payments surplus. Eager to lend, they tried to break into London by offering relatively attractive deals.[17]

Smaller American banks found themselves in a quandary. In London, it is necessary, particularly for newcomers, to have one's name seen. Some banks thus had to participate in loans on which they expected no profits in order to stay in the market. High returns could be earned on high risks—and 1973 witnessed increased credits to nonprime borrowers. (This was the period in which many currently "sour" loans in real estate, tankers, and LDCs were made.) Table 9-1 shows what happened to spreads between 1972 and 1974.

Although 1973's returns must have been considerably below those of 1972, since spreads had shrunk by one-half, a study by Andrew Brimmer shows that even in 1972, the rate of return on London operations was low. Table 9-2 puts the after tax rate in London at about 20 percent of the rate of return on total assets world wide. For a large multinational bank earning high returns in other parts of the world, such figures are probably not too disturbing; for smaller banks, they may constitute a heavy burden. Many of the syndicated loans publicized over the last few years hold maturities of ten years

Table 9-1. Typical Spread Over London Interbank Deposit Rate

	1972		*1973*		*1974*	
	Low	*High*	*Low*	*High*	*Low*	*High*
Prime Developed Country Borrowers	3/4	1	1/4	5/8	1 1/2	1 3/4
Prime LDC Borrowers	1 1/4	1 1/2	3/4	1	1 3/4	2
Nonprime LDC Borrowers	2 1/2	2 1/2	1	1 3/4	2	2 1/2

Source: U.S., Department of the Treasury, "Outlook for International Lending by Banks in 1975," *News* 15 July 1975.

Table 9-2. Rate of Return on Assets (1972)

	On Total Assets	*On London Assets*
15 Banks with London Branches	0.54	0.12
3 Established before 1965	0.53	0.10
12 Established after 1964	0.55	0.14

Source: Brimmer, "Changing Fortunes," p. 38.

or more, and will continue to yield small returns (or less). Knowledge of these factors thus contributes to declining confidence in international bankers, and to the suspicion that they have been less than "prudent men."

Maturities

A final element of risk involves the maturity structure of a bank's balance sheet. In theory, no banker could meet his liabilities on demand unless all of his loans outstanding were "at call." Fortunately, most depositors do not ask for their money. A perfectly matched balance sheet would show all liabilities due on a certain date to be offset by assets (loans) due at the same time. Maximum risk would occur when all liabilities are due on demand while all assets are only recoverable at some distant date in the future.

No simple formula exists to define the correct degree of risk. The banks have been accused, however, of increasing their risks in the 1970s. Certainly the growth of "term" credits in the Euromarkets tended to lengthen the average maturity of long-term assets. One particular source of fear arose with the growth of OPEC surpluses. The oil exporters created an excess supply of short-term deposits—even as oil importers sought long-term loans to cover their deficits.[18] By May 1975, the structure of assets (claims) and liabilities was as it appears in Table 9-3.

It can be seen that the American banks had over $7 billion in liabilities at 8 days with no comparable assets. At the long end (over 3 years) they held about $6 billion in claims covered by shorter-term deposits. How has their position changed over time? How do the Americans compare with other banks in the Euromarkets?

The best way to compare maturity structures at banks of different size and over time is to use the "mismatch" ratio which weights unmatched positions by the volume of business.[19] Table 9-4 displays

Table 9-3. Maturity Structure of Eurocurrencies at American Banks in Britain ($ millions, 21 May 1975)

Maturity	*Claims*	*Liabilities*	*Claims Less Liabilities*
Less than 8 days	10,585	18,205	–7,620
8 days-1 month	9,990	10,425	–435
1 month-3 months	16,100	16,110	–10
3 months-6 months	10,250	9,510	+740
6 months-1 year	4,325	4,385	–60
1 year-3 years	3,080	1,585	+1,495
3 years and over	7,690	1,805	+5,885

Source: Bank of England, *Quarterly Bulletin.*

mismatch ratios for the American banks and for all banks in Britain from 1971 to mid-1975. It can be seen that all banks increased their short-dated liabilities, particularly after mid-1974. The American banks tend to have a poorer record in this respect compared with all banks taken together.

In the long end of the Eurocurrency market, the banks generally have moved in tandem, all increasing their exposure since mid-1974 considerably. These figures do indicate then, a significantly more exposed market in Eurocurrencies than existed in 1972.[20] They confirm the suspicions that oil surpluses have put some strain on maturity structures.

The Bank of England studies these figures closely and pressures banks considered to have gone too far to better their balance sheets. An example of what can happen to banks with unmatched books came in 1974. Banks in Italy then lost one-half of their Eurocurrency deposits. All were relieved to find that the Italian banks had matched their positions closely. Although confidence in the Eurocurrency markets began to pick up again by late 1974, it would seem that the underlying maturity structure has not greatly improved. The Bank does have the power to pressure the banks to better their balance sheet structures; it should do so.

QUALITY CONTROL?

The last section supplied some rather depressing information about the quality of banking today. It would seem that hard times have hit the American banks in Britain after their decade-long optimism. At the risk of sounding like an arm-chair regulator, I shall contend that

Table 9-4. Mismatch Ratios

	Less than 8 Days	8 Days to Less than 1 Month	1 Month to Less than 3 Months	3 Months to Less than 6 Months	6 Months to Less than 1 Year	1 Year to Less than 3 Years	3 Years and Over
October 1971							
American banks	+5.6	–10.3	–12.6	+1.1	+7.7	+40.1	+69.3
All U.K. banks	+5.1	–10.2	–8.9	–2.8	+2.6	+40.3	+44.9
October 1972							
American banks	–13.4	–2.6	–2.9	+2.7	+2.7	+43.2	+47.9
All U.K. banks	–9.1	–4.9	–5.9	–0.1	+44.6	+44.9	
September 1973							
American banks	–19.8	0	0	+5.5	+2.5	+17.0	+49.0
All U.K. banks	–12.2	–1.6	–2.5	0	–3.6	+32.0	+42.7
May 1974							
American banks	–17.4	–6.6	0	+3.3	+9.1	+37.4	+43.8
All U.K. banks	–9.4	–8.4	–3.9	–5.1	+2.9	+42.1	+50.2
February 1975							
American banks	–21.2	–5.3	–3.1	+2.6	+6.8	+35.0	+61.1
All U.K. banks	–14.9	–9.0	–10.0	–8.2	+1.4	+41.2	+59.6
May 1975							
American banks	–26.5	–2.1	0	+3.7	–0.7	+32.0	+62.0
All U.K. banks	–17.8	–6.6	–8.0	–8.0	–4.2	+37.1	+62.0

most (but not all) of these troubles might have been avoided by sensible *national* government policies. Secondly, I believe that the interdependence of the world banking system has increased—but that governments can protect themselves from the added risk without performing major amputations of their foreign tentacles and without the necessity of supranational control. This applies to both Britain and the United States in this case.

It is true that much of today's malaise over banking soundness originates in the past; past decisions cannot be undone, they can only be avoided in the future. How can we avert these dangers? Each country must make a reasoned assessment of the degree to which it is subject to risks arising from the international financial markets. In this section, we have found risks to bank solvency from:

1. Exposure to banks abroad through interbank market placements.
2. Exposure to sudden withdrawals of volatile international funds.
3. Exposure to riskier lines of business, particularly long-term lending.
4. Exposure through "country" credits.
5. Profits pressure from overcompetition.

To the extent that banks in Britain other than the American banks engage in the international sector, they too subject themselves to increased risk. And Chapter Six showed how the new banking has indeed been adopted by the big banks in most countries, particularly in their London operations. Here, I shall concentrate on the British and Americans—but the regulators in other countries should be equally able to control their own banks' activities.

From the point of view of the United States, certain actions could contribute to a strengthening of the banking system. The bureaucratic competition among bank regulators at the federal level should come to an end. Congress has moved in this direction, but care should be taken to maintain the connection between monetary control and regulatory control. One reason for the expansion of bank powers originates in pressure from the Comptroller's office in the Treasury. The concept of an "independent" agency like the Federal Reserve still carries weight. The banks will always push for a return to the pre-1933 unity of investment and commercial banking even though historically this has been proved a shaky connection. The Fed has generally shown more awareness of the problems in this area.

A new bank holding company bill might clarify and limit further the relationships between banks and their subsidiaries. The exposure of the parent to the affiliate should be strictly delimited so that no questions arise as to the exposure of the bank to the activities of its foreign (or domestic) subsidiary. (In countries where branches are not permitted, subsidiaries which serve as branches can be treated for purposes of U.S. law as branches.)

Edge Act subsidiaries abroad carrying on activities not permitted at home should be reconsidered. The argument in favor of greater powers abroad assumes that American banks would have difficulty competing against host country banks if limited by U.S. law. (Another argument is that extraterritoriality should not be claimed. That argument is somewhat irrelevant since the U.S. *already* controls the activities of banking subsidiaries anyway.) At the least, the vast increase in Edge Act banking needs examination. The growth of "merchant banking" by Americans in London was not envisaged in the original purposes of the Edge Act; it conflicts with the purposes of the 1933 Banking Act. Given entrenched interests, of course, such a reassessment presents the politicians with interest group problems—yet surely other interests weigh in the balance.

Exposure to the vicissitudes of the international financial system presents a more diffuse problem. It means exposure to foreign deposit withdrawals, to foreign bank failures, and to foreign defaults. Some of the smaller American banks in London and elsewhere, given their assets and more limited management, should perhaps have stayed at home. With the follow the leader game as played by American bankers, more and more banks may like to put a finger into the international pie. The American regulators might take a stricter view of which banks can take on the added risks.

Foreign withdrawals, on the other hand, can affect domestic branches as easily as foreign branches. Foreign deposits are likely to increase in the United States with the progressive lowering of reserve requirements, the raising of interest rate ceilings, and the removal of capital controls. But foreign funds shifts among banks might occur with much less regularity if the federal deposit insurance system were expanded to include larger dollar deposits and liabilities to foreigners at domestic and foreign branches. Some of the shifts in funds from one U.S. bank to another of the last few years have been unreasonable and might, by this plan (or a modified version of it) be avoided in the future.

In general, the recent record has shown bank regulation to be weak in certain areas. It may seem strange to call simultaneously for a rationalization of banking agencies along with an extension of their oversight. In fact, both the Federal Reserve and the Comptroller have been reviewing their assessment procedures. Where they once concentrated on loan quality as a simple function of the borrower's creditworthiness, they now realize that they must look also at maturity structures of assets and liabilities, country exposure (in addition to loan limits to individual borrowers), industry exposure, currency exposure, and so on. Individual banks have internal control systems for these purposes, of course, but bank examinations should be expanded to include at least guidelines in these areas. The banks will naturally claim that the costs of increased reporting will be too high. The burden of proof, however, should be left to them.

As for the Bank of England, it faces many of the same problems as encountered by the United States. In a sense, its problem is compounded by the concentration of so many very large banks in such a limited place. The Bank plays its role conscientiously, no doubt. Its commitment to light-handed regulation limits, however, the pressure it is willing to apply. In addition, British commitment to London as an international financial center further restricts the Bank's potential discretion to restrict entry. But the costs of full supervision would entail monetary as well as psychic costs on the Bank. The Bank has decided, however, that more supervision is necessary, particularly for smaller domestic banks which have adopted too many of the techniques of their more powerful competitors.

It is easy enough to say that if the London banking system lies beyond British power to control it, it is because the British welcomed mass entry in the first place. American insurance for dollar deposits at all American branches would go a long way toward solving the problem of a lender of last resort in the Eurodollar market; more Bank of England pressure for gentlemen's guarantees of London subsidiaries by foreign parents might also be helpful. Other forms of moral suasion might stabilize the City's banks. Modern forms of data processing can also ease the costs of analyzing a bank's position.

Although the management of London's banks might logically seem to demand a sort of supranational system of control, it can also be argued that the London system is only as strong as its individual parts. If the American banks are weak, London is weak; if German banks are weak, the same follows. This is why the important points of pressure lie in the home countries: the Bank of England's role, therefore lies mainly in permitting entry only to those banks which are likely to remain stable. Many will counter that it is freedom of entry which makes London great. But the entrance of weak banks into business they cannot manage will only weaken the structure.

All of this places demands upon the powers of discrimination at the Bank of England—but certainly less of a burden than full regulation would be. The Bank might consider more surveillance of locally incorporated subsidiaries, however. But its main job, like that of the Federal Reserve, the Bundesbank, or the Banco Central de Venezuela, is to monitor the British banks and ensure that their participation in international activities and their dealings with foreign banks pose no unacceptable risks for the British economy. This prescription is obvious—but it is one not often considered by those who fear that all has already been lost and that the multinationals have the day. There is nothing obvious about the doomwatchers' conclusions.

We can quickly conclude that the changes called for here would likely set off a new round of reactions. Guarantees of dollar deposits at American banks, for instance, would surely act as an incentive to shift funds away from non-American banks. Would the Eurodollar market survive the act which was meant to protect it? Perhaps not. Those who have spent so much effort in understanding it would surely regret its passing. But would the world be worse for returning to its pre-Eurodollar state? The argument in its favor is the efficiency it promotes for borrowers and lenders. If efficiency can be preserved while removing the dangers, we should surely consider taking the chance.

The claim that supranational regulation provides the only viable solution to "transnational" problems remains powerful in its logic. Its weakness lies in defining too many difficulties as transnational. Many countries, from oil sheikdoms to socialist autarkies, have found that the supranational gods help those who help themselves. But if we find many solutions within national borders, we should nevertheless continue to seek international cooperation where we can. Where countries do agree, for instance over lenders of last resort, over support for national currencies—or whatever, common action will be both possible and effective. No individual, country or collectivity ever solves all its problems. If I have sounded a note of optimism here, it is not out of full confidence that money will be made sound overnight. Pessimism, however, seems more likely to breed inaction and despair when what is needed is an attitude of creativity, eclecticism, and hope.

NOTES TO CHAPTER NINE

1. The distinction between sensitivity and vulnerability to interdependence is made by Joseph S. Nye and Robert O. Keohane, "World Politics and the International Economic System," in C. Fred Bergsten (ed.), *The Future of the International Economic Order: An Agenda for Research* (Lexington: D.C. Heath, 1973).

2. "Dependencia" theorists, including many Marxists, hold to the belief that foreign investment—the backbone of modern interdependence—is exploitative, placing the costs almost entirely on recipients. "Mercantilist" theorists assume that dominant countries also undergo increasing costs from interdependence, at least beyond a certain point. They see conflict as a likely outcome. "Liberal" theorists assume that all sides gain more than they lose from interdependence. (These distinctions are made by Robert Gilpin, *U.S. Power and the Multinational Corporation: The Political Economy of Foreign Direct Investment* (New York: Basic Books, 1975), pp. 220-237.) I share Gilpin's conclusion that none of these theories deals adequately with the problem of multinational corporations.

3. 4 March 1974.

4. See Lewis Beman, "How It All Came Apart in the Eurodollar Market," *Fortune*, February, 1975, pp. 171-74.

5. *New York Times*, 11 January 1976.

6. See Peter T. Kilborn, "Crisis Hurts Cities and Banks," *New York Times*, 21 November 1975.

7. "Quality Street," *The Economist*, 14 December 1974, p. 12.

8. Statement to the Subcommittee on Bank Supervision and Insurance of the House Banking and Currency Committee quoted in *Federal Reserve Bulletin*, December 1974, p. 838. For corroborating views see Dwight B. Crane, "Lessons from the 1974 CD Market," *Harvard Business Review* 53 (November/December 1975): 6, p. 79; R. Alton Gilbert, "Bank Failures and Public Policy," Federal Reserve Bank of St. Louis *Review*, November 1975, pp. 7-15.

9. Address to the 1974 American Bankers' Association Convention, October 24, 1974, reprinted in Federal Reserve Bank of New York, *Monthly Review*, November 1974, p. 264.

10. Reported in *New York Times*, 20 November 1975.

11. A Federal Reserve examiner's report for 1974 was published by the *New York Times* (25 January 1976) and cited numerous domestic financial and management weaknesses.

12. U.S. Treasury, "Report on Developing Countries External Debt and Debt Relief Provided by the United States," January 1976.

13. "Banking: Good Money on Bad Loans," *New York Times Magazine*, 9 November 1975, p. 106. What Mayer means by this $3 billion is an open question. World Bank figures put term bank debt of 86 developing countries in 1973 at $18 billion, a figure which expanded in 1974-75. Chase Manhattan has admitted to holding $4-5 billion in loans to LDCs and Citibank is probably at about the same level or a bit higher (at least below $8 billion). Manufacturers Hanover admits to $2 billion; Morgan $1 billion; Bank of America to somewhere between $5 and $8 billion. (See Charles N. Stabler, "Banks and their Foreign Loans," *Wall Street Journal* 29 January 1976; *New York Times*, 15 January 1976.) For American bank loans to specific countries, see U.S. Senate, Committee on Foreign Relations, Subcommittee on Multinational Corporations, "Foreign Assets and Liabilities of U.S. Banks," 11 March 1976.

14. Neil McInnes, "Financial Time Bomb," *Barron's*, 25 November 1974, p. 9.

15. *New York Times*, 5 May 1975; *The American Banker*, 3 March 1976.

16. *New York Times*, 21 November 1975.

17. See Mary Campbell, "Japanese Pressure on Eurocurrency Spreads," *Financial Times*, 31 October 1973; "Japanese Effect on Eurocurrency Markets," *The Banker*, June 1974, p. 10. Jonathan Aronson, "U.S. Banks and the International Monetary System" (Ph.D. Dissertation, Stanford, 1976), points out the effects of competition from smaller banks on the Euromarkets.

18. Fred H. Klopstock, "Oil Payments and Financial Markets," *The Conference Board Record* (May 1975).

19. The formula for the ratio is: $100 \times \dfrac{\text{Claims} - \text{Liabilities}}{\text{Claims} + \text{Liabilities}}$ at each maturity. This concept was developed by David Ashby in "Analysing the Maturity Structure of the Eurodollar Market," *The Banker* (July 1973), pp. 767-72. The number represents a percentage of business volume which is unmatched at a certain maturity. Both higher negative and higher positive ratios signify increasingly unmatched positions.

20. Unfortunately, maturities of over three years are aggregated in the data. This precludes a detailed look at the length of these longer assets and liabilities.

Chapter Ten

Managed Interdependence: Banks in a Larger Context

Although students of international politics generally agree that interdependence is on the increase today, it can be argued that such is not quite the case.[1] For instance, the fall of the Creditanstalt in 1931 had international reverberations far beyond the impact of the fall of Franklin National Bank in 1974. The difference lies not in a lessening of interconnection—for it has indeed increased—but in the increased powers of states for dealing with the shock waves which interconnection transmits. Even as technological discoveries enable multinational corporations to move funds at the flick of a switch, so governments can develop comparable defenses. Current research on the sources, results and the prescriptions for the interdependence accompanying the spread of multinational corporations reflects a tendency to ignore the positive role that governments can play in the process. This study of American banks in Britain brings to the fore the significance of government policy in the spread of multinational banks and points to some possible remedies for the problems they bring. The conclusions reached here apply in large part, I believe, to problems associated with multinational corporations in general. In fact, experts disagree about the sources of the spread of multinational companies, the results of that spread and, as a consequence of different analyses, and of different values, they also disagree over solutions. The issues can be clarified to some extent, and I think some conclusions can be put forward in the light of this study.

ON SOURCES

We have seen ample evidence here that American banks went to Britain for many different reasons and that some among these banks have expanded there for even more reasons. This case does not support either the simple claim that multinational companies respond to free market conditions, or the equally simple claim that it is all a matter of politics. Both approaches prove helpful. The free market point of view corresponds to classical economic analysis, an analysis of the economic system abstracted from a larger social-political system. Economic factors alone explain flows of trade or capital according to classical economics. Economists tend to point to examples like Ricardo's trade theory where wine obviously turns out better and everyone can drink more when the English import it from Portugal in return for English woolens. Similarly, direct foreign investment is said to originate in lower labor costs say, in Taiwan, or perhaps in differential capitalization rates.[2] This approach is insufficient, although within a set of conditions, these underlying factors will come into play. While the considerations of traditional economics must be taken into account, they must first be placed in their political framework.

In explaining the causes of the spread of American banks in Britain and their expansion there, this study has had to go behind the immediate economic factors. Competitive factors, availability of supply, customers' demands, and so on were doubtless important—but insufficient to explain the sudden spurt of expansion in the 1960s. Equally important were the politically controlled factors, particularly regulations in the United States and Britain, as well as broader factors such as the structure of the international monetary system itself.

This eclectic explanation of the multinational movement could be called *structuralist*. It claims that one must assess the structure of interstate power relationships in order to explain the direction of investment and the distribution of benefits among states.[3] One must also analyze the structure of power within countries to explain the stance of both home and host countries vis-à-vis the multinational corporation. A structuralist viewpoint expects that state power will be used—be it economic, political, military or a mixture of these—to procure the maximum possible benefits from a system. And, depending on internal political structures, these benefits will be either widely or narrowly distributed within the state. Narrowly distributed benefits indicate that the state is captive to special interests; widely distributed benefits indicate that the state acts rationally in the general interest.

The best explanation of the growth of the multinational corporation must rely on a structuralist interpretation as the ground upon which economic explanations must stand. In the case of the banks, there was little question that profits, growth, and corporate survival were at stake. Occupants of company boardrooms have little time to consider their part in contributing to the power of their home states, even if their independent actions promote that end. Yet the banks' pursuit of their own particular goals depended largely on the structural conditions created by the states they dealt with.

Is the United States actively responsible for the spread of American business? In the sense that the U.S. promoted freedom of foreign investment, fostered the dominance of the dollar, allowed direct investment abroad to be made easily and profitably, and permitted large oligopolistic companies and banks to emerge, this is so. No effort was made to reverse the trend toward foreign branches by American banks in the 1960s, even when the cause of this trend was an anomalous set of capital controls. This conclusion supports the structuralist argument in that it illustrates the way in which the U.S. worked to create the proper framework for the international growth of its banks. The assertion that large, dominant, developed states create open systems, as Stephen Krasner demonstrates in the case of trade, seems to be necessary to any assessment of the sources of the internationalization of corporate life.[4]

The example of American banks in Britain not only supports the structuralist viewpoint, but also expands it. Many of those who employ structural analysis stress home country policy and assume host country policy to be relatively passive or even subservient. We have found, however, that host country policy may exert independent influence. The host country attitude toward foreign investment may be strongly determined by its own domestic structures.[5] Thus, a structuralist explanation includes not only an analysis of international structures, but also a study of the particular domestic political configurations within the countries involved. While multinationals undoubtedly bring pressure to bear on potential hosts in order to procure favorable treatment from them, it is often the strength and unity of domestic politics which determine the outcomes. American banks in Britain benefit from the support they get from British financial circles. This, it seems, has more to do with the British political system than with the existence of overweening American power.

ON RESULTS

Arguments continue over the results of the spread of multinationalism. Laissez-faire economists on the whole exhibit a penchant for optimism. This is a pleasant enough penchant, but it is often unfounded. As E.H. Carr observed, "The economic expert, dominated in the main by the laissez-faire doctrine, considers the hypothetical economic interest of the world as a whole, and is content to assume this is identical with the interest of each individual country." John Rawls in turn confirms that the problem with utilitarianism (which is at the heart of classical economics) is that it fails to look at who gets what but measures instead only how much everybody gets all together.[6] The utilitarian suspects on the whole that states are the principal barriers to the maximization of world welfare and that organizations which transcend states herald a new and better world.[7] The multinational company is therefore seen to be benign in impact, donating a bonanza in welfare to somebody, and by extension, to everybody. There results a symmetrical outcome of balanced gains, a positive sum game where all parties benefit.

Those who concern themselves more with politics worry similarly about the welfare of states, but differ about which states we should worry about. They disagree with the optimists and conclude that the effects of the internationalization of business fall asymmetrically. They tend to see these outcomes as a zero sum game where one actor's gain is another's loss. One group agrees with the utilitarians above that both home and host country have lost power to the multinational but sees the decline of the state as a bad thing. The growth of the Eurodollar market, for instance, threatens national monetary autonomy. Individual interests gain at the expense of the collective good. Hence, from this "sovereignty at bay"[8] perspective, American labor unions cry out that the multinationals export jobs from the U.S.; developing countries claim that they cannot control the infinitely flexible finaglings of the foreigners in their midst; and developed countries complain that their own home markets are being monopolized by outsiders. Everyone loses but the MNC. But even if the sovereignty at bay thesis seems persuasive at first, the case of the American banks in Britain gives but sparse support to the claim that the state need be prostrate before the corporation. This is not to say that the state never prostrates itself, for we have also seen that the United States has sometimes allowed disruptive activities to continue unnecessarily and that Britain also bends too far backwards in the service of multinational banks. The difference is that the sovereignty at bay pessimists assume that the state has no choice. We have found here not the absence of choice, but the absence of any commitment to limit the multinational banks in the first place.

Others dispute the sovereignty at bay group in claiming that it is not the MNC which gains at the expense of the state, but rather it is the home country (along with its companies) which gains at the expense of hosts. The structural approach yields persuasive evidence that strong countries do benefit from the spread of multinational business. For the structuralist, the strong set up frameworks which skew outcomes in their own favor in the first place. The structuralist will accept the economist's analysis to explain why particular companies or industries go abroad, and he values the economist's goal of joint gain. He concludes, however, that joint gain is not the natural result in a system of states of unequal power and resources. At best, the distribution of gains from a given state of affairs will be unbalanced, the actual proportions depending upon the situation. Given this orientation, it is not surprising to the structuralist that home countries and their nationals get more out of system of multinational corporations than the hosts. It is also not surprising that relatively powerful countries sometimes use the system to their own advantage.

In the case of American banks in Britain, the structuralist argument is strong. In the meantime, the acceptance of economic arguments has proved to be useful in an explanation of how the system has worked. As would be predicted, the British gain little from the presence of the Americans in the City, while taking on a huge burden of control. The United States, on the other hand, loses virtually nothing—while gaining from the world-wide network of its banking system and most importantly, from the world-wide acceptability of the dollar. To the extent that the United States can be said to have suffered a loss of monetary control or suffered from the dominance of its large banks, the country is itself responsible for not having done anything about it.

How has the United States gained from its relatively strong economic-political position? The United States has rarely used its banks in any direct way to control British policy, although the overall influence of the United States on British policy is undeniable. That influence is doubtless increased by the presence of American business in Britain, but that is only a part of the general military, economic and political ties which exist between the two countries, ties which put Britain in the position of junior partner. Significant changes toward say, the banks, would be virtually impossible as long as this kind of partnership persists. The global dominance of American banks, of which their presence in London and in the Eurocurrency markets is an important part, facilitates as well America's ability to control policy in lesser countries than Britain. Private bank credits are in practice geared to official policy as regards the creditworthiness of countries seeking loans, for example, so that government credit policies are usually seconded by private bank decisions.[9]

ON MANAGING

To manage, traditionally, means to control. In today's usage, it can mean, less confidently, to get by. The world of multinational corporations and banks shifts constantly and countries will probably do well to manage in the latter sense. Any decisions about how to do so will necessarily reflect the point of view of the analyst or policy-maker and some states might find that they are satisfied with a low level of control. But unless one accepts the harmony of interests doctrine, no one solution could possibly please all interests concerned. This is why attempts at supranational control or uniform guidelines are likely to fail insofar as this control is expected to be either fair to all countries, or effective. Competing values must be constantly adjusted.

The example of OPEC illustrates the problem of such conflicts. We champion the cause of host countries, worrying that they will be unequal to the task of extracting a just return from foreign investors. At the same time, we feel that home countries should also control their own companies, particularly with respect to company policies which affect security. Some feel OPEC won more than its fair share from the developed and lesser developed countries by using the powers at its command. Others feel that the oil nations had long cowered before the producers, accepting prices lower than the market would bear. The issue of company loyalty also arose. Should companies be expected to act like citizens of their home countries? Are they really "persons" in the sense of owing something to parent countries when operating elsewhere? There can in fact be no objective answers to these questions. We cannot find general principles to define how high a price, how loyal, how much control? We can try at least to settle disputes peaceably. In the meantime, only the people of one country can define their own needs and how to acquire the means to them.

I have emerged from this study of American banks in Britain with certain perspectives:

1. The state is the most effective agent of the collective good we have, although states vary in effectiveness in this respect.
2. Most states are technically capable of controlling multinational companies, although a developed country like Britain has relative-

ly high capabilities to apply control with discrimination and subtlety.

3. The principle barrier to state control is the lack of a unified internal structure and the dominance of local groups which have allied themselves to foreign interests.
4. International control is possible only where there is wide agreement (rare when important questions are involved), or where there is a group of more limited scope in which there is similar agreement (far more likely).
5. Controls have the best chance of success when made with the goal of preserving maximum possible freedom for economic activities consistent with security, welfare, and liberty within the state.

Not surprisingly, there are problems with these perspectives. Perhaps banks are unique and lessons learned from studying them do not carry over to other areas. It seems to me, however, that one would expect banks to be *most* difficult to control. Bankers are footloose—all they need is a place to set down their vaults and teletypes. Bankers constitute a large and varied group dealing in an especially slippery product. If even banks are subject to control, then it may be that the argument here can be applied more widely.

What of lesser developed countries? If they have fewer resources than Britain, might their powers of control be insufficient? At some point, of course, this will be so. Then some form of alliance will be necessary. What I have found is that banks can be more subject to controls than their critics would suggest; I suspect that this is true elsewhere as well. The LDCs seem increasingly to believe this too.

Another problem is more general. If as a rule, all states are encouraged to pursue their own interests, is this not a call for mutually destructive beggar my neighbor policies? It has been demonstrated, for instance, that protectionist trade policies produce losses for all parties—might not statist policies vis-à-vis the multinationals also lead to joint losses in the end? There are arguments that this need not be so, particularly if the calculations include noneconomic gains. Moreover, it is argued here that the structure of the system and oligopolistic patterns of business produced the original investments anyway. One is not necessarily tampering with the allocations of the free market but with a very different animal.

A final problem flows from structuralist analysis. A call for states to use their latent power to protect their interests applies to both big powers and small. The large state pursuing its own interest tends to do so at the expense of weaker states. But if this amounts to a serious problem, it does not result from flaws of analysis, but follows from the nature of international relations themselves.

Barnet and Müller call for a change in the global value system away from the goal of infinite accumulation and a turn to idealism by the large states. But before this ethical revolution comes about, they settle for the use of public power for public benefits and the restoration of the efficacy of national governments. Calleo and Rowland take the view that the potential for conflict is too great, that the world would be both freer and more prosperous as a "loosely related series of national and regional systems." Keohane and Nye also place faith in international organization, but tend to favor more universalistic ones than the others above.[10] The view taken here is that all of these efforts must *start* at the level of the nation-state. Supranational organizations may mobilize public opinion and elevate certain ideals, but cannot be depended upon to initiate real improvements. They may even work against the interests of less influential countries. States must act for themselves. When they see that others share their goals, they should join forces. OPEC was a success because of a simple joint interest in a higher price, after all. Such lower level international organizations may in fact prove to be the most effective in the end.

If states assert themselves, perhaps the less desirable outcomes of the spread of multinational corporations can be controlled. Our fear should not be that governments will be impotent to protect themselves should the need arise, but rather that they will lack the wisdom to do so. Walter Bagehot had the same thoughts on closing his study of London over 100 years ago, saying:

> A system of credit which has slowly grown up as years went on, which has suited itself to the course of business, which has forced itself on the habits of men, will not be altered because the theorists disapprove of it, or because books are written against it. . . .
>
> We must therefore, I think, have recourse to feeble and humble palliatives such as I have suggested. With good sense, good judgment, and good care, I have no doubt that they may be enough. But I have written in vain if I require to say now that the problem is delicate, that the solution is varying and difficult, and the result is inestimable to us all.

NOTES TO CHAPTER TEN

1. The literature on interdependence is extensive, but the most influential work on the subject must include Richard N. Cooper, *The Economics of Interdependence: Economic Policy in the Atlantic Community* (New York: McGraw-Hill, 1968); Kenneth N. Waltz, "The Myth of Interdependence," in Charles P. Kindleberger, ed., *The International Corporation* (Cambridge, M.I.T. Press, 1970); Robert O. Keohane and Joseph S. Nye, Jr., eds., *Transnational Relations and World Politics* (Cambridge: Harvard University Press, 1972), and

by the same authors, *Power and Interdependence: World Politics in Transition* (Boston: Little, Brown, November 1976).

2. The ideal types delineated here may, of course, describe no one individual, but nevertheless represent a commonly observed line of thought, even if incompletely articulated. Businessmen, for instance, will answer attacks by pointing to their contributions to production or efficiency. See for instance, Jacques G. Maisonrouge, "How the Multinational Corporation Appears to Its Managers," in George W. Ball, ed., *Global Companies: The Political Economy of World Business* (Englewood Cliffs: Prentice-Hall, 1975). For a typical economist's analysis, see Robert Z. Aliber, "A Theory of Direct Investment," in Kindleberger, *The International Corporation*, pp. 17-34.

3. Related approaches can be found in Gilpin, *U.S. Power and the Multinational Corporation*; David P. Calleo and Benjamin M. Rowland, *American and the World Political Economy* (Bloomington: Indiana University Press, 1973); Raymond Aron, *The Imperial Republic* (Englewood Cliffs, Prentice-Hall, 1974), pp. 170-71.

4. Stephen D. Krasner, "State Power and the Structure of International Trade," *World Politics* 28 (April 1976) 3: 317-47.

5. This line of thought has been more fully developed by Peter J. Katzenstein, "International Relations and Domestic Structures: Foreign Economic Policies of Advanced Industrial States." *International Organization* 3 (Winter 1976) 1: 1-43.

6. John Rawls, *A Theory of Justice* (Cambridge: Harvard University Press, 1971), pp. 26-27; Edward Hallett Carr, *The Twenty Years' Crisis: 1919-1939* (New York: Macmillan, 1939; reprint ed., New York: Harper and Row, 1964), p. 55.

7. For an example by an author who may now have modified his view somewhat, George W. Ball, "Cosmocorp: The Importance of Being Stateless," *Atlantic Community Quarterly* (Summer 1968). For an unreconstructed view about the role of states, see Harry Johnson, *International Economic Questions Facing Britain, the United States and Canada in the Seventies* (London: British-North American Association, June 1970), p. 24, quoted in Gilpin, *U.S. Power*, p. 220.

8. The evocative phrase "sovereignty at bay" was used by Raymond Vernon in his book of that name. Vernon, however, is not among those who believe that states are likely to wither away. Representative sovereignty at bay theorists are Barnet and Muller, *Global Reach.*

9. Emma Rothschild, "Banks: The Politics of Debt," *New York Review of Books*, 24 June 1976.

10. Barnet and Müller, *Global Reach*, p. 386; Keohane and Nye, *Transnational Relations*, p. 395; Calleo and Rowland, *America and the World Political Economy*, p. 252.

Appendix: The Position of American Banks in Britain January 1976

($ millions)

Liabilities		
Sterling Deposits		
U.K. Banks	3,175	
Other U.K.	2,387	
Overseas	735	
C.D.'s	1,663	
Total		7,960
Other Currency Deposits		
U.K. Banks	10,603	
Other U.K.	1,965	
Overseas	46,006	
C.D.'s	7,371	
Total		65,945
Other Liabilities		1,204
Total Liabilities		75,109

Assets		
Notes and Coin		2
Sterling Assets		
Reserve Assets	877	
Special Deposits	112	
Market Loans	3,366	
Bills	38	

Advances			
U.K.	3,853		
Overseas	81		
Total		3,934	
Investments		175	
Total			8,541
Other Currency Assets			
Market Loans		15,203	
Advances			
U.K. Public Sector	812		
U.K. Private Sector	3,441		
Overseas	45,304		
Total		50,393	
Bills		116	
Investments		91	
Total			65,803
Miscellaneous			365
Acceptances			398
Total Assets			75,109

Source: Bank of England

Index

About the Author

Janet Kelly is a Research Fellow at the Center for International Affairs at Harvard University and Assistant Professor of Politics at the University of Massachusetts at Boston. She received her Ph.D. from the Johns Hopkins School of Advanced International Studies in Washington, D.C. and is author of articles on banking and on the international monetary system.

Books of Related Interest Written under Center for International Affairs Auspices

United States Manufacturing Investment in Brazil, by Lincoln Gordon and Engelbert L. Grommers, 1962. Harvard Business School.

Entrepreneurs of Lebanon, by Yusif A. Sayigh (sponsored jointly with the Center for Middle Eastern Studies), 1962. Harvard University Press.

The Dilemma of Mexico's Development, by Raymond Vernon, 1963. Harvard University Press.

Public Policy and Private Enterprise in Mexico, edited by Raymond Vernon, 1964. Harvard University Press.

Foreign Policy and Democratic Politics, by Kenneth N. Waltz (sponsored jointly with the Institute of War and Peace Studies, Columbia University), 1967. Little, Brown & Co.

Europe's Postwar Growth, by Charles P. Kindleberger, 1967. Harvard University Press.

Aid, Influence, and Foreign Policy, by Joan M. Nelson, 1968. The Macmillan Company.

International Regionalism, by Joseph S. Nye, 1968. Little, Brown & Co.

Economic Policy-Making and Development in Brazil, 1947-1964, by Nathaniel H. Leff, 1968. John Wiley & Sons.

Europe's Would-Be Polity, by Leon Lindberg and Stuart A. Scheingold, 1970. Prentice-Hall.

Taxation and Development: Lessons from Colombian Experience, by Richard M. Bird, 1970. Harvard University Press.

The Kennedy Round in American Trade Policy: The Twilight of the GATT? by John W. Evans, 1971. Harvard University Press.

Peace in Parts: Integration and Conflict in Regional Organization, by Joseph S. Nye, Jr., 1971. Little, Brown & Co.

Sovereignty at Bay: The Multinational Spread of U.S. Enterprise, by Raymond Vernon, 1971. Basic Books.

Transnational Relations and World Politics, edited by Robert O. Keohane and Joseph S. Nye, Jr., 1972. Harvard University Press.

Organizing the Transnational: The Experience with Transnational Enterprise in Advanced Technology, by M.S. Hochmuth, 1974. Sijthoff (Leiden).

Multinational Corporations and the Politics of Dependence: Copper in Chile, 1945-1973, by Theodore Moran, 1974. Princeton University Press.

The Andean Group: A Case Study in Economic Integration among Developing Countries, by David Morawetz, 1974. M.I.T. Press.

The Politics of International Monetary Reform—The Exchange Crisis, by Michael J. Brenner, 1976. Ballinger Publishing Co.

The International Politics of Natural Resources, by Zuhayr Mikdashi, 1976. Cornell University Press.

The Oil Crisis, edited by Raymond Vernon, 1976. W.W. Norton & Co.